Through Thick and Thin

In memory of my beloved parents Now and Megan Thomas.

*Thanks to my sister Val for allowing me to write some
of her memories and for being so brave, always.*

*To my husband Embo who has been my strength throughout
our married lives and without whose support, encouragement
and patience this book would never have been completed.*

Cover photograph: My mother, my sister and me.

© *Margaret Roberts 2006*

The right of Margaret Roberts to be identified as Author of this work has been asserted by her in accordance with the Copyright Laws.

Published by: Henblas Publishers, e-mail: robertsmrg@aol.com

All rights reserved. No part of this publication may be reproduced, stored in a retrieval system, or transmitted, at any time or by any means electronic, mechanical, photocopying, recording or otherwise without the prior written permission of the publisher.

Printed in Wales by: W.O. Jones (Printers) Ltd, Llangefni.

ISBN 0-9552673-0-7
ISBN 978-0-9552673-0-76

Through Thick and Thin

BY

MARGARET

Memories of Llanfairfechan North Wales

1776 - 2005

Contents

Part 1

A brief history of my village 12

The mountains 13

The early days – a place hard to get to and a dangerous place for travellers 15

The set industry 18

Clearing the land 19

Chapels and schools 20

Thr cockle pickers 21

Glan y Mor Elias 22

Sunday afternoon cockfights 25

Beer making 25

Pen Penmaen Uchaf 26

Candles and Llanfairfechan connects 27

The danger of the sea 29

Bryn y Neuadd 30

Llanfairfechan grows 31

A place of myths and legends and stories from Dad 32

Part 2

Family Tree: Y Teiliwrs 36

Here begins the story of my Fathers family Y Teiliwrs 38

Robert Roberts (1) 38

Hugh Roberts – the first of the family tailors 39

Uncle John Roberts and the corner shop 40

Robert Roberts – another one 41

John and Jane Roberts and their family 47

My great-grandfather John Water Roberts 51

My great-grandmother Grace Owen-Roberts-Parry (1871 - 1945) 54

Huwcyn Lewis - a good friend of the family 56

Grace Fawr and Charles Henry Owens 61
Great aunties and uncles galore – the children of John Water and Grace Fawr ... 61
Grace Bach – Nain Thomas 68
My great-great-grandfather (paternal) – Alexander Ellis 74
Mary Ellis and William Thomas (2) – my great-grandparents 75
My grandfather – William Ellis Thomas (Taid Thomas) 76
Back to William and Mary 79
Fred Parry 80
And now back to Grace Bach 81
William John Thomas 86
Auntie Freda and her family 90
Uncle Ned and his crew 92
Uncle Bob and his clan 98
My Mam and Dad, Val and me 104
Finding Vera 151

Part 3

Family Tree: The Babells 166
Babells – My Mothers family – the great-great-grandparents 167
My great-great-grandmother – Nain Babell and her family 168
I will turn now to another branch of my family – who are 173
Great uncles and aunties on my Mothers side of the family 175
I will now turn to my Taid (Harry Bangor) and his side of the family 182
My loving Taid and Nain (Gwynfor) 186
My Nain (Laura Jane) 194
My uncles and aunties on Mam's side 198
And so, back to Mam 205
My sister – Val 206
Here I am with some more of my memories 215
Our Daughters 244
Our Grandchildren 250
Maps 266

Acknowledgments

I am eternally grateful to all my family past and present. Without them there would be no story to tell.

Many thanks to Lloyd Jones who has edited this book; he was the first to read it, and his help, guidance and advice have been invaluable to me.

Thanks to Hayley Devereux for being so patient with me and for giving me so much help with my computer skills.

My appreciation to Mr and Mrs Hugh Lloyd Jones for putting up with me and for giving me their time so enthusiastically; they have been an enormous help to me with their stories and memories of Llanfair and my family.

Thanks to John and Falmai Pryde to whom I went for assistance when I started this project; they have been a great help all the way through it.

My gratitude to Mr Iorwerth Benjamin (deceased). I spent numerous hours listening to Mr Benjamin's memories. It was an honour to have known such a gentleman.

It was with great appreciation and enjoyment that I visited Mrs Morfudd Jones (now deceased) at Plas y Llan. We spent countless hours speaking of bygone days. I like to think that she had as much pleasure as I did from our little chats; she was without a doubt a great character.

Many thanks to the residents at Plas y Llan who shared their memories with me, and allowed me to write them down; it has indeed been a privilege.

There have been a great deal of people who have helped me with this undertaking, far too many to name here but you know who you are. Many people have entrusted me with their photographs I am so grateful and I am indebted to you and I thank you all from the bottom of my heart.

My thanks to the archives at Caernarfon, Bangor and Llandudno (County Records Office) and also to the University of Wales Library Bangor and Llanfairfechan library.

Introduction

Before I start my story I want to tell you a few things about where my family might have come from.

History tells us that we Welsh are descended from the Brythonic Celts who came to settle in Britain many centuries ago. It is possible we come from this migration.

Another explanation is that we derive from a Spanish ship that was shipwrecked on these shores several centuries ago. During the 1600's and 1700's, French brigs involved in smuggling wine and brandy sailed as close as they dared to our rocky shores; our own fishing boats picked up the bounty and hid it along the rugged coastline of North Wales. According to the local author Elizabeth Constable Ellis (1869 - 1938) William the Tailor (one of my distant relatives whom you will hear about) could tell a tale or two about the smugglers who hid their booty in the caves on our own beaches.

A more romantic tale is that our forefathers were Romanies who wandered into our mountains and fell in love with their wild beauty and then settled here.

These explanations have been passed down the generations and any of them may be true and, they all may account for the fact that some of our family are very dark skinned and rather short.

Over the years our family were known to be, and I think still are, rather generous and passionately loyal to each other, although (as you will read here) there have been times when loyalty has taken second place to a good old-fashioned disagreement. Some members of my father's family were known to be very hard workers and equally hard drinkers.

My mother's side of the family are quite religious and the chapel has played and still does play an important part in their lives.

I will endeavour to tell the story of my family in Llanfair, reaching as far back in time as the 18th century. Some are my own memories; I will tell you about the way I remember and perceive those good old days. There are stories about my own childhood, my parents' childhood, and many other people's childhoods, which will take you back, hopefully, to your own childhoods for an hour or two.

Llanfairfechan is a small place and entwined with my family story are those of others, and so with their permission it is an honour to include them.

Part 1

A brief history of my village, Llanfairfechan

I suppose it is a village rather than a town, set in a glacial valley and cut in two by the Afon Ddu (Black River) flowing through the middle, it stands proudly on the coast between Conwy and Bangor on the fringe of the Snowdonia National Park in North Wales. We have the sea on our front doorstep and the magnificent mountains of the Carneddau on our back door. The sea and the mountains have shaped the people of LLanfairfechan.

During the Victorian era Llanfair was a great tourist attraction. We have a promenade that is second to none. The yachting pond is home to a couple of snow-white swans and a family of ducks who are always competing with the screaming seagulls for the bread thrown to them.

Along the sea front from The Towers, running for about a mile towards Abergwyngregin, is The Cob, known in the Victorian era as The Embankment; it was a gift to the people of Llanfair by Mr Sydney Platt of Bryn y Neuadd in the year of Queen Victoria's jubilee.

The Cob is a much-loved walk that attracts people from far and wide. If you sit looking out across the water towards Anglesey you feel a sense of absolute peace and well-being as the waves come rolling gently up to the pebbled beach. In the evening the sun often looks like a great ball of fire hanging in the sky as it sets, casting its flaming reflection across the water. I feel that in this magical place of mine I could actually walk across the sun's burning pathway, over to Anglesey.

When the sea is out the Lavan sands stretch for miles, and Shell Island (*Trwyn y Pyllau Gloyw*) is a haven for all sorts of birds. Many twitchers visit during the winter months. Sometimes, during a particularly bad storm, you will see waves as high as houses. When the wind howls and roars, crashing gigantic waves against the sea wall, it's difficult to stay on your feet as you walk along, taking in this marvel of nature. The spray goes high up over the tall trees at the end of the Cob. Sea birds, screeching noisily, take shelter where they can. White foam, looking like snow, has fallen all around. I love winter in Llanfair as much as any other season. The wildness of the sea and the bleakness of our mountains have a beauty all of their own. If you look northwards you will see Anglesey and Puffin Island (St Seiriol in Welsh), named after a saint who lived there many centuries ago. Its home too many thousands of birds (see Note 1).

It comes to me, and I often wonder, how did I get so lucky, to be born in a place like this?

The mountains

Turn around now and feast your eyes on our splendid rolling hills and mountains, covered in summer with glorious purple heather and the yellow flowers of the gorse bushes. Here and there you will see farms and houses dotted around the hillsides.

Cast your eyes towards the east and you will see Penmaenmawr granite quarry, once an important employer in the area. Many of our ancestors have toiled there over the years. In its heyday there were hundreds of men working there; today (sadly) only a handful. A little further along the coast lays the Great Orme at Llandudno, thrusting proudly out to sea.

Standing guard over our lovely village is Garreg Fawr (Big Rock) which stands 1150 feet high. I am sure I can say with some certainty that if you were born or brought up in Llanfair you have been to the top of Garreg Fawr. On the summit there is what looks like the footprint of a child. Mam and Dad used to tell us it was the footprint of Jesus. What a lovely warm feeling it gave us to think that Jesus had been to our little village!

Dinas on the left, Foel Lwyd in the centre and Garreg Fawr on the right.

About three miles south of Garreg Fawr lay the mountains of Drum and Foel Fras, and in the shadow of these majestic mountains lies Aber Lake (Llyn Anafon). Anafon was the source of Llanfair's water supply from 1932 until the beginning of this century. We now get our water from Lake Cowlyd in the Conwy Valley.

My Taid (grandfather) William Elis Thomas worked at Llyn Anafon when it was being dammed; he used to tell me about the terrible winding, stony track. "A long walk if you missed the truck up," he said. "Sometimes we used to have to carry bags of cement up that shocking track because the truck was full. One thing was good Margaret fach – we were never short of water for a cuppa!"

"It was a hard way to earn a crust, but we were all in the same boat. None of us had much of anything; the soles of my shoes, I remember very well, had holes in them so for most of the day I had wet feet – not something I would recommend! When it rained up there it was wet!" said Taid, screwing up his face. "Sometimes the rain was so fine it was more like a mist; it would come down so sudden – one minute we were working in bright sunlight, but twenty steps further up you couldn't see your hand in front of you." Hard days indeed. The deep, dark waters of Llyn Anafon are a good place for trout, and many anglers have used it over the years. On a hot summer's day the tranquility and serenity have to be felt to be believed; it's an ideal place to sit and rest after the long trek from Llanfair.

Opposite Garreg Fawr, on the other side of the valley, is the stony hill of *Dinas* (a Welsh word which means city). There was an early Iron Age settlement there many centuries ago.

Below Dinas is Llyn Nant Gracie, as the old people would call it – a little pool that nestles comfortably under the shade of the trees. Full of tadpoles, newts and frogs, it's a pool where generations of Llanfair children have played. Years ago the children of Llanfair would spend hours and hours up and around Llyn Nant. Oh! What fun we had. A short cut across the river takes you to the Three Streams. A more idyllic place for a picnic you would be hard pressed to find.

The early days –
a place hard to get to and a dangerous place for travellers

There is evidence of a settlement dating to the Bronze age. In 1885 an ancient grave was found at Tyddyn Llwyfan farm. It held fragments of bone and lots of broken pottery. It seems it was the type of grave found in the Bronze Age.

There is also the Roman connection. In 1883 a Roman milestone was found in a field near Rhiwiau Uchaf. The stone is at the British Museum in London. There is a replica in Cardiff Museum.

The inscription on the stone is as follows:

Imp.Caes.Trai Anos.Hadrianos Aog.p.m.tr.p.v. P.P.Cos.111 A.Kanovio M.P.V111.

It has been translated and reads:

'The Emperor Caesar Trajan Hadrian Augustus, pontifex maximus in his fifth year tribunician power, father of his country, thrice consul: from Kanovium 8 miles.'

In its more recent form the first known name for Llanfairfechan was Llanerch-y-lladron which means the glade of thieves and the people of the village are still jokingly referred to as Lladron Llanfair. The name speaks for itself. There were a few very shady characters living in and around Llanfair three hundred years ago. Owing to the treacherous coast road from Conwy it was an ideal spot for highwaymen to ambush anyone brave enough to use the headland road. Some say that our village owes its name to Mair Fechan, a lady who added a part to the parish church many centuries ago. Llanfairfechan, translated, means Little Church of Mary.

The roads leading to Llanfair were very dangerous for travellers; robbery was rife. At Bwlch y Ddeufaen (Pass of the Two Stones), high above the village, thieves laid in wait and then pounced on travellers as they crossed the lonely moors on their way to Conwy or Llanrwst. My own ancestors walked through those lonely mountains, over to Llanrwst, many times.

Close to Bwlch y Ddeufaen is one of the three streams that flows down to the valley below; this stream is still known today as Afon Lladd Sais, which means the river where English are killed. It is said that in the fifth or sixth century there

Bwlch y Ddeufaen.

was a young Welshman called Bleddyn who had fallen in love with the very beautiful Gwendud, daughter of Helyg ab Glawawg. At the time a Saxon prince called Herbert was being kept prisoner in the mountains of Snowdonia. Now Gwendud was a young maiden who wanted a little more than Bleddyn could offer her. She told him she wanted a golden torque, which was the mark of a true prince. Bleddyn heard that the young prince Herbert had been set free and was in need of a guide over the mountains. Assuring the prince that he was the best guide there was, Bleddyn offered his services and was accepted. Taking Herbert the most difficult way over the mountains to Bwlch y Ddeufaen, Bleddyn killed the unsuspecting English prince on the banks of a stream and stole the golden torque in the name of love.

Can you imagine Llanfair all those years ago? Well, it was a very desolate and lonely place, with the coast covered in bogs, marshes and trees. There were only a few inhabitants, each owning a little cottage with an acre or two of land, scattered over the upper part of the village. They kept a couple of cows, sheep and a few chickens, but their main livestock were flocks of bearded goats which roamed and grazed on the mountain sides – far easier to look after than any other animal.

In preparation for a hard winter, the autumn was a busy time, with the collection of wood and peat for the fire. The winters in these mountains were known to be long, cold and hard. The smallholders would slaughter a few goats and hang the meat on a mantle within the chimney to smoke it. The crops they managed to grow were rather inferior; the flour they produced was kept in large wooden boxes in the kitchen. In days long past the Welsh hill farmers used to live in what were known as Long Houses. These homes were shared with their livestock, the family on one side and the animals on the other. We were a hardy people and very self sufficient, with all the little community looking after one another.

The daily diet of those farm folk of long ago was a breakfast of barley bread, *bara ceirch* – oatcakes and cheese. Dinner was at around noon *tatws llaeth* or fried / boiled mutton. They would have tea at around 4pm consisting of a little junket and ground-up oatcake. Supper would be at about 8pm and was *uwd* (porridge).

A meagre light glowed from the rush light during the long dark winter evenings as the family attended to various chores. The men would spend time mending or making their farm implements, the women would, of course, be busy with the weaving and all this whilst enjoying the odd sing song or two. Thus life went on in Llanfair for many hundreds of years.

Before 1774 the only way over Pen-y-clip, to the east of the village, was along a very steep and narrow path with loose scree and rocks, and a drop of about two hundred feet to the sea below. A very dangerous journey; none but the brave even attempted it. Accidents occurred there, with lots of people (and horses too) losing their footing and slipping to their deaths. It was also a bad place for ambushes; the track was known to be one of the most dangerous places in North Wales for travellers. When the tide was out the horses and carriages used to travel across the sands rather than face the dreaded track over the headland.

There was once a Llanfair man called Sion Humphries who was sweet on a girl called Ann Thomas from Creuddyn near Llandudno. They had arranged to meet on the day of the honey fair in Conwy, but as Sion set off over Pen-y-clip he lost his footing on the narrow path and fell onto the jagged rocks below, suffering some pretty bad injuries. Ann, in the meantime, was aboard a ferry on the River Conwy when all of a sudden a storm blew up and the boat capsized; everyone was drowned except for her. Both survived and they were later married; they lived in Llanfair for many years. Ann died on 11th April 1744 aged 116, according to parish records. Sion lived for five more years and he died on 10th December 1749. They are buried at St Mary's Church.

The set industry

In around 1770 the set industry took off in Llanfair and Penmaenmawr. The stone was to be had on the beach in those days and it was cut right there into dimensions of about 18 inches by 8 inches and were known as *cerrig palmant* – paving stones. The sets were carried in small boats to Liverpool, from where they were taken to line the streets of England's new industrial towns. Eventually the sets became scarce on our beaches and a cart had to be brought in to move the sets from further inland. A man from Gerlan was said to fetch and carry the sets on his cart which was on a sledge owing to the roads being so narrow, uneven and dangerous. Of course as ever in life when the authorities found the set business was money making they took over and in 1830 leased our foreshores to a gentleman called Philip Whiteway who in turn went into business with a friend called Dennis Brundit. They saw the potential opportunity for industry; the quarry was on its way, it was known as Penmaen Quarry and Dennis Brundit built the Penmaen Mill in 1893. History shows us that it became known as The Penmaenmawr and Welsh Granite Co Ltd.

Uncle Owen Jones (Bangor) with his bugle; used to warn the men when blasting was to take place. Working with sets c 1925.

Sets and hand-broken macadam were the only products of Penmaenmawr quarry when it first opened early in the 19th century and many a street in Lancashire was paved with cobbles from Penmaenmawr. The aggregate used for concrete from the quarry was considered to be of the highest quality and was used in the construction of many famous landmarks before World War Two, including the Mersey Tunnel, Wallasey Sea Wall, and the roads of East Lancashire, to name but a few.

Clearing the land

In the late nineteenth century the local inhabitants thought it was time to concentrate on clearing the land, so that they might get a better yield of crops. Planting seeds such as oats, barley and wheat in those days, of course, was nowhere near as easy as it is today. The massive job of clearing just one field with its tree roots, thick brushwood and rocks must have taken many weeks without too much in the way of tools. It was done mainly through brute force and determination plus of course the ever-faithful donkey or ox, if you could afford one! The smallholders helped each other. Instead of payment they would borrow an ox for a day maybe, or provide a few days' labour in return. The stones and rocks that were cleared were used to build some of the dry stone walls that we see today all around our mountainside. Some of the large stones dug up were incorporated in new buildings, hence the thickness of some of the farmhouse walls.

Tyddyn Llwyfan, Henar and Pen Penmaen were among the first of the smallholdings to start clearing the land. Once the Bulkeley and Coetmor families (big landlords in the area) heard that the poor farmers had started to make the land pay a little, what did they do? Yes! Up went the rents – talk about cashing in! According to Llanfair's records in the archives for 1880, the rent for a small farm was £10 per quarter, and rent for the ffrith (upland fields or pasture) was £2/10 shillings.

It is said that the first shops in Llanfair were at Llanerch y Meirch (opposite the golf club, above the industrial estate) and at Nant y Coed (on the way to Three Streams). These little country shops sold much more than food in the early to mid 19th century; they stocked everything from farming and garden implements to candles, cloth and shoes. Red sugar was sold for 4 pennies a lb (it looked rather like red sand); at that time tea was very expensive at around 8/- (forty pence) a lb, so people rarely bought more than a quarter to half an ounce at a time. I must be getting old; I have a faint recollection of Mam buying it loose in Shop Nells. Also in the mid 19th century, matchsticks were to be bought in the area for tuppence a box. About this time in Rhiwiau lived a farmer who was known to make rope from horse hair and would mend his own shoes with used horseshoes taken off his mare, such was the poverty of the time.

Girls yard at The Village School 1900. In those days the boys used to play in the yard behind the school. I myself remember the days when the boys and girls were separated.

Chapels and schools in Llanfair

In the late 1790's there was a small farmhouse called Y Castell situated close to where the vicarage is today. It would seem that Y Castell was used as a meeting house for the newly-formed Methodists in the village.

A chapel was built on the field in front of Bryn Golau in the late 1790's. This was called Capel Uchaf. The first baptism, other than at the church, was held there in 1804. Capel Uchaf was eventually converted into two dwellings and it has just been renovated – it's near the corner of the golf course in Gwyllt Road. Members of my Mother's family lived in Number 1 (see note 2).

A Calvinistic school was formed in about 1810 and is thought to have stood in Clwt y Groesffordd, Pentra Uchaf (the patch of grass across the road from Erw Feiriol cemetery). A new school was built in about 1832 and stood close to the where the Rectory is today, this school was used until the opening of the new National School in about 1847 (Ysgol Babanod).

The old school was knocked down in 1961. Em remembers well playing there as a boy "the old building was covered in ivy and completely over grown but it didn't stop us from climbing all over it" he says. Plas y Llan, a home for the elderly, was later built there and was officially opened on June 29th 1966 by Alderman Arthur Davies. At about the time the National School was opened (1847) and the Welsh Not was brought in to force. The children were not allowed to speak Welsh in school and if they were caught the punishment was to wear a square piece of wood hanging around their neck which was to be passed on to the next offender that was caught and when Friday came watch out! For then, the child with the dreaded plaque would be dealt with very severely. In 1871 a new Act was brought in by the Education Authority and extensions were added to the school so that the village could accommodate all the children who were of school age.

The cockle pickers

In the late eighteenth century there was a good trade in cockles in Llanfair. The inhabitants would take to the Lavan sands and work with the tide. Not one of the cockle gatherers would leave their home before the cock crowed, oh no! They

Welsh cockle girls 1908.

were not about to come face to face with the ghost waiting for them at *Giat Gwyn* - the white gate. A curse had been put on the cocklers many years back, and it could not be ignored even though by now nobody even remembered what the curse was all about. They would walk down from Pentre Uchaf past Tyddyn y Coed Farm, through Pen y Bryn park; on through the fields they would walk until they reached the White Gate, which was about three hundred yards west of Christ Church. All day they would work on the sands, breaking their backs. It was a long walk out to the cockle beds, and it was a great help if you could afford a donkey or an old horse to cart all those cockles back to the beach. The cocklers would make a fire there, on the beach, then boil the cockles in large pans, pickle them and take them to Parys Mountain in Amlwch - one of the largest copper deposits in Europe, mined by thousands of men. Of course, tons of cockle shells were left over, so what use could they be put to, you ask yourself. Well, I'll tell you. The villagers would go and collect heather from the mountains, dig trenches in the sand on the beach, fill the trenches with the heather, set it alight and throw the cockle shells on the fire. Once burned, the shells could be used as lime for building. Lime was a scarce commodity in this area.

In 1877 eight cockle pickers were caught by the tide and drowned on the sands near Bryn Cambwll (an area of sand between Llanfair and Aber).

To put a net out at Penmaen for a season of herring fishing in the late eighteenth century cost 2/6 (about twelve pence).

Glan y Mor Elias

Glan y Mor Elias was named after Elias Williams born in Llanllechid in 1790 and died in 1877. Elias brought the smallholding near the beach about one mile west of Llanfair. It consisted of two cottages, a farm builing, a couple of fields and they owned a cow and a few sheep. The stream that runs alongside the cottages was diverted to its present course by Col H. Platt to create a couple of small fishing ponds. A cockle bed, which was nearby, was Elias's main income and he ran a flourishing little business there. Times were hard and the women he employed there were glad of any extra income they could earn. Elias had a shed built so that the women could clean and cook the cockles. Of course it was good for the ladies to have somewhere to shelter in the sometimes very stormy weather. Mary Jones from Llanllechid was a widow and would walk six miles to work every day to supplement the two guineas a year pension she

Glan y Mor Elias 1895.

received when her husband John Jones was killed at the Penrhyn Slate Quarry. Elias Williams used to fill his boat with cockles and sail to local harbours and as far afield as Llynlleifiad – the old Welsh name for Liverpool. He did a roaring trade there and bought earthenware pots and other goods that were not available in Llanfair. Sometimes Elias would call at Flint on the way home for a load of coal.

It is said on one occasion Elias and Richard Roberts of *Tŷ Bach* only took five hours to sail from Liverpool to the nose of the Great Orme. There is also a tale about Elias having to fight off a press gang in Liverpool in his youth.

Elias's son Hugh helped him in the family business and on one occasion sailed to Liverpool with his cargo and while he was there he bought a face mask. Now Hugh was a bright spark and liked to play a trick or two on people. One dark night he had heard that an old gentleman – a neighbour was going to walk to Aber to pay his club. This man was a big strong chap but rather nervous. What Hugh did was to hide behind a wall and as the old gentleman passed, out jumped Hugh nearly giving him a heart attack. "You are an ugly devil" said the old man as he ran for his life. On arriving home he slammed the door so hard he took the frame and the door with him!

The entrance to Christ Church for the wedding of a member of the Platt family in 1898.

Now Hugh had a son who was also called Hugh; this Hugh was born in 1858 and died in 1898, aged only 40. He left a widow Dorothy and six children. Money was scarce and there were six little mouths to feed, the youngest was only 4 years old. After a while Dorothy could not maintain the cottages as her husband had done, the roof was leaking and other work needed doing but of course Dorothy had no means of getting it done. She was approached by Col H Platt owner of Bryn Y Neuadd Estate next door. The Platt's had a suggestion that would help Dorothy out. In exchange for the two fields he would build her two new houses. One house, he hoped, she would let to his estate worker called Mr Prichard of Bod Silyn. He wanted the fields for his wife's race horses who with her friends the Penrhyns liked to exercise them along the Lavan sands. The houses were completed and after a year Mrs Dorothy Williams received a rent demand for her house and that is how Glan y Mor Elias became part of Madryn Farm. In the 1950's Mrs Elizabeth Owen (Dorothy's daughter) was approached about the buying back of one of the houses for £500 which they proceeded to do. This little story was told to Em years ago by Dorothy's grandson Mr John Owen (deceased).

Sunday afternoon cockfights

At Glan y Mor Elias are two small cottages and originally they had thatched roofs, as did many in Llanfair at that period. The inhabitants would use straw or bracken; even reeds were used when the need arose. Slate was too expensive for poor families, I suppose. Close to the cottages there was a sand pit where the men would hold cock fights – a very popular pastime. The men would gather there on a Sunday afternoon. Having been to church in the morning, they would enjoy the afternoon chatting among themselves, trying to pick out the best bird and placing a penny or two on it, spending money which most of them could ill afford. It was church, cockfighting and the pub on Sunday, in that order. In 1881 "Dry Sunday" was made law and there were no taverns or pubs open in Wales on a Sunday.

Beer making

In the mid 19th century malt-making was widespread in this area. Richard Williams was one of the first in the region to brew beer (bragu). He started in Aber and then opened a brewery in Gwyllt; he used to sell his malt to people in Bangor, Llanrwst and further afield. There was a brewery in Nant y Felin I believe, owned by the same family. There was also a brewery in Pen Lan at around that time.

A tragedy happened in the Nant y Felin brewery in the mid 1800's. Mrs Louie Jones remembers her father telling her that a child had fallen into the vats and was drowned.

The old bragdu (brewery), third building up, with the white wall of the flood yard next to it. Mill Road, early 1900's.

Pen Penmaen Uchaf

I thought this was an interesting fact and so I am going to share it with you. High above the village stood Pen Penmaen Uchaf. John Jones and his wife Sian lived there in the late nineteenth century and ran *Y Dafarn* (the pub); this was on the old road leading past the quarry and over to Bwlch-y-Ddeufaen, Dwygyfylchi and Conwy, so business was quite brisk. Years later, when the pub had disappeared altogether, my mother's family lived in Penpenmaen, a house standing a little lower down the mountain. One of my ancestors, Maggie, lived in that house (see Note 3). She had a brother called Harry living in South Wales who had tuberculosis. The family had already lost two or three children to it. Maggie decided to bring her brother Harry to live with them in Penpenmaen. It was thought the mountain air was good for what ailed him. "It must have been quite a chancy thing to do with a house full of us kids there, but that's the way it was then. We all helped each other, regardless of the consequences," says Dilys Eames, Maggie's daughter, who still lives in the village with her husband David.

One night Maggie and one of her nearest neighbours were taking turns to look after Harry. It was as black as pitch outside. Maggie and her friend were sitting in the little kitchen, a small fire glowing in the dark room, with the only candle flickering on the mantelpiece. The house was as quiet as the grave, with everyone asleep except the two of them. All of a sudden they thought they heard someone walking about in the room above them, but they knew that no-one should have been there. The footsteps carried on for a couple of seconds, then one said to the other: *Dos di i fyny* – you go up. *Dim mymryn o beryg, awn ni efo'n gilydd* – not on your nellie, we'll both go up together, said the other one. Neither budged, though the noise had stopped by now. Eventually they both went upstairs, scared stiff, but realizing that they had to face whoever or whatever was there. Bravely they went, up those dark creaking stairs, on their tiptoes, and they crept quietly into the bedroom, one carrying the candle and the other the largest poker she could find. Who do you think was there? Nobody – but they found a large pile of candles on the floor. The candles had been kept in a box high up on a shelf; someone had forgotten to replace the lid on the box, and one by one the candles had slipped down onto the floor (there were no carpets in those days) – hence the flip-flop-flip sound of footsteps on the floor.

Station Road. The young man with the horse is John W. Owen (Sion Ox), 1906.

Candles and Llanfairfechan connects

On August 23rd 1857 at 3.30pm the first English service was held at St Mary's Parish Church. It is said that it was for the benefit of Mr Richard Luck who had settled in the village with his family. He was a wealthy solicitor from Leicestershire and had been bringing his family on holiday to Llanfair since 1852. My relatives were all at that first service, in support of the many English people who had settled in our little village. It was probably around that time that the wind of change arrived here.

It was the coming of the railway that started the influx of people. In 1848 the railway came to Llanfair, or at least it passed through to Aber, where the nearest station was. This was probably the biggest change ever to come to our little village. With it came better wages and better conditions for the people of the village, who at that time were dreadfully poor. Whole families lived on smallholdings, with perhaps as many as ten people living in tiny cottages and crofts, struggling to make a living off the land. The opening of our own railway station took another twelve years, but by 1860 Llanfair had a station of its own.

In 1875 the village had gas lamps to light up the streets. Henry Platt of Gorddinog owned the gasworks, situated at Madryn.

May Day 1909.

In 1886 a new reservoir above Camarnaint was opened at an estimated cost of £6,000. Hugh and Elizabeth's son Richard was a member of the Water Board that celebrated its opening at a banquet held at the Queens Hotel. Not everyone was connected to the supply; some of the locals still used the wells and river. In 1891 the Board of Health put their foot down and made some households connect up. Pool Street and Gerizim were mentioned. It seems that the Teiliwrs were quite a respected family in the village. Richard lived at Meirion House (Old Post Office) at the time of his death in 1903. He was buried with his parents and brother Mathias in St Mary's. I include more details about this side of my family in Note 5.

I talked to Mr Hugh Lloyd Jones, a member of the Hengae family and a councillor in the village for many years. He was also Mayor for a while. "It was in October 1927 that electricity finally came to Llanfair," said Mr Jones. He was an apprentice to Victor Hughes when they wired St Mary's Church in 1928 - 1929. He went into business on his own in the mid 1930's. Hugh tells me of the days his grandmother Catharine Williams used to go to the old Horeb Chapel in Pentra Uchaf. Every Sunday morning and evening she would walk from Hengae, down Terrace Walk, carrying her Bible. During the dark winter evenings the only light came from the moon, stars, and a candle glowing inside a jam jar she carried, hanging by a piece of string tied around it; this made an ideal handle. Hugh lived in

Nant y Pandy as a boy and it was a must to go to chapel twice on a Sunday and Sunday school in the afternoon. He recalls the children of Nant y Pandy one cold winter's night in a large procession being led by a new preacher. Their jam jars were glowing brightly, bobbing up and down, the kids enjoying the darkness. "It seemed to be a different kind of darkness in those days and the stars would be so much brighter as well," said Hugh. "I remember when I was a boy living in Nant y Pandy, most houses had a pig and a few chickens." His first big job was to wire the Nant y Berllan council houses in about 1938. "A feather in my cap," he tells me proudly. It was a real boost to him, since he was still in his early twenties. Before Hugh and Louie were married (it must have been around 1936) Louie remembers walking down in the dark from Gladys Cottage (where she worked) to the bus stop. "It was the 9.30pm bus I wanted to catch," she said. "The bus company at the time was Bangor Blue and I didn't need a ride on the bus - oh no! I wanted to post some letters; the bus used to have a letter box fixed onto the back of it!"

In 1923 one of the first radios was bought to the village, by a Mr Hugh Cecil Roberts of Camarnaint. Apparently Mr Roberts liked the latest in high tech gizmos.

The danger of the sea

We were at the house of Hugh and Louie, showing them some old photos (Em is a keen collector of old photos of Llanfair), and would you believe that Hugh spotted a photo of his brother Idris who died in 1929 aged 20 - a photo he had never seen. Idris worked at the smithy (still there today) which was just across the road from where Eddie his best friend worked as a baker in The Mill Stores. The boys worked in stifling heat all day, so one day after work they decided to go to the beach for a swim. Eddie jumped in and got into difficulties - it is thought he had cramp. Idris jumped in to help him. Both young men were drowned. When they were found they still had their arms wrapped around each other. Working in the hot bakery all day at Mill Stores and then going swimming in the cold sea was blamed for giving Eddie cramp. So tragic, the loss of two young men in their prime.

Over the years a lot of people have drowned on the beach here. When I was a child a family from Valley Road went out on a boat trip around Puffin Island. They got into difficulties and all four of them - mother, father and two children were drowned. Llanfair was a much smaller village then and tragedies like that seemed to touch us all. I suppose it is one of the penalties we pay for living on the coast.

It isn't possible for me to write merely about my family long ago – there's always something happening which I want to tell you about. It's 11.30pm on April 1st, 2003. The war in Iraq is getting worse; women and children are getting killed there. Young men are losing their lives; fighting for who knows what. I hope, that somehow, it's all going to be worth it. It seems to me that there should be other ways in which so-called civilized people sort out their differences.

Bryn y Neuadd

Bryn y Neuadd has played an important role in the history of Llanfairfechan and I will briefly mention it here. A house was built on Bryn y Neuadd estate in about 1667, it was later demolished and a mansion was built in 1862 by Mr Henry Platt, a prosperous businessman from Oldham in Lancashire who bought the 130-acre estate. When a number of smallholdings on the estate were demolished, some of the smallholders took their families to America in the hope of finding a better life. However the arrival of the Platts in Llanfair also brought some much-needed work to the community.

In 1898 St Andrews Hospital, Northampton, bought Bryn y Neuadd estate to provide care for people called "lunatics and idiots." What horrible words.

Bryn y Neuadd.

Embo, Lorraine, Karen and Beaver (1970), working in Bryn y Neuadd sub-contracting for Pochins.

In 1967 the mansion itself was demolished and the site was used to construct a long stay hospital (at a cost of two and a half million pounds) to provide a service for 520 "mentally handicapped" patients from all parts of North and Mid-Wales. The hospital was opened in 1971; and is still home to many people.

Llanfairfechan grows

In 1801, the population of Llanfair was 470. During the next fifty years the population almost doubled. In 1851 there was a total of 809 people living in Llanfair; the number of dwellings was 182. It was, I imagine, rather upsetting to have to fill in the census forms in those days, as most of the people could not read or write. Their homes were small cottages and farms scattered around Pentre Uchaf (near St Mary's church, Pen y Bryn), Nant y Felin and close to the beach. The only substantial house in the village was the vicarage.

According to Mr Lloyd Hughes my family was one of the three biggest families in the parish in the mid 1800's. It is not surprising that so many of us are related here. Although the family surname is Roberts, we are all known as the teiliwrs because my forbears were tailors.

A place of myths and legends and stories from Dad

Our mountains are full of old stories. Dad used to tell me that long, long ago two giants came from far away across the sea. The giants were looking for a new land to make a home in. When they arrived at our mountains they felt the serenity and saw the beauty of the place, and immediately fell in love with it. They cut two large rocks out of the mountains and stood them on their heads as markers, for fear that they would not be able to find the same spot again. Away they went to search further afield, in case the grass was greener elsewhere. "Alas," said Dad, "they were never to return. Perhaps they found their new home further away. I don't think they would have found anywhere nicer than this, do you girls?" Val and I would love listening to that story every time he took us up to Bwlch y Ddeufaen. That was his explanation for Bwlch y Ddeufaen – the pass of the two stones. I'm sure there's a more sensible reason for the naming of Bwlch y Ddeufaen. I know which I would like to think is correct! These tales, of course, were enchanting for us when we were kids.

Another legend I remember was about a family living close to Tan Graig. They were only poor farmers, struggling to make a living from the land. The lady of the house had a recurring dream; she dreamt that she was out walking in the mountains and found a pot of gold. Her dream was so real that she decided to go to the exact spot she had dreamt about. Taking her shovel with her early one morning, she crept out of the house before anyone could ask her where she was going. Having walked for a few miles she came upon the spot she'd dreamt about. She was sure she would find something there and started digging. Deeper and deeper she went, but she found nothing. She was getting tired and almost gave up, thinking that her dream had been just like any other dream. But she decided to dig for just a few more minutes before giving up and going home with nothing to show for her morning's work. At last the shovel hit something hard! Her heart beating fast, she started to claw at the earth with her hands. There was a large stone buried in the ground. Her excitement was mounting; she couldn't move that stone quick enough. When she did it was with great delight that she saw a metal box and guess what was in it? Yes, it was full of gold.

Dad loved stories and he was a great one for family lore. Once upon a time, many years ago, in the olden days, said my Dad to Val and I when we were girls, one of our very old Neiniaid (grandmothers) went over to the fair in Llanrwst with her son. It was indeed a long trek over the mountains, up past Bwlch y Ddeufaen, down to the Conwy Valley and on to Llanrwst – a six-hour walk at least. She left her youngest child at home as it was the middle of winter and the mountains were bleak, barren and far too cold for a child. They had a good day at the fair, meeting their family and friends, having a chat, selling their home-made produce to people who were just as poor as them, probably enjoying a glass or two of beer. But there was a long walk back over treacherous mountains ahead of them. Tyrd mam bach said her son, *rhaid i ni fynd* – come on, we must go. Their friends and family tried to persuade them to stay overnight. "No, I must get home to my family," said the mother. Half way home it started snowing. You must remember that it was pitch dark and the narrow tracks were soon covered by snow. Once past Bwlch y Ddeufaen, she was getting slower and slower. Her son said: "I am going to carry you Mam bach," and he lifted her gently onto his shoulders. They would, of course, have been speaking Welsh. On they went, through the driving snow, the cruel winds cutting through their inadequate clothing. They'd gone too far to turn back; the only way they could go was forward. Later on, noticing that his mam had gone very quiet, her son said: *Mam, wyt ti'n iawn?* Mother, are you all right? No answer. He laid his mam down gently on the cold white snow – she was dead. Her last journey over her beloved mountains was over. With tears in his eyes and a sad, heavy heart, her son picked her up and carried her home.

My Dad said to me many times: "Remember, when you grow up and have little children of your own you must tell them all these stories, so that they all remember the old Nains and Taids of long ago." Some of these tales I am writing about have been handed down over the generations, some I have read about, and some I have picked up along life's pathway.

Our village has indeed grown in size since I was a girl, with the building of new roads enabling people to commute – and making it easier for them to settle in our little corner of the world. No more can you wander down our streets and know everyone as Uncle and Auntie. Far away, locked in our memories, is the close-knit family community of long ago. What does that matter? The people of Llanfair are friendly, welcoming and helpful, and I like to think that our inviting little village is as lovely as it ever was.

Wil Williams (centre), and his mates working on the Pen-y-Clip project in 1933. The tunnel was opened in 1935 after taking 5 years to complete at the cost of £250,000.

The new Pen-y-Clip project nearing completion in 1993 at an approximate cost of £51,000,000.

Part 2

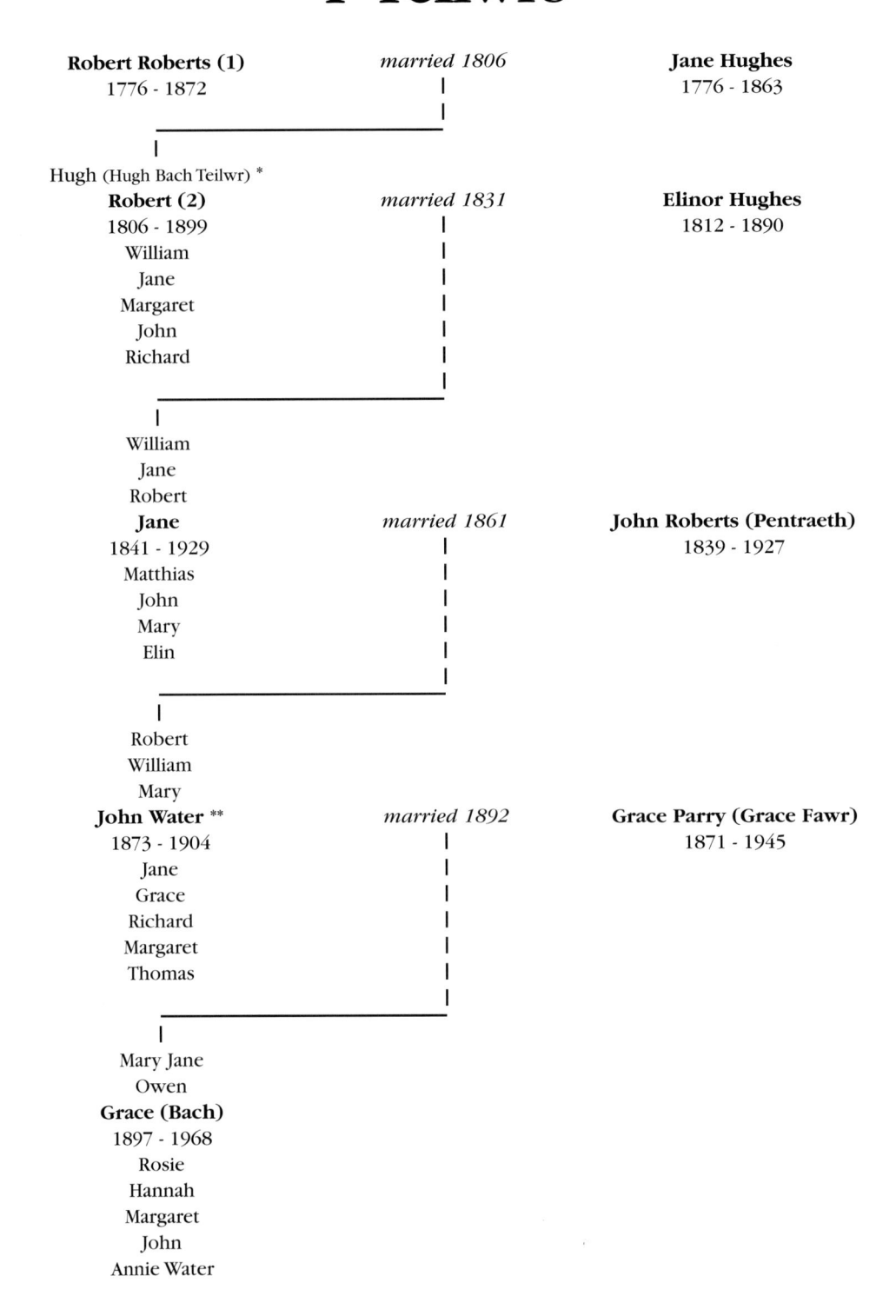

Y Teliwrs

Robert Roberts (1) *married 1806* **Jane Hughes**
1776 - 1872   1776 - 1863

Hugh (Hugh Bach Teilwr) *
Robert (2) *married 1831* **Elinor Hughes**
1806 - 1899   1812 - 1890
William
Jane
Margaret
John
Richard

William
Jane
Robert
Jane *married 1861* **John Roberts (Pentraeth)**
1841 - 1929   1839 - 1927
Matthias
John
Mary
Elin

Robert
William
Mary
John Water * *married 1892* **Grace Parry (Grace Fawr)**
1873 - 1904   1871 - 1945
Jane
Grace
Richard
Margaret
Thomas

Mary Jane
Owen
Grace (Bach)
1897 - 1968
Rosie
Hannah
Margaret
John
Annie Water

Y Teliwrs

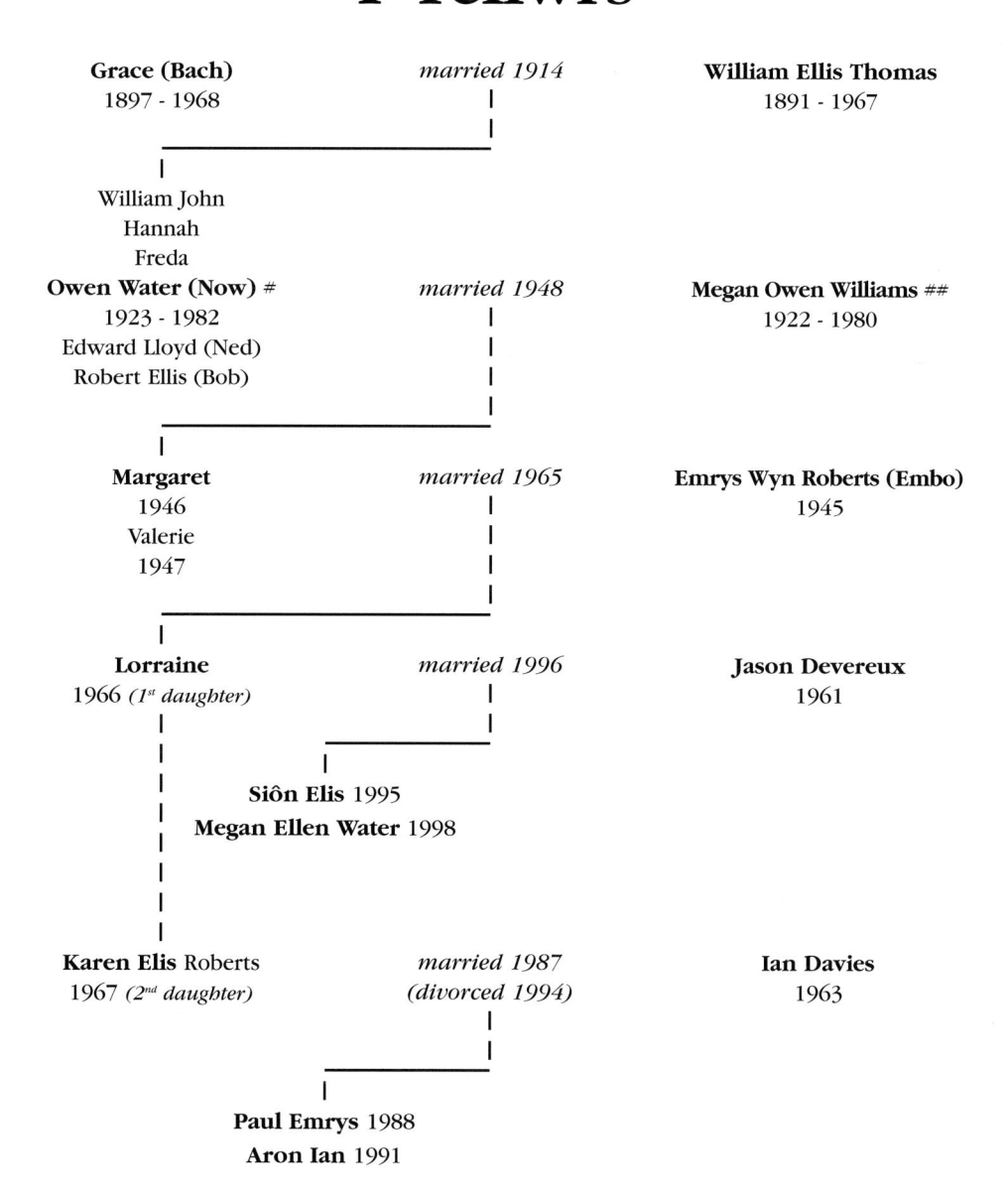

Grace (Bach)   *married 1914*   **William Ellis Thomas**
1897 - 1968   1891 - 1967

William John
Hannah
Freda
Owen Water (Now) #   *married 1948*   **Megan Owen Williams** ##
1923 - 1982   1922 - 1980
Edward Lloyd (Ned)
Robert Ellis (Bob)

Margaret   *married 1965*   **Emrys Wyn Roberts (Embo)**
1946   1945
Valerie
1947

Lorraine   *married 1996*   **Jason Devereux**
1966 *(1st daughter)*   1961

                     Siôn Elis 1995
                     Megan Ellen Water 1998

Karen Elis Roberts   *married 1987*   **Ian Davies**
1967 *(2nd daughter)*   *(divorced 1994)*   1963

                     Paul Emrys 1988
                     Aron Ian 1991

---

*   Hugh was the founder of the family tailoring business.
**   John Water died aged 30. Grace Fawr remarried and had a further 5 children.
\#   Owen Water had previously been married in Vancouver.
\#\#   Megan had previously been married in Llanfairfechan.

Here begins the story of my father's family:
Y TEILIWRS

Now this may get a bit complicated but bear with me and hopefully all will be clear in the end:

Robert Roberts (1)

My great-great-great-great-grandfather Robert Roberts (1) (1776 - 1872) lived in Pen y Comins, a croft in the grounds of the present day Bryn y Neuadd.

At that time, of course, there were no roads, only little tracks leading from one small cottage to the other. Recently, when I was picking blackberries along the Cob, I couldn't help but wonder how many of my ancestors had passed that way over the years.

In 1749 the estimated population of Llanfair was 480. In the census of 1841, Robert Roberts (see Note 4) was an agricultural laborer aged 55, living in Comins Isa with his wife Jane, aged 55, and their children Margaret, aged 20; John, a quarryman aged 20, and Richard, a stone cutter aged 15.

Robert Roberts' wife Jane would go collecting firewood along the beach and carry it in bundles on her back. What a hard life people must have had! Carrying her sticks on her back, her basket on her arm, sometimes with berries in it, she would stop at Wern Bach to buy some of the butter that Mrs Morris was so good at making. Mrs Morris – a relative of my family – was married to John, a constable, though he was not a policeman in the modern sense.

Hugh Roberts – the first of the family tailors

Hugh and Elizabeth, my great-great-great-great Uncle and Aunt (see Note 5), were married in 1806. Hugh was the one who established the family's tailoring business in the village. At one time there were at least six or seven members of the family working in the business. It must have been a busy little village as there were also at least a couple of other tailors here at that time. In days gone by some tailors lived a little like nomads, not having a home to call their own. They would wander around from farm to farm, making clothing for everyone who lived there. When they were done they moved on to pastures new, looking for another farm which would be their base for a short time. The clothing was mostly made of rough wool spun by the farmers' wives themselves. Hugh and Elizabeth lived in Bryn Meirion - also known as Erw Fair and Erw Feirion - for most of their married lives. It was, in those days, a smallholding. Eight of their ten children were born in Erw Fair, which has been there since the days of Cromwell (early 1600's).

I have been told that when Cromwell's army were making their way over our mountains, three of his soldiers killed an elderly man at Erw Fair, then robbed him and ran off. The man's sons gave chase, caught them at Aber and killed all three of them. This is a story, not a historical fact but there is some evidence that Cromwell's army did march through Bwylch y Ddeufaun down to Llanfair and damaged the Parish Church about that time.

Hugh had a *cwpwrdd* (cupboard) made for him in 1855 at a cost of £3/8/2, also a new lid for a cauldron at a cost of four old pennies. You would pay five pennies for new soles on a pair of clogs and two shillings for a new wooden door; in 1832 the cost of an adult's coffin was 15/- (75p) and a child's was 7/6.

In 1857, after living there for over thirty-five years, Erw Fair was conveyed to Hugh Roberts for the grand sum of £160 from the Bulkeley family of Baron Hill, Beaumaris. Erw Fair at that time was part of the Plas Estate. The surviving Roberts children - Richard, William and Elizabeth, all unmarried, continued living with their parents, running the tailoring business. In 1869 Hugh their father died, leaving a will in which he left everything to his "beloved wife Elizabeth." The effects were under £200. Elizabeth died in 1873. In 1878, the children sold Erw Fair to the Llanfair Burial Board for £800. The field was to be used as a cemetery, known today as Erw Feiriol.

The words on Hugh and his family's grave are really touching. It seems that this verse was written after a son, Mathias, died in 1864 aged 29 years. I wonder who wrote it. Was it one of the family, or a friend?

Ffarwel fy Nhad rwy wedi'm rhoddi

Mewn tywyll wely yn y pridd

Ffarwel fy Mam, paham yr wyli?

Caf ddod i fyny'n iach ryw ddydd

Ffarwel fy mrodyr, a'm chwiorydd

Myfi sy'n ddedwydd iawn fy lle,

Draw mewn canu mawl i'r Iesu

Byth yn nghwmni teulu'r ne.

(Farewell my father, I have been put in a dark bed in the soil. Farewell my mother, why do you cry? I will return healthy one day. Farewell my brothers and my sisters. I am blissful where I am, singing and worshipping Jesus, forever in the company of heaven's family). They were obviously very religious.

Uncle John Roberts and the corner shop

My great-great-great Uncle John Roberts (1820 - 1879) married Elin Hughes, whose mother kept a shop at the top of Cae Ffynnon Road, near West Coast Antiques. After his mother-in-law's- death John built onto the shop and ran it with his wife. It was known as 'top shop' or 'Corner Shop' as it was up at the Groesffordd, Pentre Uchaf. John was a bit of a handyman. He called himself a "shop-keeper" in the 1851 census.

A little tale about John now. There was a man who had complained to the powers that be that the rector and his family did not keep Sunday as they should. Of course, in those days the Sabbath was strictly a day of rest and worship. However, milk was brought from Bryn y Neuadd every Sunday for the rector's children and that was just not the done thing! The one who complained was John Roberts. So to solve matters the rector, Philip Constable Ellis, bought some cows and hired a man as his gardener/cowman and his wife as a dairy maid. They served him for many years.

John died in November 1879 aged 55 and is buried on his own in St Mary's. We found his grave – the gravestone, covered in ivy, must be over 10 feet tall. We tidied it up a bit. Ken Roberts, Licensee of the Pen y Bryn Hotel, bought St Mary's Church in 2003. He has repaired all the stone walls around the churchyard. We bumped into Ken and had a long chat with him. We showed him the family graves and he asked me to write a story about my ancestors which could be featured in an exhibition at the church. It seems that Ken wants to make the church into a heritage centre for the village.

Robert Roberts – another one

My great-great-great-grandfather Robert Roberts (1806 - 1899) spent most of his life in Ty Coch y Comins in Nant y Felin. To avoid confusion I will refer to him as Robert (2). Robert married Ellin Hughes on October 28th 1831. On the parish register of marriages they both signed their names with an X. One of the witnesses to this marriage was Hugh Roberts, probably Robert 2's brother. The other was Mary Hughes, Ellin's sister perhaps.

Robert (2) was a tailor by trade, apparently a very good tailor and a very capable basket and rope-maker. He used to make hooks out of thorns and prickles for catching fish. As well as making them for his own use he made a fair living out of hooks – a proper little cottage industry. Robert (2) and Ellin were to have 10 children (see Note 6). In the census of 1841 they lived in Bryn Rhedyn with their children William, Robert and Jane. To make ends meet and despite the cramped conditions in these small houses/cottages lodgers were taken in and lodging with them was John Hughes, an agricultural labourer.

They were later to move to Ty Gwyn where Ellin was known by many to keep all sorts of herbs and potions to help with ailments. There was no doctor or pharmacy in those days. The first chemist's shop in the village was opened at Bron yr Allt by a Mr R B Roberts in 1863. As I write this, in October 2004, our chemist's shop opposite Ysgol Babanod is to close and move to Plas Menai, the new Health Centre. A good idea I suppose, but what a shame – another shop has gone from the centre of Llanfair.

Ellin (teiliwr) as she was known was the salt of the earth and a typical Welsh plain Jane. She and her faithful old donkey used to go gathering cockles on the Lavan sands. Fishing for herring with hooks made by her husband Robert was another of her many activities. She would return from the shore with reed baskets (made by her husband) hanging on each side of the animal, filled with the fruits of her labour. She took her produce many miles away if need be. She would set out very early in the morning to make the long journey over the mountains – up past the quarry (it was quite a busy road in those days), sometimes leading the old donkey and sometimes managing to get on him to give her legs a short break from the climb up. Quite often her sister Mary would accompany her, over Bwlch y Ddeufaen to Llanrwst and further afield. In all weathers they would go to sell their cockles and herrings. The villagers who were in the fishing trade would inevitably get into debt in the summer months and pay it all back during the winter when the herrings were more plentiful. There was a great abundance of herrings on our shores in those days. After a day's walk over the mountains, then selling their produce, never mind the picking and catching the previous day, they must have been exhausted. Sometimes it would be as late as nine pm when they crossed the river by barge at Tal y Cafn with another three or four hour walk back to Llanfair over those cold wet mountains. Their wage for the day was £1 between them. I suppose they were lucky they could afford donkeys – what a hard life, toiling from morning till night just to keep your family fed and clothed, and not much else.

On one of those occasions, after her day was done and the donkey was loaded with all sorts of treasures which she had bought or swapped, including metal cups, measuring jugs, and pots and pans all hanging loosely from the weary old animal, Ellin was challenged to a race by Mr Hughes from The Bull Inn at Llanbedr y Cenin. "I will pay you one shilling if you beat me, you on your donkey and me on my horse. I will even give you a head start," he said. "*Iawn Mr Hughes*," said Ellin as she jumped on the donkey, shouting and screaming for the animal to get going, holding on for dear life. The old donkey seemed to know that this was important to his mistress and was off like wildfire, the pots and pans all making a terrible din. She had gone but a few yards when Mr Hughes's horse took fright with all the noise and bolted the opposite way. Consequently he lost the race and Ellin was delighted with her day's work. She had won not just a shilling, but a good meal at Y Bedol as well.

Another little story tells how a father and son went from Llanfair, up past Bwlch y Ddeufaen to Llanrwst to the fair to do their trading. Having finished for the day and with his wages tucked in his pocket, the son went to buy himself a *teisen ceiniog* – a penny cake – to eat on the way home. His father was very cross with him for wasting a penny. Before too long they reached the pastureland near Bwlch y Ddeufaen and decided to have a drink of water and a rest. The son pulled out his cake and started eating it; smacking his lips together he said *mae hwn yn dda dad* – this is good Dad!

Beth am ddarn i minnau? – what about a piece for me, asked his father. The son's reply was *dos i fwyta dy geiniog dad* – go and eat your penny, my father!

There was a massive cottage industry right across Wales around that time, knitting woollen gloves and stockings, weaving baskets and making clogs, to name but a few trades. The clogs were made from the alder tree – a soft wood that was ideal for the job and grew in abundance in the boggy areas of Llanfair. In parts of Wales the clogs were cut up into square blocks of wood and then transported to England to be finished. Some of the English were so poor they couldn't afford a proper pair of shoes, said a Welsh woman in 1853. Was it surprising that people worked from dawn till dusk?

Christmas wasn't too far off when Robert (2) got a job at Tyddyn y Coed farm, behind where the old Horeb chapel stood in Pentre Uchaf. Like many people then, the old tailor had to subsidize his tailoring with anything that came along. *Chwipio'r gath* was the job; the direct translation is whipping the cat, which was the term they used in those days for beating the barley, corn, or wheat by hand with a flail. It was hard, strenuous work. For this, Robert was paid sixpence ($2^1/_2$p) a day. The old farmer asked: "Well, Robert bach, have you got your goose sorted for Christmas?"

"Not yet, I suppose I should order two," said Robert. The cost of two geese was five shillings (25p); but of course, Robert was guaranteed ten days work to pay for them.

Robert was a great prankster and loved playing tricks on people. He was known as the 'old tailor' in the village, hence the nickname Teiliwrs or Tailors in the family. It was a name that was to follow us down the generations to this day – the old families in the village still remember the name. There are still an awful lot of us around!

Sometimes though, his pranks went wrong as on this occasion. Ellin and her sister were rather late getting back from Llanrwst one time, and Robert the old tailor was getting quite concerned. He went as far as Bwlch y Ddeufaen to meet them, a walk of about three miles. The sun had just gone down over Anglesey. It was that time between day and night when everywhere you look seems to be in shadow and behind every shadow is something to scare you. Nonetheless, Ellin and her sister had decided to leave the narrow little track in search of the mounds of peat they had spotted, drying out, earlier in the day. Peat was wet when first dug up in small squares and had to be left in piles to dry out on the mountainside; it was then taken by sledges pulled by donkeys to be sold in Bangor and further afield. Wheels weren't used on the mountainside; it was far too boggy.

The old donkey already tired and weary from the long walk and the heavy supplies he was carrying was about to be burdened with yet more supplies. Whilst they were helping themselves to some of the peat (not theirs I might add) they saw a tall, dark figure in the distance - keeping low to the ground, dodging in and out of the gorse bushes and bracken, and making some very eerie noises. Worse than that, it was making its way towards them. *Tyrd Mary fach, rhed am dy fywyd* - run for your life, yelled Ellin. Whoever or whatever it was, they didn't wait to find out, for it frightened the living daylights out of them. Off they went like bats out of hell. Down the mountain they ran, stumbling and screaming; never mind their acquisitions or the poor old donkey, it could find its own way home! The old tailor shouted after them, pleading with them to stop, but they didn't hear him - his voice was carried away on the wind. The exhausted women didn't stop till they reached home.

Ellin was one of the last women in this area to keep leeches. She would travel over the hills and across all kinds of rough ground on her own until she reached Anglesey on the back of her faithful old donkey in order to find them. The way she collected them was rather disgusting. Oh dear me, the thought of it! Ellin would walk into a dark murky pool in her bare feet. She would wait for the leeches to latch on to her feet and legs and when she felt she had enough leeches stuck to her, out she came; she put them in bottles and brought them home. Ellin would make a small charge for treating locals with the leeches. She also used the leeches to treat blood poisoning. Not so silly when you think that they sometimes use leeches in medicine today. It seems that the old ways were not always so daft.

People in those days were poor and found many a way to use the local resources to earn money. The heather which grew in abundance on the mountain would be collected to pack slates from the quarries. The villagers would load their donkeys with as much heather as they could carry and travel to Port Penrhyn near Bangor. There the slates from Bethesda quarry would be packed with the heather and loaded on to the waiting ships. Between Llanfair and the port there was also a toll gate called Tan y Lon. If there was no money to pay the toll, the poor inhabitants would have to walk up the old highway, which was up through Cremlyn and Llanllechid, to get to the port, a detour of about three or four miles - a long journey for six pennies (2$^{1}/_{2}$p) per sack.

About that time, a local man called John Griffith did a lot of collecting and decided perhaps he would get a little more for his efforts in Conwy. Now John, having no donkey, carried as much as he could on his back (remember, this was a round trip of about sixteen miles). Arriving at Conwy, his payment was eight pennies. To buy one pound of butter and a candle would cost you about six pence then. Would we work as hard for such little pay?

Late in the nineteenth century a local woman called Mari Jones would earn 6 pennies for collecting bracken and laying it on the church floor; such were the floors of the time.

As I return to my family I have a very sad tale to tell you. In 1850 Robert (2) and Ellin lived at Ty Gwyn in Nant y Felin with their five children they had lost two of their children previously. On January 8th 1850 Robert (2) and Ellin buried three more of their children on the same day: Robert (3) aged 12; Mathias aged 6, and little John aged 3. They all died of scarlet fever. The fever was the cause of so many deaths in those days, especially in children. How terrible, to have lived in fear of losing your children, to have nursed them through fevers and rashes, and after all that, to lose three of them together, and have to bury them on the same day. You cannot imagine; can you, the terrible hardships they went through, and the grief they must have felt. I feel that I know the people I am writing about and indeed share a little sadness at the death of three little boys all those years ago.

The villagers had to carry water from the river for all their uses, and of course the river was where all the waste and raw sewage was dumped. I'm sure the water was the cause of a lot of their health problems.

Five years later, in 1855, Robert and Ellin were to bury another son Robert (4) aged 1. In 1858 they buried their daughter Ellin aged 6. Five of their children were buried in the same grave. God only knows how people got over tragedies like that.

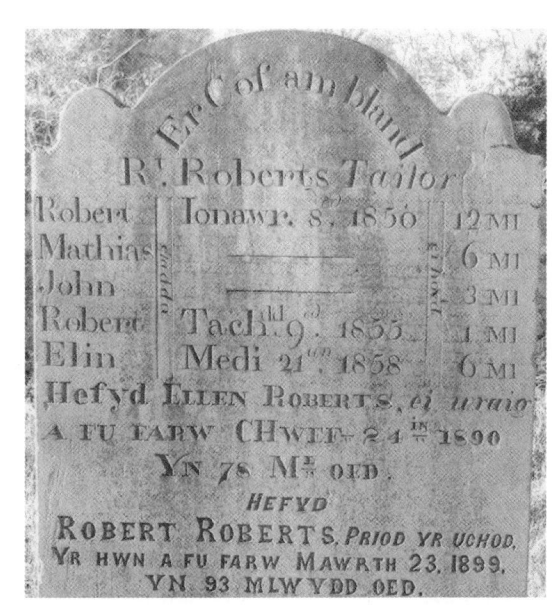

The grave of Robert and Elin (Tailor) and their 5 children in St. Mary's.

The census of 1851 shows us that Robert and Ellin lived in the village with their children. In 1861 they lived in Nant y Felin with their two daughters, Jane (my-great-great-grandmother) and Mary. Also living with them were three boarders and a servant whose occupation was described as a tailor. How in the world did they all sleep in one small cottage?

In the census of 1871 there were 11-12 tailors living in the parish and at least 4 of them were from the Roberts family.

The census of 1871 shows that my great-great-grandmother Jane, her husband John and four of their children lived in Ty Gwyn, Nant y Felin, with her parents, Robert and Ellin. Times were hard and John was out of work. There was no unemployment money then, so it was up to the whole family to pull together. The Welsh, I suppose, as in many cultures, have lived for many centuries in clans and tribes and perhaps that makes us what we are today, very clingy towards each other. I feel that we are a people who think almost as much of the dead as we do of the living, and we are at our best when we can be of help to other people. Words my Dad used to say to us come to mind: "It is better to give than to receive."

By 1881 Robert (2) and Ellin lived on their own in Ty Gwyn. On 4th February 1890 Ellin died aged 78.

In the census of 1891, Robert, aged 85, an unemployed tailor, still lived in Ty Gwyn. Living with him was his nephew Thomas Roberts aged 9 (see note 7). On March 23rd 1899 Robert (2) the old tailor died at the grand old age of 93. He and his wife Ellin are buried with five of their children in St Mary's.

A death in those days affected the whole community, as everyone was related to one other. I think we Welsh are a morbid lot. About two hundred years ago, on the night before a funeral a *gwylnos* or a wake was held; you would see a white cloth draped over the coffin of an unmarried person and black over a married person. On the coffin stood three burning candles. Family, friends and neighbours would gather together in the home of the deceased. Inevitably a jug of ale and pipes would come out, and in a mist of smoke they ate heartily; their reason for being there was to comfort the close family. There was no harm in eating and drinking while they did so, was there? So the wake started early.

Next day, before the funeral procession started, a female member of the family put some bread, cheese and often a few coins in a dish on the coffin and invited the poor and beggars of the neighbourhood to eat from the dish. This was supposed to help the deceased on to the next world, with a last good deed. The mourners, of which there were many, all carried some rosemary which they threw into the grave. It was traditional for members of the family to carry the coffin; this showed the highest respect for the deceased. We in Wales are blessed with lots of rain, and for rain to fall during the funeral procession was considered lucky – it was the dew of heaven. It was felt to be really important in those days for us Welsh to be buried close to our relatives in our own village. "The Welshman clings to these family graves as to his ancestral cottage," said Julius Rodenberg in 1858. Julius wrote a charming book about this area. I can understand the Welsh family bond, as I myself have left instructions that I want to be buried not only with my husband but also with my parents.

John and Jane Roberts and their family

For information on Jane Roberts (1841 - 1929) and John Roberts (1839 - 1927) (see Note 8). John and Jane Roberts (teiliwr), my great-great-grandparents, married on November 16th 1861 at Bangor Registry Office. At the time of their marriage Jane lived at Ty Gwyn, Nant y Felin, with her parents. John lived at Tan y Graig,

John and Jane Roberts, taken at Erw Feiriol Cottage, 1920's.

Pentraeth, and was a farm labourer. It is probable that John came to Llanfair looking for work in the quarry, at that time the main employer in the area. He met Jane (teiliwr) and settled here. There were nine children in all.

My great-great-Auntie Jane Davies (1875 - 1957) was born in Nant y Felin. She was the only one of Jane and John's children that I remember. As far as I know, she lived all her life there – she died in 1957 at the grand age of 82. Auntie Jane was a general servant before she married William from Bethesda. Jane and William had ten children, four of whom died at an early age. I remember her living in Tan y Ffordd in Nant y Felin. That would have been in the early 1950's when we lived in Tan y Bonc. By this time Auntie Jane was a widow and lived on her own. I did not know at the time how we were related.

I remember well, we used to walk home through Nant y Felin, especially in the winter, because there seemed to be more shelter from the wind and rain than in Valley Road (happy days!). There were no cars in those days to run us about, at least not for us ordinary people! In the summer months, Auntie Jane would be sitting on her chair outside on a very narrow pavement. She would always have on a clean apron with a few sweets in her pocket for us kids on the way home from school. A cup of tea was offered to Mam and Dad. Auntie Jane was a bit of a character. She knew everyone, and indeed all the village gossip. She was a kindly soul and would help anyone, I'm told. Iorwerth Benjamin told us a little story about Auntie Jane. She had been chatting to his wife Aisne (who was Auntie Jane's niece) one day in the village and excitedly told Aisne that she had bought a new Hoover. Vacuum cleaners must have been quite new and a luxury in those days. *Rhaid I mi frysio I wneud y whorio* – I must hurry away to do some whoring, she said, getting her words mixed up (she wasn't a great one for speaking English). Mr Benjamin chuckled to himself as he told us about it.

My great-great-Uncle Robert Roberts, born in 1864, lived in 14 Mona Terrace. Robert (5) lost his first wife and then married again. He had one of the allotments along the Cob. He used to have a cart on two wheels which he used to push to the plot and he would come home loaded with all kinds of vegetables that were in season. We have found out today what we suspected – that Robert was Will Deido's father. "Will Deido was the living image of his father," said my Uncle Elfed. When Robert's second wife died he went to live in Stoke on Trent with her family and died there shortly after. I remember Will Deido as being a small man who wore a flat cap and always smoked a pipe. Will Deido was Peris, Ian and Delyth's grandfather.

My great-great-Uncle William Roberts (1867 - 1939) married Elizabeth Ellen and lived at Llwyn Celyn, Nant y Felin. They had six children (see Note 9). William went to America as a young man, working his way around. Their son William (1893 - 1946) also went to America when he was a young man. William and Elizabeth's youngest daughter was Kitty; she went on to run The Skerries pub in Bangor. We met Bill Skerries (Kitty's son) and his wife Ann recently. "He's a Tailor through and through," said Ann laughingly. "He really enjoys his pint!" Bill is a builder and he built his own house in Bangor; he is retired now. Bill told me a little tale that his Uncle Dai told him. "It has been handed down from father to son over centuries and that we must never forget we were related to *Cochion Pen Mynydd* – the Tudors, said Uncle Dai. Penmynydd is a little village in Anglesey associated with Henry the Seventh. Uncle Dai was a Sergeant Major in the Army.

My great-great-Auntie Margaret Evans (1886 - 1946), or Maggie as she was known, lived in Pentre Ucha. I am told that she was a great one for playing pranks, like her grandfather before her. There was a prank she would play on anyone and everyone she could catch out. She had made up a dummy and dressed it in men's clothing. The toilet was at the bottom of the garden. It was a cold and wet wintry evening when Owen Evans and Glyn Gamin were doing a job for her at home in Pentre

John Water's brother William, third from left. The tailor family married into the Quinn's who were licensees at Llanfair Arms, 1922.

Uchaf. Now Owen needed the toilet and made his way home, telling Glyn he wouldn't be long. He was back in no time and got cracking on the job in hand, trying to get it finished before it got too late. Unfortunately, Owen needed to use the toilet yet again. *Dos I'n ty bach ni* – use our toilet, said Maggie, but not before she'd been there first. On the toilet she had sat the dreaded dummy, with his trousers round his feet. Poor Owen, rushing down the garden path in darkness, saw that the toilet door was ajar and pushed it open further. To his shock he saw that the toilet was already in use – there was a strange-looking man sitting on it. "Oh dear me sir, I'm so sorry," he said, backing out of the toilet. Running back up the path, he could see Maggie standing at the back door. "There's a strange man in the *lle chwech*," he told a delighted Maggie. Of course, by this time she couldn't hold back her laughter. Once again her prank had fooled someone. Owen Evans was not impressed.

On occasion the kids of the area used to play among the gravestones in the cemetery, messing around and making hoo-ha. In those days there was a path leading to the cemetery past the side of Maggie's house (Erw Feirion), so the kids disturbed her sometimes. Maggie would gain revenge by putting a sheet over her head and creeping around the gravestones, scaring the living daylights out of the kids; then peace would reign for a while again.

Maggie was left to bring up her children on her own, and she would take in washing to help feed her kids; her ginger beer was much sought after – on Sunday mornings she would do a roaring trade, selling it to the locals. I knew her daughter, Megan Dunkley (Megan Teiliwr). I worked with Auntie Megan in a sewing factory in Llanfair. Pauline, one of Auntie Megan's daughters, lived until recently in The Old Post Office, also known as Meirion House. It was the home of the Teiliwr family in 1873 and for years after. Like her mother before her, Pauline was always game for a laugh. Sadly, she died in July 2005. She was only 58 years old and had not been well for a long time. Auntie Maggie is buried in Erw Feiriol with her parents John and Jane (Teiliwr) and her son Peter (1914-1988).

My great-great-Uncle Richard Roberts (1882 - 1951), known as Dick Teiliwr, married Jane and had a daughter they called Aisne, after a river in France where he served in the First World War. He was said to do a bit of boxing in the Army. He liked a pint and was always quite jolly after it – he was also true to the family tradition of enjoying a good scrap now and then. Dick was known to be generous to a fault. Most of the Tailors were known to be kind-hearted people. Dick lived in Pen Lan until Aisne was eleven years old, and then moved down to Bryn Meirion in the late 1920's, possibly to look after Dick's mother and father John and Jane.

Dick had a dog called Toto, according to Auntie Catharine of Tan Rallt Isaf. The local kids were always on the mountain or the ffrith playing, but if it was wet they were kept indoors. The only way out would be to beg their mothers to allow them to go for a walk with Dick and his beloved dog Toto.

Uncle Elfed remembers walking down Pen y Bryn hill one Saturday afternoon and Dick was having a real good time fighting with one of the other locals each one trying to throw the other over the wall. Dick and his wife ended their days in Bryn Meirion (old name Erw Fair or Erw Feirion) and are buried in Erw Feiriol Cemetery.

Mr Iorwerth Benjamin, Aisne's second husband, told us that he and Aisne had bought Bryn Meirion from the council in the 1970's for £800, the same sum as it had been sold for in 1878. Can you believe that! He sold it in the 1990's for £43,000. It had been lived in by the family for over 150 years. Mr Benjamin said he didn't do any DIY on it. All he did was paint it and keep it looking nice, he told us proudly. Em and I were in Mr and Mrs Hugh Lloyd Jones's house recently when they had a phone call telling them that Mr Benjamin had died. He was 92. I had said to Em just a few days earlier that we would have to go and see Mr Benjamin. A lesson in that, as my dear Mam used to say: Never leave until tomorrow what you can do today.

My great-grandfather John Water Roberts

My great-grandfather John Water Roberts (1873 - 1904) was born in Nant y Felin. He was the fourth child in the family. When I was girl, my Dad (Now) used to tell me a story about his 'Taid' John Water, born in a flood. I suppose it was just a tale Dad used to tell us. Between my Dad's memories and some research I have come up with this little story about Llanfair and the flood.

When John was born in April 1873 there was a great flood in Llanfair. At that time Robert, William, Mary and their new baby brother, John Water, lived with their parents in Nant y Felin. John had been christened on April 17th that same year, and just a few days later, on April 23rd, after hours of heavy rain and hail in the hills over Bwlch y Ddeufaen, a torrent of water flowed down the mountainside, destroying everything in its path. As the water surged through Terrace Walk a bridge was completely washed away. There was much damage at Cae Carw and

Nant y Felin, where the great flood of 1873 occured.

Pen Lan. Massive boulders rolled like chippings, such was the force of the water. Great big trees which had taken hundreds of years to reach maturity were ripped up like matchsticks – and still the rain fell. Much damage was done in Nant Pandy, the upper part of Valley Road, and in that general area. Down through Nant y Felin the torrent carried everything it could away with it. Houses disappeared under the water as if by magic; furniture bobbed past the amazed, frightened inhabitants.

John, at the time, was in his cradle (a drawer from the dresser) on the floor. The water started rising very quickly. His mother Jane, who was in a panic, had to lift the cradle onto the top of the dresser while she gathered the other terrified children together as fast as the flood water would allow her, pushing them in front of her onto the roof. With the help of friends and neighbours they were able to get to safety up the hill to Terrace Walk. Further down the road, near where the smithy is today, there were five little cottages. Two of the families who lived there had emigrated just a fortnight before the flood. The only things that were left in the old cottages were a couple of old iron beds. It seems that the flood water was still hungry and had swept them and the old dwellings away. There was also a malt house swept away. Damage went into the many hundreds of pounds. In those far off days there was a floodgate – above the top end of Pool Street – between Nant y Felin Bridge and Bont Goch Bridge. Bont Goch was also known as Methodists' Bridge. These floodgates were to turn the water from the river to work the mill farther down. On the left of this spot there used to be a lodging house for rovers called Fflodiart that was swept away. Britannia House was totally demolished. Bryn y Neuadd estate suffered the loss of many young trees, and the chicken runs were carried away with the loss of many chickens.

The water could be seen pouring down the hills towards the village, following its own course; even the station yard and offices were under water. "So bad was the flood," said Mr Morgan the station master, "that we had to stop the trains for a while."

The railway line was under torrents of water and the bridge across the line was swept away. The only safe place was in the signal box. Trains were stopped until the lines were deemed safe. It is said that many families were left homeless that day, including baby John and his family. I wonder who took them all in. Rowen in the Conwy Valley also suffered greatly from the flood. If a large part of the flood water had not flowed towards Rowen and Llanbedr, Llanfair might have disappeared under the water completely. There were no lives lost that day (so it is said) but a great deal of hardship was caused.

The day after, many people came from neighbouring villages to see the desolation caused by the flood. From that day onwards, John was known as John Water. Indeed it has been a family name ever since – my own Dad was called Owen Water. Why ever I didn't give one of my daughters the name I don't know! As far as I know there are only two people left in the village with the name Water: Shane Water Jones and Megan Ellen Water Devereux.

The old folk of the village said that Llanfair was cursed owing to the wrongdoing of an old lady and blamed the terrible disaster on her. This little lady owned a donkey and made her living by charging the tourists for donkey rides on the sands. Sometimes she would use the donkey for carrying gorse or heather in the ffriths. This particular Sunday her donkey had given birth. She had drowned the baby donkey immediately it was born. It was said that the old lady didn't want her donkey to rear the foal. It was the job of the donkey to get on with earning a living for her mistress, and not to spend time rearing her young!

Some help came from Lord Penrhyn, a local landowner, who was in London at the time, saw a paragraph in one of the papers about the flood and quickly made arrangements for £50 to be sent to help the poor people who had suffered in the flood. His gift was one of many – other people sent gifts of money and clothing.

As I wrote about the flood of 1873, we had a night of heavy rain in November 2002 that caused another flood which came from beyond Tyddyn Angharad, carrying the bridge nearby away. The waters, grey and murky, came rushing down past Ysgol Nant, all the way down Valley Road and Nant y Felin, carrying all kinds of debris with it, turning the roads into rivers. It was; of course, nowhere near as bad as 1873. I spoke to one of the ladies who live in Valley Road and she said that the water had got into her house and ruined most of her carpets. Some of the houses further down suffered rather more damage. There is now a new bridge near Tyddyn Angharad.

My great-grandmother Grace (Fawr) Owens-Roberts-Parry (1871 - 1945)

Grace was a member of the Cockles family; I will refer to her as Grace Fawr. She was born in Gwyllt. In the census of 1881 she lived with her parents Owen and Mary Parry (nee Hughes) in Pen y Fordd, Llanfair. Owen was born in 1842 in Anglesey and Mary in 1843 in Aber. Owen and Mary were married in about 1862. Owen worked as an agricultural labourer. Grace Fawr was the fifth child of nine. She worked as a housemaid in Priory House on the Promenade. In 1891 it was a lodging house run by a Margaret Thomas. By what I've been told about Grace Fawr I gather she was a hard worker and somewhat larger than life. She was, I believe, a very formidable lady who liked her own way.

My great-grandfather John Water Roberts (Teiliwr) married Grace Fawr in about 1892 when he was only 17 or 18 (see Note 10). This was a marriage between two very

Grace Fawr

large families in Llanfair – the Tailors (Roberts) and the Cockles (Parry) families. The newlyweds lived in Tudor Terrace in Nant y Felin where four of their eight children were born. They lived in 16 Gerizim Terrace in 1901 with their five children. John Water was a Stone Quarry Miner. The wages for quarrymen in the early part of the 20th century were about £1 a week, working 10-12 hours a day, six days a week. The men didn't have lorries to take them up in those days. It was about a mile and a half of steep walking from their little cottages, in all sorts of weather, and even a longer one back, I'm sure. It's a good job we don't know what's around the next corner, isn't it. Poor John only had three years left to live.

When the police station (completed in 1902) was being built, John Water worked as a labourer there. It was a good gang and as well as working hard they had a bit of fun. One day the men decided to have a bet. *Pwy fydd y cyntaf I gael ei gloi I fyny* – who'll be the first one to be locked up? - asked John. True to form, it was John Water himself! One Saturday night John and a friend drank a bit too much and had a squabble; the next thing they knew they were both locked up for the night. After a few pints he really enjoyed a good scrap, so what's new! John Water also worked on the construction of the bridge just past Ysgol Nant. John Water died when he was a young man of 30. He was in the hospital very ill when he decided he wanted to die at home. He hadn't been home for Christmas that year, hadn't seen his little children open what meagre presents they had. It was freezing hard outside but John had decided that, by hook or by crook, he was going home. He dearly wanted to be at home to bring in the New Year, probably the last he would see. He arose from his hospital bed in Bangor, dressed in only the scantiest of clothing, and went out to face the cruel weather. He walked part of the way and managed to hitch a ride on a cart the rest of the way. "He was a very determined man," said my Auntie Freda. A couple of hours later, and in a state of near collapse, he reached his parents' house at Erw Feirion. *Diolch I Dduw am ddod adref* – thank God, he was home at last. A saying my maternal Nain used to say comes to mind. *At pwy af ond at Mam* – whom will I go to, if not my Mother?

John was ill for quite a while and his good friend, Huwcyn Lewis from Tyddyn Weun, would take turns with the family to sit with him. He died on February 18th 1904. His death certificate cites valvulas disease of the heart, and hepatic congestion. Auntie Freda tells me it was a heart attack. At that time Erw Feirion was a small, one-storey cottage. Present at his death was his father John (my great-great-grandfather), who also registered his death.

Auntie Rossie remembered being called home from school that cold day in February because her father had taken a turn for the worse. She and her brother and sisters ran all the way home, with no time to even button up their coats, and gathered around their father's bedside. "The curtains were drawn across the small window and the bedroom was very dark, with only an oil lamp on a small table in the corner of the room; it really scared us kids," said Auntie Rossie. Grace Fawr sat on the edge of his bed; the little children went to their mother's side and stood rooted to the spot until their Nain, Jane, took them out crying, not really understanding what was going on. Grace Fawr was with child at the time. The baby, born a few months later, was named Annie Ellen Water. How sad – and him such a young man. He was never to see his children grow up, and indeed, he never even saw one of them. What a shame, to leave all those little children fatherless. We must not forget Grace Fawr, left on her own, pregnant with six young children to provide for. We can only imagine what hard times lay ahead of them all. I remember Dad taking me to Erw Feiriol cemetery when I was a young girl, to show me his grandfather's grave. His words were: "Margiad, I want you to know where my Taid (John Water) was buried, because as the years go by there will be no-one left who knows." There is a small slate marking the grave with the letters J.W.R on it (see note 11). I took our daughters to see it many years ago.

Huwcyn Lewis – a good friend of the family

I am going to tell you a little about Huwcyn Lewis – John Water's best friend. I know he was not family, but he was a very good friend, according to his daughter Morfudd. She was related to me through marriage and I have known her most of my life. I used to visit Morfudd at Plas y Llan. She was indeed a character. Sadly, she died just before Christmas 2003 aged 96. She was one of nine sisters who lived in Tyddyn Weun with their father Huwcyn Lewis and mother Isobella in the early 1900's. Tyddyn Weun was a smallholding up behind Garreg Fawr, one of the furthest dwellings in the community. Huw used to come down to the village with a donkey and load it up with all sorts of provisions. He would hang a sack each side of the poor donkey and make his way home in all sorts of weathers, up past Hengae or Bryn Golau or sometimes up past Tanrallt he would go. On weekdays, Huw would do his chores on the smallholding before starting on his long trek across the mountain to do a day's work at the quarry, then walk all the way

Huw, Isobella and their nine daughters.

back to do some more chores; at the end of a long day he would fall into bed only to be woken up before dawn next day by his wife. *Newydd fynd i gysgu rydwi, Bella Bach* - I've only just gone to sleep, he would say. Morfudd and her sisters had their own chores to do before school: feeding the chickens, collecting eggs, fetching some wood or peat in for the fire and so on. All this was before 8am. How hard times were then. *Wnaeth o ddim drwg i ni* - it did us no harm, said Morfudd.

Huw and the family were all hay-making one year, hoping to get all the hay in before it rained. All the girls were helping, singing along as they worked. Suddenly Morfudd gave a scream. She had stuck the fork right through her foot. Isobella her mother ran to get something to wrap it in and Huw took the fork out of the screaming girl's foot. His daughter was crying hysterically, with blood running everywhere. Her sisters were upset and thought she had cut her foot off. He wrapped the wound up in an old sheet and ran with her in his arms, all the way to the doctor's surgery in the village miles below. What a long way to carry someone!

Huw, Isobella and two daughters in Tyddyn Weun c. 1910.

Another little story about Huw. When Isabella was expecting one of the babies Huw laughingly told the midwife that if this one was a girl he would drown her at birth. The time came for the birth. With great excitement and anticipation Huw and the family waited eagerly. After many hours of labour, at last they heard the familiar sound of a new baby's scream. Out of the bedroom came the midwife with the new baby in her arms. *Dos i nol llond bwced o ddwr Huw* - fetch a bucket of water, she said. "What for," asked Huw. *Hogan eto yr hen Huw* - another girl, she said, laughing at him. He couldn't believe what he was hearing - whoever heard of anyone having nine daughters!

Morfudd was left handed, says her daughter Heulwen; when she was a girl she was forced to use her right hand. Children in those days were just not allowed to be left handed.

One story that stuck in Morfudd's mind in particular was the one about her and her sisters getting stuck in the snow. Morfudd, who had far better Welsh than I, had to stop and explain what some of the word meant, telling me with a smile that I ought to be ashamed of myself, not knowing what they meant! Anyway, she told me the story - in Welsh I might add, since we never spoke anything else to each other. One cold winter's day, early in the First World-War, the older girls were in school. The snow started to fall thick and fast. Their teacher, knowing how far they had to walk, thought it best to send them home early. Up they went, through Pentre Ucha and past Llanerch y Meirch, turning left just before Llys y Gwynt, the snow blinding them; they were freezing cold, holding tightly to each other's hands, the little ones crying. The blizzard was getting worse and the little girls were really terrified by this time. As they opened the mountain gate leading to the old golf links, what did they see? A message written in the snow: Huwcyn was here. Their dad had only just passed that way. The girls started shouting and screaming at the top of their voices, and despite the howl of the wind in the trees, Huw heard his daughters and turned back. How relieved they were to see him. Morfudd remembered her father getting them all to hold hands and make a chain, with a warning not to let each other go lest they be lost for ever. Off they went on the rest of their journey home, behind Garreg Fawr; finally, in the distance, they saw a candle shining through the blizzard. *Adre o'r diwedd, diolch i Dduw* said Huwcyn - home at last, thank God. They lived there until the early 1920's. Tyddyn Weun was used as target practice in the Second World War. All that's left now is the two stone garden gateposts and a pile of stones; little enough to show that lively, happy families had lived there once.

I have a few tales to tell about my great-grandmother, Grace Fawr

When all her children were young, Grace Fawr used to go cockle-picking – not only to feed her family, but also as a way of making some money to help them live. There was a good cockle bed on the Lavan sands; however, conditions were treacherous so a lot of care had to be taken in case you were caught by the turn of the tide. Grace used to leave the house, walk all the way to the beach, and then across the sands. Remember, there were no lamp posts in those days; the only light was from the moon and the stars. In 1876 a lamplighter was employed for one shilling (5p) a night to turn all the gas lights out by 11pm. It would all sound quite romantic if it wasn't for the fact that she had to stoop for hours picking the cockles and then carry them all the way back home to Nant y Felin. She had to get home in time for the children's breakfast and to send the older ones off to school. The children used to have a bowl of boiling water ready, but not as you might think for the cockles Oh no! It was for their Mam to soak her aching feet, the minute she got in.

As I write this in February 2004, 19 people have been drowned picking cockles in Morecombe. There were over 30 cockel pickers trapped by the tide in Morecombe Bay more than 20 were drowned in the freezing cold waters. The bay is well known for its quick rising tide and treacherous quick sand. It would seem that most of the pickers were young Chinese people who were possibly working here illigaly. What a terrible tragedy: so many lives lost.

Here is a story from Robin Parry, a window cleaner for many years in Llanfair; retired now (also a relative). He remembers a tale about two young men going cockling on the sands. It was a bright sunny day when they started off, quite early in order not to be caught out by the tide. Anyway, they had nearly come to the end of the day; they had filled their buckets and it was time to go home, when all of a sudden a mist came down and caught them unawares. They couldn't see their noses in front of them and were walking around in circles. They started to panic, thinking that this was the end. All of a sudden they heard a sound in the distance – the church bells at Abergwyngregin, a noise they could follow! What a welcome sound: it was as if the bells came from heaven to guide them home, they said. Had it not been for the bells that misty afternoon, long ago, the sea would have claimed two more lives.

I myself picked cockles many times as a child with my Dad and my sister Val. I hate cockles, although I used to love collecting them. Val didn't enjoy it at all. I couldn't wait to see the little holes in the sand, through which cockles breathe, and then dig like mad with my spoon to try and find a cockle and shout triumphantly: "Look Dad, I've got another one!" Happy, happy days. There's a tear in my eye just thinking about it all. Of course, when it was cold and wet, which it quite often was, I used to hate it. Dad would carry the cockles home in sacks which used to be soaking wet, the water dripping down his neck and back, soaking him to the skin. We lived in Tan y Bonc at that time and it was a long way home. When we got back we all mucked in to boil the cockles in a galvanized bucket that was already black from the coal fire. The flames in the black lead range were jumping, the sparks flying everywhere as Mam or Dad put the bucket on the fire. Mam would spend hours cleaning that old grate. You could see your face in it. I used to love watching the shells open slowly and the little cockles peep out as the heat got to them. Now for the job of shelling them – I didn't like that at all, they were so slimy! My dear Mother washed them in the sink over and over again to make sure there was no sand left in them. We would then put them in clean jam jars and add the vinegar, which Mam would buy from Shop Nell's. The cockles were ready for their final journey. It was Val and me who sold them around our neighbours; people couldn't get enough of them. Looking back, I can't help but think how really cruel we were, boiling those cockles alive in our living room.

I will return to Grace Fawr. I'm told she was the first to open a chippy in the village, in the same place as Glyn's chippy (Tan y Fynwent) is today. It was built in 1850 and was the first Post Office in the village. In the late 1800's the outbuildings were used by the council for their meetings.

Grace Bach used to help her mother serve in the shop. Grace Bach must have been about fourteen at the time, so it would have been about 1911. Grace Bach was a kind-hearted soul and of course it was inevitable that she gave more chips away than she sold. The customers would bring in bowls and ask for a few coppers worth of chips. Nain being Nain, she would fill the bowls to the brim, never mind that Grace Fawr, her mother, needed to make a living. It was one of the reasons why Grace Fawr had to shut the shop. I suppose Grace Fawr was renting the premises, so whether or not they carried on living there after the shop closed I don't know.

Grace Fawr liked a glass of beer and used to go to the Virginia Inn; she also liked to go to the little side door of the Llanfair Arms (facing the chippy), where you could buy your beer to take home, or if you preferred you could have a drink there to save you going into the pub – a sort of off-licence. I remember, in the early 1960's, having to go there quite often for a couple of bottles of mild beer for my Dad. I would go with two empty lemonade bottles and Dick Sansom (the licensee) would fill them straight from the pump; I was about 16-17 at the time. I hated going there, but we all have to do things we don't like sometimes, don't we. Eirlys (one of her grand-daughters) was telling me that everyone in the family was a little afraid of Grace Fawr. She used to stand by the garden gate at 7 Nant y Berllan and watch out for anyone in the family: the unlucky one who was caught had to go to the Llanfair Arms to get her some beer. No-one dared to say no to her!

Grace Fawr and Charles Henry Owen

Sometime after John Water died; Grace Fawr remarried Charles Henry Owens and lived in Bryn (a row of four houses facing the river at the bottom of Bryn Road). Charles was a painter and he fell off a ladder whilst working on the Llanfairfechan Hotel; he never worked after that. Auntie Freda recalled visiting Grace Fawr (her grandmother) as a girl. "There was always something nice to eat in Nain's," she said. Grace Fawr and Charles had five children together: a son born in 1913 (who died in infancy) was followed by Lea, Robin, George and Tommy. Grace Fawr had 14 children in total. Charles died in 1939 aged 69. Grace Fawr moved from Bryn to 7 Nant y Berllan when the estate was built in 1939 and lived there until she died on January 10th 1945 aged 73. Her son Robin and his wife Louie lived there after they were married. Blodwen, one of her grandchildren, remembers the funeral well. She recalls sitting in the car outside Grace Fawr's house, ready for the funeral procession. Blod was breaking her heart, the church bells were ringing loudly and someone told her not to be so silly, saying that we all have to die sometime – a comment that was meant to cheer her up but only made her cry harder. It was such a big family that the church was packed that day. Grace Fawr was buried in Erw Feiriol cemetery with her second husband Charles and their baby son. Also buried there are her daughter Mary Jane and her husband Robin (Llys).

Great aunties and uncles galore –
the children of Grace Fawr and John Water

Great-Auntie Mary Jane Williams nee Roberts (1894 - 1951), the eldest daughter of John Water and Grace Fawr, worked at Camarnaint farm as a girl; I don't remember much about Mary Jane (see Note 12). She married Robert Williams, known as Robin Llys. I remember my Dad telling me that when he was a young man, Mary Jane – who was a very generous lady – often gave him the price of a pint, followed by a strict warning to behave himself. It seems to me that Dad went through his life receiving warnings that he ignored! Auntie Mary Jane was in a wheelchair for the last few years of her life; she died aged 57. Her husband Robert (Robin) died in 1962 aged 70. They're buried in Erw Feoriol. The family name Water was passed on to Mary Jane's great-grandson Shane.

Speaking to Eric Lewis, Mary Jane and Robin's son-in-law recently, he told me that he, Robin Llys and Jim Bryn used to go to watch every home game that Bangor City played. "We were football mad," he said. "Robin lived with Vera and I for a few years after Mary Jane died, and in all the years we knew each other he never interfered between Vera and me. I don't remember us ever having had a cross word," Eric said. He went on to tell me a few stories from his childhood.

His mother Maggie Lewis (Madryn) was in charge of the margarine factory at Aber. The factory also made butter, said Eric, and any waste was turned into soap. On one occasion she had to reprimand one of the workers and received a load of verbal abuse in reply. Maggie wasn't happy but couldn't do anything

Margarine factory at Aber in the early 1900's.

about it in the workplace. The end of the day came and Maggie waited for the woman; making sure there were no witnesses, "my mother gave her a good hiding," said Eric, laughing as he told me the story. Owen Lewis (his Taid), who lived in one of the Madryn Cottages (a row of 4 or 5 houses near Madryn demolished for the new road), was head horseman for Major Platt, who owned both Madryn and Gorddinog. Among Owen's duties was the job of delivering an occasional cartload of turnips from Madryn farm to Gorddinog; practically everything they needed was grown on the farm. He would take the long way round so that he could drop off a few turnips for the poor folk of Tan y Clogwyn and various other homes on his way. "By the time he reached his destination there was not much more than half a load to drop off. He was taking a big risk; had he been caught it would have been the end of his working life with Major Platt," said Eric.

Eric himself worked in Madryn Gasworks as a young lad and recalls the hard job of filling the hungry furnace with coal and later with coke. "The boiler was very long and to reach the back we would have to shove the coal in. What a hell of a job it was. We would get into terrible trouble if the coal wasn't pushed far enough. Occasionally, when it overheated, we would have to throw buckets of water in to cool it down. You couldn't begin to imagine the smoke, the water spray, and the coke particles which the furnace spat at you from within; what a hell of a place to work."

Eric used to go the village shopping with his Nain Ellen Lewis and the last stop before getting the bus home was Mrs Williams's shop on Bont Castell – Castle Bridge. There would be a sweet for Eric and some chewing tobacco for his Nain. "She used to chew as good as any man," said Eric proudly. The baccy was kept in an open jar on the shelf and was sold by the ounce. On this occasion Eric and his Nain went back home to Madryn Cottages with their shopping; and having stored the food it was time for Ellen to have a chew of her baccy. Spitting it out of her mouth, she said *Dos a hwn yn ol i'r siop a dywed wrth y ddynes yno i roi bacco fres i chdi* – go back and tell that woman I want my baccy fresh, she said, reaching for a penny-ha'penny, his return fare to the village. "I will change it for you," grumbled the shopkeeper as she went to the back of the shop to get a fresh jar. "I didn't know it was dry!" As well as keeping a sweet shop and tobacconists, Mrs Williams was some sort of agent for a parcel delivery firm: if you wanted a parcel delivered to Bangor or Penmaenmawr, or even further afield, you would take it to Mrs Williams and for a small charge she would send it on by bus.

"There was no water inside my Nain's house at Madryn," said Eric, "it was my job to fetch and carry it from the stream, *Ffynnon Wen* – the white well, about fifty yards along the main road towards Aber. On Saturday nights I would have to carry enough water to last until Monday morning as we were not allowed to do anything that resembled work on the Sabbath. The water was kept in a huge earthenware urn in the kitchen, covered with a slate to keep it clean and cool. On the side of the fire there was a massive cast iron kettle, it was always topped up with water and placed close enough to the fire to make sure there was always enough warm water for household needs."

Richard Thomas from Madryn Farm and Will Owen from Henfaes Farm, as well as the milkman from College Farm, all used to deliver milk to Aber and Llanfair when Eric was a boy. Early every morning, with their horses and milk carts, come rain, hail or shine, they would be out and about on their rounds. On the carts there would be large old urns with a tap. The milkman would measure and pour a pint or a half pint into the waiting jugs; occasionally people could only afford a quarter pint.

Great Uncle Owen Roberts (born 1895) was the only son of John Water and Grace Fawr. I know very little about him. He worked for the coastguard service for many years in Holyhead. I met him only once or twice. Uncle Owen lived in Penmaenmawr after his retirement. He married and had one daughter. They are both dead now; I do not know where they are buried.

I will tell you about my paternal grandmother Grace Thomas nee Roberts (1897 - 1968) later in the story.

Great Auntie Rossie Jones nee Roberts (1898-1983). She was named after the rose because there was one rose still blooming in the garden of the family home in Nant y Felin on the day Auntie Rossie was born. I remember her very well. She was a busy lady and loved to go from house to house having a jangle. When we lived at Britannia House, around 1960, Auntie Rossie was in our house all the time. She would be there when I got up for work at 7.30am and had my breakfast (a plateful of thinly sliced bread and butter dunked in my tea!) and she would be there when I went home for lunch at 12.15pm; of course, she would have gone home in between to do all her work. Sometimes she would be there at 5pm, after I'd finished work. I must tell you that she never came empty-handed, bringing 5 Woodbines perhaps (at that time both Mam and Dad smoked) or a quarter of tea, a loaf of bread, and very often a couple of shillings for Mam. She would lend Dad a couple of bob, after first checking that it was OK with Mam. Auntie Rossie was very well liked and respected in the village.

Blodwen, Auntie Rossie's daughter, told me that when her mother was a girl she used to walk to Aber every morning to work in the margarine factory and after a hard day's work she would have to walk the three miles home. One day after work, when it was getting dark, she was walking home and she felt there was someone following her. Auntie Rossie said she ran all the way home with her heart in her mouth. Whether or not she had imagined someone was after her, it scared her so much that many, many years later she still remembered the terrible fear that overcame her that night. Auntie Rossie married Evan from Bethesda. They had two sons and two daughters. Stanley, one of the sons, met with a fatal accident when he was 40 years old. He was doing some work on West Coast Knitting in August 1962 when he fell through an asbestos roof. I don't think Auntie Rossie ever got over it. Annie went to live away. Blod still lives in Nant y Berllan with her brother Cyril.

Great Auntie Hannah White nee Roberts (born 1900) ran a second hand shop in 5 Buckley Terrace in Mill Road in the 1920's. It was a busy street in those days, with shops selling all sorts of goods. Auntie Hannah emigrated to Australia with her husband and daughter Rose, taking her half brother Charles with them. Rose has been over here a couple of times over the years. Em and I went over there in 1990 and had a great holiday. We met Rose's children Stewart and Joyce and had a love-

Buckley Terrace, early 1920's.

ly welcome wherever we went. We also visited my cousin John and his family and had a weekend with Noel – a friend of ours, with whom we went to Pant y Rhedyn School – and his family.

Great Auntie Margaret Griffiths nee Roberts (1902 - 1982), known as Auntie Maggie, married Ted and had nine children. Uncle Ted, a rather quiet man as I remember, was a gardener at Bryn y Neuadd for many years. They lived in Pen y Bryn when I was a girl. I especially remember one of their sons, Hayden, who was in our house quite a lot when we were growing up. He used to work with my Dad occasionally; we always had a laugh with him. He was a friendly bloke and liked a pint. Uncle Gwyn (Mam's brother) remembers Hayden from school, saying he was handy with his fists. Hayden would knock lumps out of anyone picking on him, said Gwyn. Sadly, Hayden died a young man, aged 39.

Two of Auntie Maggie's boys emigrated to Australia and both died there: Danny aged only 24 and Teddy aged 47. Three of the brothers all died before reaching fifty – so, so sad. They are buried with their parents in Erw Feiriol cemetery. My Dad and I went a few times to visit Auntie Maggie at Plas y Llan; she was a cheerful lady. One of her daughters, Auntie Nancy, lived in Llanfair all her life I believe. Auntie Nancy was a character, always full of fun. My Dad and Auntie Nancy had many arguments but always remained friends. When my Mother died Auntie Nancy came to Mam's house with a bunch of daffodils. After speaking to Dad she came to me and said: "How are you del? Put these daffs in the house." I was very touched.

My great-uncle John Roberts (1903) died when he was just a few weeks old.

Great Auntie Annie Water Owen nee Roberts (1904 - 1980) was the baby John Water never saw. She married Gwilym, whom we knew as Uncle Cwil – a quiet, friendly, pleasant man who worked in the quarry for a time and then as a general handyman at St. Winifred's School for Girls in the village. Its founder was Miss Eleanor Douglas Pennant. The school, which opened its doors with one pupil in May 1887, began in three houses in Garth, Bangor. The fees for girls at St. Winifred's School in Bangor in 1904 were £35 per year with a special £5 reduction for the Welsh and Irish. Doing their bit for the First World War effort, the girls used to collect foxgloves in and around the woods of Bangor and Penrhyn; the seeds and dried leaves were used to make the drug digitalis. The school moved lock stock and barrel to a building which stood in the general area of Parc Henblas, Llanfairfechan, in 1922 (one of the entrances can be detected in the wall opposite the Village Inn); in its heyday it had over a hundred pupils. Judith Chalmers is among the ex-pupils. Hockey was a favourite game and occasionally they would organize a game between the Celts and the Saxons – the Welsh and Irish against the English (all very friendly). The school chapel was a very beautiful building which was scandalously destroyed when the estate was built: what a shame all those beautiful buildings were knocked down, and we call it progress! The school even had its own little hospital which was referred to as the sanatorium. Dr and Mrs Thomas Bellis made a gift of the drugs and medicines to start it off. St. Winifred's was a good employer for the people of Llanfair for four decades. The pupils used to wear a green uniform with a green beret perched on their heads, and our name for the girls when we were kids was Green Cabbages. Kids can be so cruel, can't they!

St. Winifred's closed its doors for the last time in Llanfair, after over 40 years, in July 1968, for financial reasons. The 15-acre site was sold in lots, by auction, at St. Winifred's School on July 26th 1968. Here I am, nearly forty years later, living on what was part of St. Winifred's School.

Auntie Annie had two children, a boy who died in 1933 aged 18 months, and a daughter, Venice, who lives in Stratford upon Avon. Auntie Annie used to own two of the cottages in Tan y Bonc, numbers 2 and 5. Her husband Gwilym Gerfor Owen bought the two in 1948 from Richard Semple Williams. They paid £60 for each cottage. She also lived in Pendre at one time. They moved up to Bryn Mair in 1955 and lived next door to Uncle Ned until they died. She spent many hours in Auntie Glad's house. When our girls were about twelve and thirteen years old, we lived at Woodlands, next door to the golf club. The girls and their friends organized a jumble sale at our home and raised £45 for Plas y Llan. Auntie Annie wanted to come to the jumble. She loved a good root around. I picked her up in the car at the same time as I went for my Mother; neither one got out much any more owing to their failing health. They had a good natter that day and a good root around in the jumble. I can see my dear Mam now, sitting by the table looking out of the window, with her legs folded under her, arms leaning on the table and struggling for breath, and shouting out her instructions to the girls, and what a voice she had! I would give anything to hear it one more time. She thought the world of both girls, and since they were her only grandchildren, it's not surprising is it? I recall Auntie Annie had a large funeral, which is what you would expect with such a big family. It was the first and last funeral I ever went to in which the mourners walked behind the hearse to the cemetery, as they did in the old days. It was a quiet and somber walk from Bryn Mair to Erw Feiriol that day.

Grace Bach – Nain Thomas

My paternal grandmother Grace Thomas nee Roberts (1897 - 1968) was known to one and all as Grace Bach. She was a real character! Val and I called her Nain Thomas. Nain was born in Nant y Felin and she died there too. Nain, I'm told, worked on the farm Tan Rallt Uchaf when she was a child – she used to carry milk to some of the houses in Nant y Felin; whatever the weather, Nain would turn up for work. I don't really know a lot about Nain's childhood. It's not something you bother asking about when you're young, is it? Then, before you turn around, you're not young any more, the older members of your family are gone, and it's too late! I do remember a tale she used to tell us. "If you hear an owl hooting it's a sure sign that someone close to you is going to die," said Nain. To this day, if I hear an owl hoot I think of Nain and it makes me a little nervous. Here are a few tales I have heard about Nain Thomas.

Em my husband told me a little tale he remembers from the early 1960's. He has an excellent memory. He and his mate Clifton (known as Beaver) were in the Virginia. I'm sure they must have been under age, at about 16-17. They were sitting in front of a big roaring fire in the small front room with Auntie Alice Fflodiau (Mrs Coleman). She was one of the senior citizens. "It was Christmas Eve and rather quiet in the pub," said Em. He had just walked me home. I had to be in by 10pm, even up to the day we got married. Auntie Alice knew we were courting, therefore took great delight in teasing Em about it. She was a great character also, and a lifelong friend of Nain. Anyway, she was telling Em and Beaver about a pub called The Harp that used to be across the road from the Virginia years ago. It's a house now, renamed Ty'r Delyn (Harp House) – it's good to keep the old names isn't it? She remembered how she and Nain, as girls of around 12, used to go there and stand on boxes to reach the bar so they could drink a glass of mild beer! There was no such thing as worrying about how old you were then. "If you wanted some refreshment and could pay for it, then there were no questions asked," said Auntie Alice.

Will and Grace Bach and their daughter, (Auntie) Freda.

Auntie Alice (floodyard) c. 1960.   *Harp House poster.*

She and Nain were both rather small, even as adults. I was talking to Mrs Dilys Hughes (Waen) the other day and she told me that Grace Bach used to work as a maid for her mother and father when she was a very young girl up in Waen. "In those days, as soon as they were able, the children went out to earn," said Mrs Hughes. Grace Bach's words after finishing her day's work and having a bite to eat were: "when the scram is gone Grace Bach is gone," and off home she went, running like the wind, said Mrs Hughes laughingly. What a long walk for a child after a full day's work. Weun is behind Dinas and Grace Bach lived in Nant y Felin!

I have just seen a poster about the Harp. It seems that on Tuesday September 2nd 1919 Harp House (formally Harp Inn) together with a commodius coal yard, which was then occupied by Mr William Hughes at the low rental of £10 8s 0d per annum, was put up for sale by public auction.

Grace Bach and her sister Rossie went to Barrow in Furness during the First World War to make shells and bombs. There must have been a factory there. Blodwen told me that her mother had said that Grace Bach was always game for a laugh and always up to some mischief or other! Auntie Rossie's words were *diawl drwg oedd Grace* - Grace was a little devil! Grace Bach was married at the time and Will, her eldest son, lived the early part of his life in Bangor with his grandparents. Grace Bach met Taid (Will) when he used to come down from Bangor to play football.

I have a rather funny tale to tell now. What is true and what has been added over the years I will leave for you to decide. When some members of the family were children they were playing on the beach one summer's day, in the early part of the twentieth century (there was no sea wall then, or nice lawns, or cafés). Beachcombing was a popular pastime and all sorts of goodies were washed up. You never knew what you would find owing to so many shipwrecks. Their shoes at the water's edge, the kids were all up to their knees in seawater, enjoying the day. All of a sudden one of the children spotted a large wooden box which had been carried up onto the stones by the tide. It was with great excitement that they all ran shouting and yelling y *fi welodd y bocs gyntaf* - I saw it first! It was a struggle to get it open, despite bashing it with stones and pieces of driftwood. All the children gathered around the box trying to be the one to open it. "Hurry up," they shouted to one another. When they finally got it open they not only found lots of coins in it, but also some sparkling jewellery. Not one of the children really knew what to do with it, or what it was worth. Along came a man who spotted the children with the box and said *mi roddai hanner coron i chi am y bocs* - I will give you half a crown for it (you must remember that 2/6, or $12\frac{1}{2}$p, was a lot of money in those days); the children jumped at the chance and ran home to their mothers so that they could share the windfall. The man who bought the box and its contents that day was a man who ran one of the shops in the village. He indeed knew what it was worth!

Nain did a lot of bilberry picking when she was a girl. As a family they went up the mountains quite often in the summer months. In those days there were many other families that went also, and the children used to have loads of fun. Nain was always one to play a prank on the other kids, I'm told. Of course, there was always a day or two off school for this venture. In July it was to Penmaenmawr Mountain that they all went, because the bilberries there were ready first. Then in August it was *Foel Special* which is up past Camarnaint, past the new water reservoir which gave Llanfair its water. Quite often during the summer months it would dry up. They would leave the house early in the morning, stay out until late evening and then they would go home to try and sell the bilberries. "On the way home from the mountain we were all very tired, yet were singing at the top of our voices, *It's a long way to Tipperary*. What good days they were," said Mr Robin Parry the window cleaner. Mr Parry is about 82 years old. "They weren't only used for pies and jams," he said, "but made an excellent dye." People couldn't get enough of them. Another favourite place to pick was around Aber Lake. Of course that was a lot further than *Foel Special*. My Dad would pick about 1lb in half an hour and he was a fast picker. It was a hard, back-breaking job.

Another little tale about Grace Bach. The whole family was coming down Tan Rallt Uchaf ffrith, everyone tired from a long day's picking. With the baskets and tins full of bilberries the kids, as kids have done for centuries, were playing up and teasing each other. Grace Bach, at that time, was expecting Uncle Bob, so it must have been around 1928. Anyway, she was so busy shouting at her boys: *byhafiwch eich hunain, hogiau* – behave yourselves, boys! – that she lost her footing. The next thing everyone knew she was rolling down the ffrith. "My poor old mother was more worried about her bilberries flying all over the place than anything else," said Auntie Freda. She did not stop until she reached the bottom. She couldn't move her leg, it was bent under her and she was in agony. Will Bach her son ran for help. It took quite a few men to carry her down the mountainside. When the ambulance finally got there she was taken to hospital and was found to have broken her leg rather badly.

I have been talking to Blodwen (Auntie Rossie's daughter) about those days. She told me that Grace Fawr and the rest of the women who used to go picking bilberries had a kind of stall by the side of the road at the top of Nant y Felin, next door to a little shop known as Siop Dowell. People from Llanrwst used to come and buy the bilberries to make the dye used at the woollen mill in Trefriw. The women were all really glad to sell them in bulk. It saved a lot of selling on the stalls and round the houses.

I remember doing exactly the same thing when I was a girl: I loved picking bilberries, and loved eating them. Most of all I loved the long hot summer days on the mountains with Mam, Dad and my sister Val. We would leave our house, 5 Tan y Bonc, quite early so that we would get to the mountain before it got too hot. Val and I ran ahead shouting and yelling, looking forward to the day ahead. We loved it. Mam would make tomato sandwiches with fresh bread, my favourite. They were lovely and soggy by the time we ate them. There was also some home-made lemonade, made from a recipe that Mrs Avis Bellis gave to Mam. I will print it here, with Mrs Bellis's kind permission, in case you want to try it.

Home Made Lemonade

2 lemons (grated rind and juice)
1/2 oz citric acid
1/2 oz Epsom salts
3/4 lb sugar
2 cupfuls boiling water.

Method:
Mix well together, stir until sugar is dissolved, cool then strain. Add water to taste.
I tried it and it was exactly as I remembered it.

We also enjoyed some of my dear Mother's apple pie on those mountain jaunts. Mam was a wiz at making pastry. Mam Bach – I miss her as much today as I ever did, and indeed I still talk to her. By the time we were up the mountain Val and I wanted our food. There was no chance: Dad would say *rhaid i chi ennill eich cinio yn gyntaf, heliwch lond piser o lys a wedyn gawn ni ginio* – you must earn your dinner first, so collect a jarful of bilberries and then we'll eat. "Come on Dad, don't be so mean," was our reply, but we always had to wait! Dad would collect bilberries in a 1lb jam jar, that way he had an idea of how much he was picking. It was boiling hot, the sun shining down on us; my Dad had a snow white hankie on his head, knotted at the corners to stop the flies from nibbling at him. Of course it didn't work! Why do those days seem to have been always lovely and hot? The picking nearly done for the morning, my Mam would shout "come on girls; let's make Dad a cup of tea." We would collect a little dead gorse wood and start a fire; before long the flames were dancing and jumping, with sparks flying everywhere. What wonderful days they were, how happy we all were.

When we got home Liza Zack – Nain next door as we used to call her – who lived in 6 Tan y Bonc would have gone into our house, made a fire and ensured there was something ready for our tea. Front doors were rarely locked in those days. In the early part of the twentieth century Liza Zack was referred to as the Queen of Nant y Pandy, which was the upper part of Valley Road. She was Em's grandmother. Life's funny isn't it: here I am, over fifty years later, married to her grandson. What would she have to say about that? She was a real character – a really strong, old-fashioned Welsh lady, with a heart of gold. But if you upset her – watch out! Her youngest son Owen (Em's Dad) was a little boy in 1918 when he ran all the way home from school to Tan y Bonc. Crying his eyes out, he managed between sobs to tell his mother what had happened. His teacher had forced him to sit under a table in the corner of the classroom,

Liza Zack, Tan Bonc 1949.

facing the wall, with blackboards placed at both ends of the table to block out the light. The teacher ordered him not to move until playtime. Poor Owen, on his own in what seemed like total darkness, was scared stiff and playtime seemed a long way away. At last, playtime came and Owen could escape from that horrible place. By the time he'd finished telling his mam why he'd returned from school early, she was fuming that a teacher could do such a thing to her child. "He's not getting away with that," she said as she threw her cape around her shoulders. Liza marched down to the school, went straight into the classroom, got hold of the teacher by the scruff of his neck, and told him in no uncertain terms what she would do if he ever did anything to upset her son again. The children sat in amazement, enjoying every second of it.

Jacob (the shepherd) and his wife Liza with their children Peter and Margaret in 1899.

Liza's husband, Jacob, was a shepherd who was born in Llanfair. His parents had died when he was a young boy in the 1870's and his siblings had moved away, to look for work in the coal mines of South Wales. Young Jacob had no family left in Llanfair to care for him. A family from Glyn Farm, Abergwyngregin, took him in and cared for him until he was old enough to pay them back by working for them, which was the custom in those days. Jacob spent weeks at a time tending his flock on the mountains.

One particularly cold spring, Jacob, a young man with a family by then, and living in Llanfair, was up on the mountains of Aber, caring for the little lambs and watching over them as shepherds had done for centuries past. They had a late snowfall that year, a blizzard as bad as any he had ever seen. The wind was howling and blowing so hard he could hardly stand up in it, let alone tend his flock. The snow came down thick and fast and soon everything in front of him had turned white. Jacob was stuck up on those harsh, cold mountains – what could he do? The wind was causing drifts five to six feet deep. The poor sheep were clinging to the walls, trying to get some shelter. Jacob knew he couldn't make it home that night and decided to take a leaf from the sheep's book. He dug himself a shelter of sorts, and with his faithful old dogs managed to survive that shocking, freezing cold night. Many sheep and lambs were buried alive in the snow. Morning came at last, and Jacob knew that if he had to spend another night there he wouldn't live to tell the tale. It was with great determination that he made his way down that beautiful but hostile mountainside. Past Aber Falls he walked, with his dogs close to his heels. Suddenly the dogs started barking; they had heard the rescue party, and all was well again. Later in the year it was decided that never again were the shepherds to be stranded in those conditions so a hut was built, about three miles south of the Falls, and it's still standing today, a little hut known as Cwt Jacob. So, whenever you make your way up to Aber Falls, spare a thought for young Jacob, the shepherd who nearly lost his life in the snow many years ago. Liza Zack and Jacob died in the early 1950's.

Cwt Jacob

My great-great-grandfather (paternal) – Alexander Ellis

My great-great (paternal) grandfather Alexander Ellis (1837–1916) was born at Bangor, in all probability. Alex could read and write, and he spoke both English and Welsh. He was a potter in the census of 1871 and lived at 39 Kyffin Square, Bangor; they were large houses with a few landings and lots of rooms which housed many people, with one toilet between half a dozen families. In the census of 1881 he was down as a hawker, born in Bangor, aged 53. His wife Jane's age was given as 42 (sic). They were still living in Kyffin Square. Looking at the 1901 census, we find that Alex, aged 64, and his wife Jane, aged 62, were lodgers living at 55 High Street Penrhyndeudraeth with their daughter Margaret and her husband William, who was the head of the household. William, a labourer, was down as working from home. There were a total of ten people living in the same house, all related to each other. In those days, I suppose, people shared houses and had a room or two each. I'm sure that Alexander must have been a bit of a gypsy – they moved around such a lot. We went in search of Alex's grave and traced it to Glan Adda cemetery in Bangor. The grave was unmarked, but with the help and kindness of the superintendent of Bangor Crematorium we were able to find it. One day I hope to put some kind of marker on it.

My great-grandmother Mary Ellis (1867-1928) was born in Llanerchymedd. She was a rag gatherer when she was 14, living in Kyffin Square, Bangor. Mary is buried with her parents and brother in Glan Adda, Bangor. Other members of this generation are listed in note 13.

Mary Ellis and William Thomas (2) – my great-grandparents

My great-grandparents Mary Ellis (daughter of Alexander) and William Thomas were married in Bangor on June 26th 1891. I will refer to this William as William (2) (see Note 14 for more on this generation). They both lived in Kyffin Square at that time. William (2) could not read nor write; Mary signed their marriage certificate herself. The 1901 census tells us that Mary Thomas, and her son William (Taid Thomas), aged 10, lived at 50 Kyffin Square. There was no mention of her husband William (2) so I can only assume that he was working and living elsewhere at the time. Having done some more research into this I have found out that on the night of March 31st, 1901, in Fleetwood Quay, a William Thomas (2) worked as an able seaman on a vessel called *G A Savage*. It is probable that this William was Taid Thomas's father. I have been told by one or two people that William (2) always wore a sailor's cap.

Auntie Freda had vivid memories of her Nain Mary limping up Nant y Felin – she had one leg shorter than the other. She would walk up from the village in all weathers, with her black felt cap sitting crookedly on her head and a little cape wrapped around her shoulders in a vain attempt to keep out the cold. "She always came bearing gifts," Auntie Freda said. "We would wait by the gate for our Nain, knowing full well that there would be a treat for us all; we were her only grandchildren so she would spoil us when she could afford it."

When Dad (known to everyone as Now) or one of his siblings were ill with the whooping cough their mother (Grace Bach) would get up early and prepare the children for the train journey to Bangor. What excitement indeed, a ride on a train – the kids could hardly contain themselves. There was an ulterior motive for some of these train rides. Not only would they all get to see their Nain and Taid and probably have a feast there, but Mary (their Nain) used to live near the gasworks and this was one of the reasons for the day out – long ago it was thought that if you stood in front of an open furnace door, and inhaled the sulphur fumes, it would help alleviate the symptoms of whooping cough.

Auntie Freda told me that when her grandmother Mary was very ill in bed in Dean's Court, she remembers all the children going there to see her and sitting around her. Uncle Bob was a baby at the time and Mary took great delight in bouncing him up and down on the bed despite being so ill. As I have said, she is buried with her father and mother.

My grandfather – William Ellis Thomas

My grandfather William Ellis Thomas (1891 - 1967), or Taid Thomas as we called him, was born in Kyffin Square, Bangor He was an only child and I'm told he was spoiled by his mother Mary. Taid Thomas was born three months before his parents married, hence the story in the family that we should have all been named Ellis and not Thomas. Taid Thomas met Grace Bach in Llanfair when he used to come down to play football for Bangor City before the First World War. Uncle John Morgan told me that Taid Thomas was an excellent footballer who may have played for West Bromwich. He and Nain were married in 1914. Taid served with the Caernarfon Battery of the Royal Garrison Artillery in the First World War, in France and Flanders. Taid represented the British Expeditionary Force at several football games abroad. He was shot in the leg and was invalided out of the war in 1918; he was left with a pronounced limp. Despite his injury, he was determined to try and play a little football for Llanfairfechan Town, but not for long. His injury would not allow it. He loved the game and did not want to give it up.

A little more information about Llanfair's football history: I recall my Dad reminiscing about how, when he was about six or seven years old, he went to a big football match in Llanfairfechan on his father's shoulders. Dad remembered that it was a big day in the village. He had never seen so many people in his short life. Having done some research I came across this story. For the first time in Llanfairfechan's history they had reached the semi-finals of the Welsh Amateur Cup. On March 16th 1929 Llanfair played Cardiff Corinthians at Bryn y Neuadd Park (the field on your left as you enter Bryn y Neuadd). Llanfairfechan colours were "red jerseys and white knickers." People came from far and wide to watch the game. The trains were packed with passengers of all shapes and sizes. Off they went up Station Road, streams of men, singing and shouting merrily on the way to the first pub they could find. There was a carnival atmosphere in the village, with cars and charabancs parked anywhere and everywhere. It was standing room only in the pubs and men could be seen out in the streets with their pints of beer and wearing their rosettes proudly on their chests. There was singing and joking, with plenty of friendly banter in both English and Welsh thrown back and forth between the supporters. Then, down to an uneven Bryn y Neuadd field they went in their hundreds, in plenty of time for the kick-off. The supporters from both sides were full of great expectations that their team was going to win. The Rt Hon David Lloyd George was extended a very warm welcome, as were all the visiting team and supporters. Mr Lloyd George kicked off at 3.15 pm. One of the lady supporters thought he was going to play the whole game and said "How can he play? He is just not fit enough." Also present was Mr Ted Robbins, Secretary of the Football Association

Llanfairfechan F.C., 1920's. Back centre - Tommy Jones,
Middle centre - Taid Thomas, Front centre - John Sam.

Program for Llanfairfechan V Cardiff Corinthians 1929.

of Wales. Despite Llanfairfechan's best efforts they lost by four goals to one. It was all over. They had lost, but never mind – there's always another time! A dance was held at the Caradog Café (sailing club) to celebrate the occasion. Mr Nightingale and his jazz band entertained from 7pm-11pm, admission 1/6. The people of Penmaenmawr and Aber, not to mention the people of the village, especially the young in all their finery, were not going to be cheated out of a good time just because their team had lost. They danced the Charleston, the quick step, and didn't stop bobbing and shaking all evening.

A little tale about Glyn (Gamin) Jones the chimney sweep. Glyn was Gwenda's father. I must tell you that Auntie Gwenda is an honorary auntie to most of the children in the village. She has worked in the village school as a dinner lady for many years and the kids all love her. Our little granddaughter Megan thinks that Auntie Gwenda is lovely and there is no one like her.

In the early part of the twentieth century Glyn lived in Pentre Uchaf. Before school each morning it was Glyn's job to go up to Bryn Golau farm to get milk. The farmer used to deliver the milk by horse and cart to the people who wanted it delivered. However Glyn's mother insisted on having fresh milk so Glyn would make his way up to the farm with a large pitcher, which was quite heavy for a little boy. None the less, he did his chore without any complaints. Eventually his mam had a sneaking suspicion that the farmer was adding water to the milk. This went on for quite a while and Mrs Jones said *dyna ddigon* – enough is enough! So up she went to Bryn Golau to give the farmer the length of her tongue. *Naddo yn wir Mrs Jones* – no indeed, he would never do such a thing. The next day, young Glyn went up for his usual quart of milk. The farmer, knowing full well that it was not he who was watering the milk, decided to follow Glyn home. Now between Bryn Golau and Glyn's house was a water trough, used in those days as a communal water point for the people of the area.

Having made sure young Glyn had not seen him, he watched from a distance as Glyn drank some of the milk. How was the little rascal going to explain that to his mother? Never fear, Glyn had a good idea. Yes, you're right – he bent down by the trough and added some water to the milk. The farmer followed Glyn the rest of the way home and told his mother what he had just witnessed. Poor Glyn had a good licking off his mother that day and never played that particular trick again. "Glyn was a great one for a tale and had a story to tell for every occasion," said Em.

Bryn Golau rebuilt in 1736, photo taken c. 1906.

Back to William and Mary

When Mary died her husband William (2) came to live in Llanfair. He lived for a while with his son and daughter-in-law (Taid Thomas and Grace Bach) in Laburnums. Demolished now to make way for the Expressway, it was in a row of large houses between the Victoria Inn and Pendalar. He then moved next door and had a room of his own; he used to eat at Nain Thomas's so they were all happy. William (2) always wore his sailor's hat on the side of his head and looked rather comical. His little white dog followed him faithfully wherever he went. Uncle John Morgan tells me that William (2) was a really heavy drinker and used to cause all sorts of trouble after his drink. "The only problem was, he was too drunk to handle himself. Poor Grace Bach had a rough time of it while he lived with them," said Uncle John. William (2) and Taid Thomas (his son) would fight on a regular basis. What a family! What chance did the boys have, seeing all this as they grew up? Auntie Freda didn't like William (2) very much: her memory of him is that he always pulled her mother's plats and Grace Bach hated it, so she was always shouting at him. She remembers him as a grumpy old man – he lived the latter part of his life with Nain and Taid Thomas in 3 Pen y Bryn. He died in Dolwaen, Conwy, aged 80. Dolwaen (on the site of the recently-demolished Conwy hospital) was the old workhouse. As a matter of interest, the fee paid for an internment in 1943 was £1/16/8. Twenty years later in 1967 the cost of internment was £4/5/6. In 1977, when Uncle Bob was buried, the cost was £32.50. I do remember Nain (Grace Bach) saying that her father-in-law was a nasty drunkard of a man and she didn't like him at all. My poor old Nain was buried with him and must be forever more in his company.

Fred Parry

I'm sad to report that a friend of ours has died as I write this family history. Fred Parry hadn't been ill for very long; he died in Walton Hospital, Liverpool, on May 5th 2003 aged 64. We had been to see him only a few days previously and gave a lift to a couple of his friends. He was so pleased to see us all. Em used to enjoy a chat with him in the pub – he was a gentleman! Fred was born in Conwy and had lived in Llanfair for many years. He was a quiet, inoffensive man and a bit of a philosopher. He enjoyed growing his own vegetables and had an allotment along the Cob. He often brought me some of his homegrown vegetables with the words: "The best in Llanfairfechan, Margaret." Quite often, over the last few years, he came to our house for a bite to eat, sometimes for a spot of breakfast and other times for lunch. Indeed, on New Year's Eve 2002 Fred joined us all for our lunch; there were eleven of us here. Who would have thought it would be Fred's last New Year's lunch. After Fred's funeral his daughter Helen gave Em a letter her father had written to us in the last few days of his life. How sad! We sat in the parlour and I read the ten-page letter out loud to Em and Karen; I had to stop every now and then with the tears pouring down my cheeks. It was, I think, the saddest letter I have ever read (parts of it are reproduced in Note 15). To think of Fred, at his lowest ebb, writing down his innermost thoughts to us in the middle of the night in the hospital. There we were, reading it only hours after his funeral. I hope he is in a better place now.

And now back to Grace Bach

To return to Grace Bach: what else can I tell you about her? I suppose I must tell you some of the tales my Dad told me. He remembered his mam going out and spending all day doing whatever she did, perhaps going to Llandudno for the day, having a few drinks with her friends, spending hours chatting. Calling at the Virginia, rushing home and putting a load of clothes in the sink and then on the line and pretending to Taid that she had been busy washing all day. Sometimes she would get away with it, sometimes she wouldn't. Grace Bach used to keep lodgers at Laburnums, Marine Terrace. She let some rooms to the summer entertainers who used to work in the pavilion on the beach. The family lived in the basement and slept in the attic; the best rooms were of course for the paying guests. When Auntie Freda was about 13 years old her mother, Grace Bach, used to run a small chip shop in the front room of the house. Taid Thomas worked in the quarry for a while; his wages were £2.50 a week to keep a family of seven. Taid Thomas's father William (2) was partial to a pint of beer and used to walk over the mountains to Llanrwst to visit his family (and as an excuse to get drunk of course). He would stay there for a few days and then make his way back to his son and daughter-in-law with his tail between his legs. Eventually William (2) moved to a room in the house next door and things were a little easier for all the family; he was to live on his own for a few years. Grace Bach was a porter at Llandudno Junction railway station in the Second World War. She was a woman who'd try anything! Taid Thomas worked on the council for many years as a labourer. I remember my father telling me that Taid had dug his own father William (2)'s grave in Erw Feiriol.

I have fond memories of Nain and Taid Thomas. My first memory of them was living in 3 Pen y Bryn. My sister Valerie was born there, in a small room at the back of the house that no-one really used. I remember the little back kitchen with the white sink and a well-worn wooden draining board which was always full of chipped dishes. Under the sink was the gas meter, which was constantly hungry for a penny. It had a small flowered curtain round it, in an effort to make it look nice. The cast iron cream enamel triplex grate usually had a small coal fire in it. There were always a few logs by the side of the grate, brought by their sons; any old shoes, I remember, were burned too. Nothing was wasted then. On the table were a bag of sugar and a bottle of milk (half used, sometimes on the turn). If there was no milk we had to resort to Nestles condensed milk from the can. The teapot was always hot, even if it was stewed and so strong you could stand a spoon in it. There was always a half eaten loaf of bread and some butter or margerine there for anyone who was hungry. I don't think the table was ever cleared completely in most houses then; the essentials were put tidily on a corner of the table, ready for the next meal. I used to enjoy a sugar buttie there. Yes indeed! There was a welcome for anyone who called at my Nain's. There was a big "parlwr" at the front of the house with overly stuffed chairs and sofas all covered with flowered fabric, which in turn was covered with more covers on the arms and the backs "just in case they got dirty". Not that we sat in the front room often! There were loads of pictures of all shapes and sizes on the walls. I remember one in particular – a poem entitled *Mother*. It was on a silk square which my Dad had brought home from New York, and Nain had it framed. The words went something like this:

M is for the million things she gave me

O means only that she is growing old

T is for the tears she shed to save me

H is for her heart of purest gold

E is for her eyes with love's light shining

R is for right and right she'll always be,

Put them all together
They spell Mother, a word that means the world to me.

More tears! I didn't realize I was such a softie. It's funny – the more I write the more I remember. They were such happy days. It's a shame that you don't appreciate it more at the time, isn't it?

Taid, as I recall, used to stand for hours by his gate in Pen Bryn watching the world go by. Anyone passing was well used to Taid's words: *oes gennych chi Woodbine i sbario os gwelwch yn dda* – can you spare me a fag? Not very nice to cadge fags in the street was it? But that was Taid Thomas for you. Whenever I went to Nain's I had the run of the place. I used to love rooting around everywhere to see if there was anything new that Nain had brought home from Ball and Boyds, the Llandudno auction rooms. Perhaps a chain for my neck, a brooch, or even something for my dressing table at home; I wasn't fussy, it was indeed a house of many treasures and I knew that if I asked Nain for it, it would be mine!

Many years ago my Dad told me a rather unpleasant family tale, but then not all family tales are pleasant, are they? Taid Thomas worked as a labourer for the council for 27 years – he was a hard-working man was my Taid! One Friday evening after a hard day at work Taid came home with his wage packet and it seems that Nain had had a drink or two in the day. Taid said *dim mymryn o beryg gei di'r cyflog yma* – he wouldn't hand his wage packet over to Nain. Nain instructed her sons, who were only boys at the time, to take it off him. Poor Taid didn't offer much resistance, and who could blame him, with his sons holding him down on the floor and his wife going through his pockets.

One day after school Dad and his brother saw their Mam coming from the pub. Come on Mam, *beth am geiniog neu ddwy* – can you spare us a few pennies, they said. *Dim pres* – no money, she said. 'Well if you don't give us some fag money we'll tell Dad that we saw you in the pub,' they told her. "What naughty boys we were," said Dad as he told me this story.

I was talking to Gerallt (who farms at Tyddyn Angharad) recently. He told me a little story about my Nain. When he worked on the council he was in Nant y Felin building a wall with Arthur Morgan and Nain said to them: "Come in for a cuppa and a sandwich, you've worked hard." My Nain wouldn't take no for an answer! "Your Nain was a very kind woman," said Gerallt.

I think I was one of Taid's favourite grandchildren, because I saw quite a lot of him I suppose. Taid was a good one for putting his hand in his pocket and bringing out exactly what he intended. He used to give me a threepenny bit, or if he was flush it would be a sixpenny piece (just over 2p) and warn me not to tell anyone he'd given it to me. I always went home and told Mam that Taid had given Val and me some money. Taid was not as generous as Nain; she would indeed give her last. Taid was a smoker and always after a fag or a stump. I don't think Taid ever had much money of his own; who did in those days? I remember them mostly living in Maes Helyg in Nant y Felin. When I was a girl I used to help my Dad to decorate their house, although Nain was a dab hand at it herself when she was younger.

In the late fifties and early sixties, Nain and Taid worked as a cook/dishwasher in a couple of hotels called Paynes and the Ritz in Llandudno. Nain got me a weekend job there waiting on tables. I absolutely hated it. I was only about 14 and I'm afraid I only stuck it for three days. I was really not suited to the job, being the shy, rather quiet girl that I was!

Every Wednesday there was an auction at Ball and Boyds. Nain used to love going there to spend her hard-earned money. She would buy any old junk and come home and share it with the family, whether they wanted it or not. I recall Nain's pantry, or *spensh* as we called it, in Maes Helyg. It was really just the space under the stairs. There was a marble slab there on which Nain used to keep her Welsh butter or Stork margarine, cold meat, and all sorts of foods which we would help ourselves to. There were always jars and jars of home made pickled onions, red cabbage and jams that I loved. The slab was supposed to keep everything cool. There was a small net-like canopy which was put over the food (when she remembered) to keep the flies off in summer. Nain never cooked her meat enough for me, it was always rather bloody. My Mam used to say that Nain murdered the meat, which was cooked on the outside but raw on the inside.

Taid used to watch Nain like a hawk, making sure that she didn't drink too much. They would come down to the village: Nain would be half a mile in front, with poor Taid hobbling behind, trying to keep up, which of course he couldn't, owing to his bad leg. Nain would get to our house complaining that Taid had a melancholy cob on again. Nain was such a cheerful person and Taid didn't laugh very much, so it must have been hard for her sometimes. In Taid would come. *Oes yna baned Megan?* he would ask. My Mam would pour him a cup of tea; he would pour the tea from the cup into the saucer and start drinking (or should I say slurping) from the saucer.

Their local pub was the Virginia Inn. Nain would leave Taid's war pension book there as security and they were able to borrow money on it, for whatever they needed at the time (although I suspect it was used quite often to fund a night out). These things were done in those days; personally, I can't think of anything worse than sitting in pubs for hours on end. I suppose I'm the odd one out! Nain and Taid would go to the Bryn Coed Club in Penmaenmawr for a game of bingo. I never saw either of them the worse for drink, or was I too young to notice? Taid wasn't as fond of his pint as my Nain. On their way to the Bryn Coed Club on the evening of November 17th 1967 Nain and Taid were crossing the road near the English Church, Llanfair, to catch a bus. Had they gone a little further there was a pedestrian crossing (there were no traffic lights in those days). Nain had made it across. As usual, Taid was lagging behind her. Nain shouted to him: "Will – don't cross now!" Taid saw a gap, took a chance and crossed, but couldn't walk very fast, so even if he'd seen the car coming he wouldn't have been able to get out of the way. He was thrown in the air, over the top of the car. The man driving the car never saw a thing until it was too late. Taid died of multiple injuries. He was 76 years old. My Dad (Now) was working in Home Loaf, Conwy, at the time and had called at the Castle Hotel for a pint on the way home. As he approached Siop John

Dick, the newsagents in the village, someone told him that his father had been knocked down. He ran back to the crossroads and the last thing he was able to do for his dad was to close his eyes. The coroner's verdict was one of accidental death. A couple of days before he died, Nain and Taid had called at our house, as proud as punch. They had bought a lovely silky-white pram cover from a jumble sale for our new baby. Karen bach was born in 2 Glan Ffrwd on November 15th 1967, two days before Taid died. He never saw her. I remember listening to the church bells toll for Taid and watching the funeral cars from Glan Ffrwd bedroom window. Karen was given Ellis as her middle name, after my Taid. All Uncle Bob's kids have Ellis for their middle name.

After Taid died Nain wasn't much good on her own – they had been married for 54 years, a long time. My Dad (Now) used to take Nain a little food up to Nant y Felin as she didn't look after herself very well. One morning, about seven months after we lost Taid, my Dad was taking a bag of groceries up to Nain's. There was no answer and Dad couldn't get into the house; he was worried. He looked through the letterbox, and saw something or someone at the bottom of the stairs. By this time Dad was in a bit of a state, as you can imagine. He went into the road and saw Norman Parry; he asked Norman to go with him to his Mother's house, since something was obviously not right there. Norman went round the back and the door was ajar. In he went and saw poor Nain at the bottom of the stairs. She had been dead a while. He shouted to my Dad: *Aros lle rwyt ti Now* – stay where you are. Norman told me many years later that my Dad was shaking like a leaf, and he'd never seen anyone so pale in his life. Not surprising really, is it? One of the neighbours called him in and gave him a cup of tea. Norman went for a policeman. I remember Dad coming to our house later that day – we still lived at 2 Glan Ffrwd at the time. "Em," said Dad to my husband, "will you come to my mother's with me – something terrible has happened there." It seems that Nain had taken a man home from the pub the night before. Why, is anybody's guess? I like to think that she took pity on someone who had nowhere to stay and things went horribly wrong. The outcome was that Nain was dead! I don't remember much about that day but Em said that my Dad went to get his brother Will who lived in Nant y Berllan.

Following Nain's funeral (see Note 16) my big tough Dad took to his bed and I remember he couldn't eat anything and didn't go out for weeks. There was an inquest on Nain but my Dad couldn't bring himself to go, so Em and I went. I have no memory of it at all. Em and I went to Llandudno archives and found a newspaper story about Nain Thomas's inquest. The verdict was accidental death. After

Nain had enjoyed a drink with a married couple with whom she'd been friends for years a man had joined them. He was from South Wales and was working on a road construction locally. They had a few drinks in the Virginia and Nain had invited him up for a cup of tea. Having got home, Nain took her coat upstairs. This is very hard to write, simply because I only have one version of the story. I suppose I only want to see what I want to. Anyway, there were no signs of any interference with Nain's clothing and it seems that nothing untoward had happened. On the way up the stairs Nain must have tripped and fallen, the man was at the bottom and Nain fell on him. He didn't remember much about the fall and found himself outside in the road minus a shoe. He reported the accident next day. Death was consistent with a fall, and Nain died of shock and a haemorrhage. My Dad's brother Will and his wife Auntie Rose sorted out Nain's house in Maes Helyg. There was nothing there of any real value. I did ask for a little frame with a photo of me as a girl. I still have it somewhere, I think. Will and Auntie Rose, I remember, made a fire in Nain's back garden and burned loads of Nain and Taid's belongings. What a shame. According to Auntie Freda there were a few photos of Taid in the Army. Never mind, that's the way it goes!

William John Thomas

William John Thomas (1914 - about 1988) their first born was known as Will Grace Bach. He spent a lot of his childhood with his grandmother Mary in Bangor. He was a regular in the Army and used to box and play football for his regiment. On one occasion before the Second World War he went absent without leave. It was a very tight-knit little village, and nobody was going to tell the Military Police anything – it wasn't a done thing, shopping one of your own. The MPs went to his parents' home at Laburnums to ask them if they'd heard any news of him. His mother and father were fiercely protective of him and totally loyal. Whatever Will Bach had done they would protect him. "No indeed, we have no idea where he is," said his father, shaking his head. "If you hear from him remember to get in touch with us immediately," said one of the officers very sternly. "Yes, certainly we will Sir," said Taid. In the meantime Grace Bach was pushing her son out of the little back kitchen window. *Dos I fyny'r mynydd Will Bach, fyddi di'n saff yn fano* said his mother as she stuffed his pockets with food – go to the mountains and hide! Having established that his family had no idea where he was, but believing that he was still in the village somewhere, the Military Police organized a search of the area.

Llanfair being a fairly small village at that time, the search was over quickly – the MPs got very little help from the local inhabitants. No sightings of Will Bach anywhere! They left the village in the hope that someone would spot him and inform the local police. Will lived rough in the mountains above Llanfair for a few weeks, with members of his family taking food, drink and cigarettes to him. A whisper went through the village that Will Bach had been spotted on Garreg Fawr. The local police got wind of it. Once again Llanfair was crawling with the military. The inhabitants had never seen the likes of it! Red Caps and Military Police all over Garreg Fawr. Will was ducking and diving among the gorse and heather. Having spent most of his childhood playing in these mountains, he knew every nook and cranny, and with his Army training he was really fit so he was proving to be very elusive.

Looking up at Garreg Fawr from the village you could see all those Red Caps bobbing up and down. "Far more excitement than had been seen in Llanfair for many a long year," said a local resident. Eventually Will Bach gave himself up and was brought down from the mountain in handcuffs.

Will Grace Bach married a lady called Rose. She was from Altringham. One thing in particular I remember about Auntie Rose was that she had very long hair which she rolled up around her head. When she let it down it reached her waist. It was a lovely shade of grey mingled with dark brown. She and Mam remained good friends through

The Luxor Cinema in the 1930's, was central to our village life for many years.

On the left of the picture is Auntie Rose with Mike and Ann.
Val, Mam and me are on the right. In Bangor, on a day out, about 1950.

all the hard times, even when the brothers fell out. I have many good memories of Auntie Rose, even though she often gave me a clip round the ear – I used to sniff a lot as a child (still do, I'm told) and Auntie Rose would shout: "Margaret, I'm warning you!" The next thing, a hand would come flying out and she'd struck again! Auntie Rose was scared of spider's big time and she would be rooted to the spot if she saw one. We spent a lot of time at Auntie Rose's house in Nant y Berllan when we were kids. We'd call there on the way home from the first house at the Luxor Cinema (the Town Hall) where we went with Mam. Dad would come with us when there was a good cowboy film on. Tickets cost seven pence (about 3p); there were some double seats, so of course that is where we kids made a bee line for with our sweethearts. The best seats in the house were half a crown (12p). Mostly the courting couples sat in these, or the people whom we thought to be rich! You must remember that there were very few TV's around then and computers were unheard of.

We lived in Tan y Bonc then, so Auntie Rose's house was a half way stop for us. We all sat in the kitchen; I recollect sitting around a little fire that burned low in the triplex grate. You could bet your life that there would be a pot full of tea stewing by the side of the fire. It was in Auntie Rose's house that I saw cheese being fried on an open fire for the first time. They used to love it (but I didn't – I was a fussy eater!). In the corner near the window was a big white sink with a wooden draining board; with five children living there it was often full of dirty mugs and plates. Under the window there was a table, always with a sugar bowl and a pint of milk on it; it was a household full of tea addicts, the stronger the better – they would even drink it stone cold. Em was also friendly with Auntie Rose's son Michael (Mike). He remembers calling for Michael in the mornings and he wouldn't even speak before he had his gigantic mug of tea. I was especially friendly with two of the children, Ann and Michael, both of whom did a paper round for Hinchliffs in Station Road. I remember Auntie Rose telling me that Mrs Hinchliff was very kind to them and would occasionally make them a cooked breakfast. We would go pinching apples in the orchard (plot) near Auntie Rose's house – it was such fun, out in the dark doing what we shouldn't, running home like mad in case we got caught. Mam used to play hell with us. "You should not steal, Margaret," she would say, smiling to herself. Our punishment for this act was a stomach ache the next day, from snaffling too many apples. If we were at Auntie Rose's house we would head for home before what they called "chucking out time" in the pubs, which was 10pm in those days. Auntie Rose would come up to top steps with us, talking and laughing, chiding us kids for making too much noise.

Dad and Will weren't particularly good friends – over the years they must have had many a fight. I remember one in particular. They had been fighting outside Will's house in Nant y Berllan; of course they were both the worse for drink. The brothers had a "hell of a fight", both being sturdy and stubborn men; neither would give in to the other. Even in their drink they managed to kick each other to kingdom come. Dad came home in what can only be described as a bloody mess. He had two black eyes, a swollen mouth and his nose was twice its normal size. How he used to walk home from those punch-ups I will never know. My poor Mother! What a life, you might say, but let me tell you, before we go any further with the story, that my parents loved each other very much. Anyway, next morning Dad sent Mam down to see how his brother was. "He's in bed in a hell of a mess," said Auntie Rose. Mam came back home and told Dad this. Dad was so worried that he went down to see him. Will's words were: *dos I'r diawl o'm golwg* – go to Hell out of my sight. Will wasn't a pleasant man. He wasn't very kind to Auntie Rose. If he had any money left after a night out in the pub he used to hide it in a hole in the wall ready for the next day's drinking session. When Em and I lived in Bryn Glas in the 1970's Auntie Rose often called in on her way home with some sweets for Lorraine and Karen. We would have a chat and a cigarette together and put the world to rights. Em recalls that Auntie Rose used to like watching *Up Pompeii*. Frankie

Howerd, the comedian, was in it and she would split her sides laughing at him. Life got easier for Auntie Rose as the children grew up. They were all so good to her, three sons and two daughters; eventually she went to live in Cornwall to be near her daughters. She divorced Will and had many happy, contented years. She died just before her eightieth birthday.

I can hear her now: "The devil takes care of his own, Margaret," she would say. "I hope to God that he (Will) dies before me so that I get a little peace and quiet in my old age." Another of her sayings was "When beer comes in the door, wit goes out the window." How true. My father's words for his brother were: "He is not my brother, just my mother's son."

Auntie Freda and her family

My Auntie Freda Pearson nee Thomas (born 1921) is 84 years old and still going strong. Being the only girl, she was the apple of her father's eye. Of course her brothers were very protective of her. "I couldn't do a thing without one of them watching me," she said. Auntie Freda married Uncle Howard when she was nineteen years old and went to live in Sutton Coldfield. Her Welsh is as good today as it ever was. Uncle Howard, I remember, was a quiet man who worked hard. My dear Mother was particularly fond of Uncle Howard, who used to run a coal haulage business with his father many years ago. Later on they bought a garden nursery in Sutton. "It was a hard way to earn a living," said Auntie Freda.

When I was about ten or eleven years old my Dad worked at a garage in Aber and contracted dermatitis; as a consequence he received some compensation. Mam went straight out and bought two double wooden beds instead of our iron ones (I think it was the first time we had slept on a spring interior mattress – what a treat!). My parents decided we would have a holiday in Auntie Freda's. I remember going out through the door in Tan Bonc; I was so excited – a holiday in Birmingham! I have no idea how we got there but what stuck in my mind all these years ago is a memory of my dear Mam throwing some money onto a high shelf in the back kitchen before we left. "For a rainy day Mags," she said, putting her finger to her lips: it was our secret! Mam and I shared many secrets over the years. Auntie Freda and Dad would have many disagreements, as brothers and sisters often do, but I don't remember them having a proper falling out, although Auntie Freda would always be telling Dad off for his silly behaviour after a few pints. In the mid-60's Dad worked for Uncle Howard in Sutton and stayed with them. On one occasion Dad had done something he shouldn't have and Auntie Freda was really cross with him. "He went out and bought me a lovely china tea set with red roses on it," says Auntie Freda. "Roses for remembrance, Freda bach," Dad told her. "How could I stay cross with him?" she said as she gave me the remaining pieces of the tea set. She never gets tired of telling me that story.

Freda and Howard had two sons, and they all came to Llanfair for their holidays every year – the boys, Glyn and Derek, used to love it here. I remember particularly well the summer I was 13. We all went up to Garreg Fawr for a picnic. Loads of kids screaming and shouting, running around like fools, enjoying their freedom. Auntie Freda and Uncle Howard had brought some friends – the Barlows – with them from Birmingham, so there was a really big crowd. We decided to take a short cut home through one of the ffriths, over one of those hardy dry stone walls, and then we went through a field full of cows. Half way across the field one of the adults shouted: "There's a bull over there, run for it!" Never in my life have I seen people move so fast. Through reeds and bogland we ran, sinking and slipping our way across, with the menfolk pushing screaming women and children over walls. I recall being scared stiff but still giggling as I watched the ladies climbing up those loose stone walls. Everyone made it home safely, though we were all soaking wet and muddy. We made our way to Nain Thomas's house in Nant y Felin to dry out. Nain had a big pot of lob scouse simmering on the stove for us. However many there were for tea Nain would say: "There's plenty to go around". Derek remembers vividly the time when the two boys were desperate for one of the pups in Uncle Ned's shed. The holiday was over and it was time to go back to Sutton Coldfield, but they couldn't go without a lovely cuddly puppy! Their parents were adamant that it was a no puppy situation. Goodbyes were said, and the lads had to leave Llanfair with long faces. After travelling for a while they heard a strange whimpering noise coming from the boot (Uncle Howard always drove a big black car, as I recall). Anyway, they pulled up at the next lay-by and checked the boot. Yes, you're right – they had a lovely snow-white puppy on board! The boys couldn't believe their eyes or their luck; Uncle Ned had sneaked it into the boot when no-one was looking.

For the last twenty years or so Auntie Freda has stayed with us for a week every year. It's a great pleasure to have her, and all the children enjoy her visits; she is such good fun to be with. There's only one problem with our Auntie Freda: she has so much energy she wears me out! She loves to go around the charity shops, always looking for a bargain!

Last year Auntie Freda wasn't well enough to visit us, and in March she was taken to hospital with serious heart problems. Em and I went to visit her and there she was, sitting up in bed as large as life. We wouldn't stay the night and she was really cross. "When I go home I'll send you some money for a meal because I've not been able to look after you," she said. Two weeks later Auntie Freda was home and we received a letter, containing a twenty pound note, telling us to go and have a meal on her.

Uncle Ned and his crew

My Uncle Ned - Edward Lloyd Thomas (1925 - 1990) - was quite a character. It's hard to write about this side of my family. Why, I don't know; perhaps it's because many of them were rogues - likeable rogues, but rogues nonetheless. Uncle Ned was quite a large man who used to grow his hair long. I remember him having a perm in the days when it was the done thing, and an earring too. We used to tease him about being the oldest swinger in town. He loved it! Uncle Ned worked in a bakery after leaving school. I spoke to Mr John Lloyd Roberts MBE and he said: "Yes indeed, Ned and I were the best of friends and spent many happy hours working in Shop Jonnies on Mill Road." Mr Roberts is one of the oldest surviving tailors in the village.

Uncle Ned holing slates, c. 1950.

Uncle Ned was a member of the Home Guard at the outset of the Second World War and joined the Army when he was old enough. He would do anything for you. I asked Uncle Ned for many favours and he did them without question. He was a man who couldn't say no to anyone. He ran a roofing business in Llanfair for many years. In the early years after the war the brothers worked quite a lot together, as well as doing a lot of fighting among themselves.

He was named Edward after his great-grandfather, a blacksmith born in Caernarfon who later moved to Llanrwst. It seems that the family, on all sides, were quite handy with their hands, and I don't mean just their fists. Oh dear me! This is really hard. Uncle Ned and my Dad (Now) were good friends - most of the time. Of course, brothers do fall out over one thing or another. The Thomas brothers more than most - they led very colourful lives!

Eddie was telling us a tale about his father Ned: "He used to tell us kids that if we didn't behave ourselves a big bad man with a beard would come and take us away," said Eddie. "Out of the seven of us I was the one who was most scared!"

I remember one occasion when Dad had taken offence over something Uncle Ned had said or done that day: who was right I don't know. Anyway, if something upset Dad he'd go out and get drunk. After a bellyful of beer, which was usually only six or seven pints of the *cwrw melyn* as he called bitter, he was roaring drunk. If he drank mild he'd take a little longer, but Dad didn't go out just for a chat and a pint, he went out to get drunk. Late that same night Dad, who had a full black beard, was banging at Uncle Ned's door with a shovel in his hand shouting: *Ned, tyrd allan i gwffio fel dyn* - come out and fight like a man. Poor Auntie Glad and the kids must have been scared to death, for here was the man with a beard. It didn't stop my father from causing a big commotion in Bryn Mair; half the street turned out, and the other half watched him from behind twitching curtains. Uncle Ned said *myn uffarn mi lladdai di* - I'll kill you! Off he went to the shed to get his shovel. Bryn Mair was used to the brothers' antics, but never anything quite like this - Now and Ned having a duel in the street, shovels swinging and clashing, both men ranting and raving at each other. Uncle Ned drove Dad down the street and took a swing at him, grazing him on the head. Dad dropped his shovel and pulled an iron gate off its hinges as he passed. He tried to belt Uncle Ned over the head with it and missed, so he threw it at him. Needing a weapon, off came another gate and again he missed. Meanwhile, Uncle Ned was still trying to bash Dad with his shovel, missing more often than not. Eventually both men had had enough and went home, bruised and bleeding. "The next morning, the street looked like a battlefield, with gates and shovels strewn all over the place," said David Eames. The neighbours had a difficult job trying to claim the correct gate. On the morning after such fights Dad would be worried, and was hard-faced enough to go round and say sorry. If it happened today I'm sure there would be serious consequences.

Eddie, one of Uncle Ned's boys, called the other day. He wanted a few photos of my Dad to copy. He has a computer and like me he spends a lot of time on it. Anyway, he told me a story about his dad working in Pwllheli. Eddie, Uncle Ned, my father Now and a couple of others were slating some roofs. They'd finished work but as usual they couldn't go straight home. They called at a few pubs. The evening passed pleasantly enough, but as it came up to closing time Dad was getting drunker and drunker and making a nuisance of himself, as he always did after too much beer. Off they went in the van. On the way home Dad became argumentative and started to throw punches in the back of the van. Agor y drws - open the door, said Ned to Eddie. Eddie did as his father asked. The next thing Eddie knew, Uncle Ned had kicked my Dad out of the door of the van and he had to make his own way home. Next morning Dad turned up for work at Uncle Ned's house. "God knows how he got home that night, it was about forty miles," said Eddie laughingly, "but there he was, fit and ready to go." Dad was always up early after he'd drunk too much beer the night before. Poor old Dad. He probably didn't remember himself how he got home.

Uncle Ned was rather deep. I will quote you something Auntie Rose used to say: "The sea is deep, but my God Ned is deeper." I hasten to add that we were all very fond of him. He was generous to a fault, and as I've already said, he'd do anyone a favour, any time. He was forever young! One thing he used to do after the pub was to take a box of crisps and some lemonade home for the kids, even though perhaps there was no money in the house for food.

When I was a girl, my sister Val wasn't well. She suffered from mental health problems. We didn't have a car, and the North Wales Hospital at Denbigh was a long way to go. Uncle Ned was there for us and used to take us whenever he could, always with a smile on his face, never complaining. He and my mother were great friends, even when the brothers had fallen out.

My friends and I were walking home from school one summer's day in the late 1950's. Pant y Rhedyn in those days was a secondary school, so I must have been about twelve or thirteen years old. We walked along the main road singing and laughing as we went. Sometimes, if any of us had money, we would go into Spiers for a cream doughnut; situated on the crossroads, it was the best bakery in the village - in fact the only one! Here, some of us would say 'tara' and turn for home down Station Road. The rest of us would carry on up past the Co-op. In those days it had two floors of merchandise, with furniture, bedding and shoes as well as a grocery and food section. On this occasion, still acting the goat and teasing the boys, we were enjoying our day and planning what to do that evening. Nearing the police station, we could see a small crowd and one of us shouted: "Come on! Let's have a look!" Of course, as in all small villages, everyone knew everyone else. To my absolute horror, as the crowd opened up, one of my friends screeched to me: "Margaret, hurry up! It's your Dad and he's in a hell of a state."

I couldn't believe what I saw. Sitting there on the police station steps was my father with his head in his hands. The blood was pouring through his fingers; his clothes were torn and covered with blood. I said "Hello Dad, are you OK?" What a daft question to ask! Dad picked his head up; his eyes were mere slits, the swelling was terrible – his lips had swollen to twice their normal size and he was black and blue. My Dad bruised easily. He couldn't see me but he replied: *Dos adra Margiad fach* – go home, Margaret. I can see him in front of me now – my poor, handsome, silly Dad. How many times will I say "poor Dad" before I finish this, I wonder? My eyes are misting with tears as the memories come flooding back. I left him sitting there on his own. I was so ashamed, with all my friends and half the village seeing him like that. My friends, especially the boys, thought my Dad was a real tough guy and thought he was great. I was used to my Dad's antics, but it was another thing coming face to face with it all, in front of everyone. I suppose it was the typical reaction of a young girl. Val went up to him and put her arms around his neck, but Dad sent her home, saying to her: "Don't worry Val; it's not as bad as it looks del." I ran all the way home to Tan Bonc to tell my Mam. She was well used to seeing Dad like that and often told me: "Don't worry del, while they're talking about us someone else is getting some peace." That was no consolation to me.

We found out later that Dad and his brothers had been working on an old cottage called *Yr Ynys* in Mill Road – where Gospel Hall stands today. "Many, many years ago," said Dad, "the river was split in two and a little stream was diverted around the cottage, in order to run the mill and brewery further down Mill Road, and that is where the name *Yr Ynys* (The Island) came from." The brothers had spent some time in the pub that day and when they went back to work a row broke out among them. This time Dad was on the receiving end. He had a real hammering. I do remember Dad saying that they had used shovels on each other. They tore into each other good and proper. Dad was in a state, but believe you me when I tell you that Uncle Ned and Uncle Bob didn't look too good either. The brothers were all as strong as oxen; my father was as stubborn as a mule, and he wouldn't have given in easily, I'm sure. Eventually Dad decided to report it all to the police and went away to lick his wounds: he sat on the steps of the police station to wait for a policeman. When he arrived the policeman asked: *Beth ddiawl wyt ti wedi'i wneud rwan Now?* – What the hell have you done this time, Now? Of course, when the policeman asked if anyone should be charged, up Dad got and said: "Sorry to have wasted your time, officer," touching his forehead as a sign of respect as he departed. There was no question of the brothers ever pressing charges against each other. Uncle Ned and Uncle Bob were perhaps a little closer to each other than to Dad, owing to being closer in age, or perhaps owing to Dad being unable to keep his tongue between his teeth. Can you imagine brothers doing that to each other, and in a few days time being the best of friends again? What a funny lot!

Uncle Ned married Auntie Gladys, granddaughter of a man called Evan Rolland Williams, known as Evan Roli. Evan had fought in the Boer War. Although he had no formal education he used to teach in the village school. He was quite an educated man and a great personality. When Mr Timmins a new headmaster came to teach in the school in the late 1880's, Evan Roli and he couldn't get on. Evan Roli had his own way of teaching and wouldn't do as he was told by the English headmaster, so off went Evan to work in the local quarry, where he loved to debate with his workmates about anything and everything.

Auntie Glad told me that when Uncle Ned had too much to drink she used to goad him and this always led to an argument. Auntie Glad is loved by us all, especially the children of the family. Lorraine and Karen enjoyed going there with my Dad when they were little; they were always sure of a sweet or some little treat at 18 Bryn Mair. She is a very kind lady and would, like Uncle Ned, give you her last.

There have always been dogs in Uncle Ned's house – all white. Generations of the same family of dogs. One was named Pig; who, I ask you, would name a dog Pig!

When we were kids times were hard; many a time I would go to Auntie Glad's and there she'd be, smashing up some old furniture for the fire because there was no coal. Auntie Glad is a collector of ornaments; there are thousands of them all around the house. When she was younger and more able she loved to paint anything and everything red. Their daughter Kash was very kind to my Dad, especially after he had lost Mam. Many's the time she put a few quid into the top pocket of his jacket.

Uncle Ned went to France on a trip one year with the Virginia Inn. He brought back two Rupert the Bear teddies, one for his grandson Francis and the other one for Paul (who still has it). Karen remembers sitting in her friend Sandra's house when Paul was a baby and in walked Uncle Ned with a giant cuddly toy for Paul. Just another good memory of Uncle Ned.

His children grew up and the boys joined him in the roofing business in Llanfair. They worked together until Uncle Ned retired in July 1990. Alex and Cedric are still roofers in the village, and recently Uncle Ned's grandsons David and Edward started up on their own. They did a very good job on our roof. Edward was telling us that they'd both gained a National Vocational Qualification (NVQ) in roofing. The wheels of life keep turning.

Alex bought a two up, two down terraced house in a derelict state in Pool Street in June 2005, and having finished the work inside it was time to think about the outside. The house has no garden so he put his thinking cap on. Recently he invited Em and I to see his latest project – he wouldn't tell us what it was until we went up. When we arrived at the house Alex was upstairs. "Come on up," he shouted. I don't know what we expected to see, but one thing's certain, it wasn't a rooftop garden! There we were, with spectacular views over to Puffin Island and Anglesey. Looking over the rooftops towards Valley Road and the quarry we had a completely new view of Llanfair from Pool Street. Alex was smiling from ear to ear – he was so proud of what he'd done, and well he might be.

When my Dad was very ill in hospital, Uncle Ned went to see him. He broke down and cried; he was so upset, Em led him to another room. Uncle Ned said: "Your father has fought in the war, been torpedoed in the North Atlantic, was in the freezing cold water for many hours, and to end up like this! What indeed is life all about?"

In 1990 Em and I went to Australia for a holiday. I remember going to see Uncle Ned and Auntie Glad before we went. Uncle Ned was not very well, complaining of pains and weakness in his legs. "Remember to get the doctor up, we'll see you in a few weeks," I said as we left. While we were away Uncle Ned's illness got worse and our girls kept mentioning in their letters that he wasn't half well – they didn't want

Ned and Bob Thomas outside the Pen y Bryn Hotel 1975.

to alarm us, but they did want to prepare us for bad news. We got home on December 17th and were told that Uncle Ned was very ill indeed. We went to the hospital the next day. Uncle Ned was dying. What a shock! I remember, as if it were yesterday, speaking to his daughter Kash outside his room. His children were devastated. They had nursed him at home for as long as they could. He had cancer of the spine. He recognized Em and I, gave me a smile and very quietly he said: "Hello del." I believe that Uncle Ned waited to see us – he died a couple of days later.

Uncle Bob and his clan

My Uncle Bob – Robert Ellis Thomas (1928 - 1977) was the baby of the family. He had moved from Llanfair many years before he died. He was as strong as an ox. He was rather small and stocky and not as dark as his siblings. He was, as I remember, quite a handsome man. I don't think I would have wanted to step on his toes! I'm sure he would have made a bad enemy, though to me he was Uncle Bob – always smiling, and always with a cheerful word to say to me. He lied about his age so that he could join the Navy during the Second World War. He was torpedoed, as were thousands of others, and he was reported missing in action a couple of times. I'm told that on one occasion he saved three lives by swimming with the men, one at a time, to some sort of floating debris in the sea. Toward the end of the war Uncle Bob went missing for a whole year; his parents didn't know whether he was dead or alive. Grace Bach (his Mam) went a couple of times to Liverpool in search of him, but to no avail. After the war Uncle Bob turned up alive and kicking – who knows where he'd been! William (his son) told me recently that Uncle Bob had been in Liverpool and Birmingham just after the war. He used to be a prize fighter in the fairgrounds and he worked the circuit, bare knuckle fighting. Uncle Bob also did some sparring with Randolph Turpin in Gwrych Castle, Abergele, in the early 1950's.

Uncle Bob married a lady from Bala, Auntie Ann, and they had ten children. There was also a son, Griff, from a previous relationship. They lived at Nain Thomas's in 3 Pen Bryn for a while. After Robert their first son was born they went to live in Ireland for a while and that is where William was born. Later on they came back to Wales and lived in a little cottage in Aber. In the garden there were all sorts of fruit trees, just asking to be climbed, and how I loved to climb! I would scramble up them like a squirrel, not considering the danger. My Dad would run out of the house: *Margiad, tyrd i lawr y munud yma* – come down this minute! They had a house full of children, so you can imagine how much chaos there was; one of them was always hungry, the table was never cleared, with cups of tea everywhere, and there was always a child looking for a shoe or a pair of pants. The shouting and laughter and indeed the crying was great and I loved it. You always felt like one of them all; of course, our house was really quiet compared to Uncle Bob's so it was a real treat for us to go and visit Abergwyngregin and my Dad's brother and his family. His son William remembers that their house was one of the first to have a television set in Aber: "I remember all the kids from Aber would come and watch, and some even watched through the window when the house was full," said William. With eight children (two not yet born) and two adults in a two up, two down little cottage the winter months were particularly hard, with no money to buy coal and no wood left in the shed. Auntie Ann would gather her children together and off they'd go with an old skeleton of a pram and a saw, up to the woods to chop and saw what branches they could. The kids would enjoy the ride home on top of the logs. "She must have had some strength," said Olwen, one of her daughters. There was no such thing as a holiday; the mountains, woods, fields and rivers were their back garden, and a day up Aber Mountain to pick bilberries was a treat. Sliding down the mountainside on tin trays, the children were indeed content. Then they moved to Tal y Bont near Bangor and lived there for a couple of years. Not far from their house flowed the river Ogwen and during the summer months the kids used to swim in the cool clear water. "The river being well stocked with salmon and trout, my father made a huge silver hook (gaff) and would often swim in the deep pools in search of dinner," said Olwen. There was one occasion when Uncle Bob caught a salmon as big as she'd ever seen. There were no freezers then so it was shared, and most of the village feasted on it.

My earliest memory of Uncle Bob is of being with him on the old golf links up near Llys y Gwynt in the early 1950's. The golf club had been opened in the early part of the 20th century but had closed down by then. The green fees for visitors in the early 1900's were: gentlemen 1/6 a day or 10/6 a month; ladies 1 shilling a week or 8 shillings a month. I recall it was a very hot summer's day; the sun was shining, or hiding occasionally behind a cotton wool cloud passing by. My Dad, Val and I had gone up there with Uncle Bob, a couple of dogs and his kids. I suppose there was only Robert, William and Olwen around then, although I seem to remember loads of us kids there, running, shouting and hiding among the rhododendron bushes, which were so thick that it was dark below them (and we made such good dens there). Uncle Bob and Dad had snared and skinned some rabbits which we promptly put on a spit over a fire. I can still see Uncle Bob sitting there in his shirt sleeves, the sweat pouring down his face beside the fire, turning the spit, smoke rising gently in the breeze. The smell from the meat was mouthwatering; we couldn't wait for Dad to share it among us. What happy days they were. A pan of water from the little stream that flowed quietly beside the track, boiling ready for a cup of tea. Oh! how wonderful it was to grow up in beautiful Llanfairfechan by the sea. I'm told that Uncle Bob swam from Llanfair to the Great Orme, a distance of about eight miles. On another occasion Mam had arranged to meet Dad on the beach and he was rather late. Uncle Bob was doing something to his boat and asked us if we'd like to go out in her. "Please, please, Mam," begged my sister and I. Against her better judgement, Mam said: "OK girls, let's go – to heck with Dad!" Uncle Bob took us around Puffin Island with no life jackets; we didn't worry about this of course, we had the time of our lives. It was a lovely day, not a ripple in the sea; it was as flat and calm as I ever remember seeing it, and were we having fun! However, the fun was short lived. My father, in the meantime, was on his way to the beach, and had

Clubhouse at the old Golf Links 1924.

been told by someone: "Bob has taken Megan and the girls out on the boat." God help Bob! Dad went mad. He met the boat at the jetty. When Dad was in a temper he went as white as a sheet and you knew not to answer back. He wiped the floor with Uncle Bob. With his finger poking Uncle Bob's chest, Dad was shouting and swearing in Welsh. Lucky they were both sober! Dad warned him never take us on that "bloody boat" again. Dad then turned to my poor Mother and played merry hell with her. "Thank God you're all safe," said Dad after he'd calmed down. Under no circumstances would my Dad take chances at sea, especially with us.

Left to right: Dolly, Auntie Ann, me Sian (welsh hat) and Didds, in Sheffield in 1967.

In the early 1960's there were some terrible storms in the South Yorkshire region and Uncle Bob and his family moved lock, stock and barrel to Sheffield where there had been much damage to roofs, and work was plentiful. When Em and I got married they sent us a lovely canteen of cutlery from Sheffield. Where on earth do these things all go to? Em says I'm too quick to get rid of things.

Em and I were chatting to George Roberts y Gof (the blacksmith) and he was reminiscing about the good old days when he was working with his father in the smithy in Mill Road. He told us a tale about the *engan camp* - anvil feat. In the late 1950's, when Uncle Bob lived in Tal y Bont near Bangor, he bought a donkey from someone living in Penmaenmawr. Bringing the donkey home was another thing, said William. "We couldn't get the donkey through the tunnel at Penmaen Bach. Whatever we tried, it wouldn't go into that tunnel; after some time trying to persuade, push, and bribe it with a carrot, we had to give up. We had to get Ned there with a van. It took Ned, Bob and Hayden (a cousin) to get that stubborn old donkey into the van," said William, "and that was how we got it home to Tal y Bont." There was a field by the side of their house, where they kept the old donkey and a pony. The donkey had been limping for a couple of days and needed some treatment to his feet. After a great deal of kicking, pulling and pushing, Uncle Bob and a couple of the kids managed to get the old donkey into the van; having reached Llanfair they went straight up to the smithy and left the donkey to be treated and shoed by Wmffra Gof and his son George. Uncle Bob went to the Virginia Inn and sunk a few beers with his brothers. One thing led to another and Uncle Bob was faced with a challenge. Could he lift the anvil? Uncle Bob was known to be as strong as an ox, and a bit of a showman – and he definitely couldn't refuse a dare. So they all piled into the smithy to see if he could do it. Wmffra Gof had been a smith in the village for many years, and during that time only one man had picked up that anvil. He was Dyfi Humphries from Penmaenmawr, said George. Wmffra gave Uncle Bob a few tips before he started. There was a certain way the anvil could be picked up, he said, which was to slide it up at an angle, slowly, onto your shoulder, and balance it a certain way. The men from the pub were there with their pints. Everyone liked a show! It was as hot as Hell there, as you'd imagine in a smithy. The men made a circle around the anvil, placing bets with each other on how high Uncle Bob could lift it, or even if he could lift it at all. Bob, in his shirt sleeves with his muscles bulging, and the sweat running down his back, was determined to lift it. After some more leg-pulling it was time for the serious business.

Siân Ellis Thomas (Bob's daughter) and her sons Larry and Luke with The Anvil.

Up went the anvil, as far as his chest. OK, that was the easy part – now for the job of lifting it to his shoulders. The veins in his neck bulged with the strain. His breath was coming in short gasps, but still he went on. With his face as red as a tomato by now, and roaring like a mad bull, he tried to lift it a little further, with the men all edging him on. Up it went to his shoulders – Bob had lifted the anvil! "Believe me, that was no mean feat; he was only the second man, for me to know, who has ever done it," said George. When the family moved to Sheffield the faithful old donkey (Paddy) and the pony (Robin) moved with them. They were sent from Bangor by train.

One Sunday afternoon in the early 1970's Em and I were on the beach with our two little girls. The sky was clear, and the waves were rolling gently up to our feet as we sat on the stones near the jetty. Our girls were having a good time throwing stones into the water, and of course arguing with each other as to who could throw the furthest. We were having a picnic, which was rare on a Sunday because Em usually worked; he was a baker at Home Loaf in Conwy at the time. Em pulled out the remainder of the chicken we'd had for lunch and started to eat it. Who popped up but Uncle Bob. Where he came from or indeed where he went afterwards, I don't know, but he was starving. He scragged the chicken carcass, ate some thin bread and butter, and gulped at our warm bottle of orange squash. *Roedd y bwyd yna'n ddigon da i frenin* – that food was fit for a king, said Uncle Bob. Em says that Uncle Bob lived in Llanfair for a while in the 1970's. He had a flat over where the bookies are today. By this time he and Auntie Ann had split up. We had a long chat with him on the beach about his family and who was doing what in the village, and we put the world to rights. It was probably the last time we saw him alive. He suffered with heart problems and had undergone some heart surgery; he died of bronchial pneumonia aged 49 on November 1st 1977 at Cleaver Hospital, Heswall, Rock Ferry, Birkenhead. He was buried with his parents and grandfather in Erw Feiriol on November 5th 1977. His son Robert was to die young also, aged only 40. He had known for a few years that he was quite seriously ill, and had followed medical advice, but he died of organ failure. Uncle Ned sorted a mini bus and we all went as a family to the funeral in Sheffield during the mid 1980's.

A little story about Robert, Uncle Bob's eldest now. When my Dad (Now) died in 1982 we were all in 8 Llwyn y Gog, ready to bury him. The house was packed, with people standing in the street. I remember like yesterday that Lorraine started to cry. "We will never see Taid again," she said. Karen started crying too. The three of us were standing in the hall and Em was at the door seeing that all was going well, when in walked a man with a long bushy beard and fair hair down to his shoulders. I had no idea who he was. "Hello Margaret," he said. I knew instantly I heard his voice that it was Robert. His words to my little girls were: "Uncle Now wouldn't like you to upset yourselves, you must be brave." He gave us a hug. "Remember, Robert, to come back after the funeral," I said. He had hitch-hiked all the way from Sheffield. I was so touched – we hadn't seen him for years and there he was to bury my Dad, who would have been so glad he came. That sounds crackers, doesn't it? I never saw Robert again.

My Mam and Dad, Val and me

My father Owen Water Thomas (1923 - 1982) was born at 2 Pant y Carw, Nant y Felin. I could write a book on my Dad alone, about all his antics – some good, some not so good. One thing I know, he loved "Meg" and his girls very much. I have written about my Dad's siblings, so now it's time to write about my dear Dad. This is going to be really difficult. All this was going to be a bit of fun, but suddenly it has grown into a massive thing which I sometimes think is alive.

Owen Water Thomas (Dad) aged 17.

Dad was just under six feet tall, and in his youth he was as handsome as a film star (so I'm told). He had dark hair, although it always seemed black because he used Brylcream. He had deep blue eyes. He was not a humorous man; rather dry, I suppose you would say. He was a nice man and a gentleman, with a great liking for young people and lots of respect for people older than himself. He was generous to a fault and would do anyone a favour if he could. Dad was most comfortable in a pair of jeans, and always had a white handkerchief sticking out of his back pocket. He could speak on any subject and he could hold his own with anyone. Dad could turn his hand to anything, from knitting to roofing; there was nothing he couldn't do with his hands. However, he was a very poor speller and always urged me to "make sure you learn in school Margiad." He would say: "If you're not sure how to spell a word just write the first letter and scribble the rest; more often than not it'll be understood." When I was old enough I was a dab hand at writing Dad's estimates for him, and between us we made a pretty good job of it. He was not a religious man, but after a few pints he used to say: *God is all-seeing*. I am painting him to be a saint I think. Well believe me, he was a million miles from that and I knew exactly what he was. When he had been drinking, if you had any sense at all you kept well away from him. He was like Jekyll and Hyde, a lovely man sober and a pain in the neck when drunk. When I was a little girl my favourite thing to do was to follow my Dad everywhere, always with a hammer and a piece of wood. I wanted to be "just like Dad." I suppose I should start with what I know of him as a boy. How sorry I am that I didn't ask more questions when he was alive. Whoever reads this, take a lesson and make sure you ask all your questions today. His father's words on his son were: "There couldn't be a better son than Now, he was one of the kindest people I have ever met, but watch out when he was drunk." He went on to say that Dad had been up to some mischief one Saturday night, when he was a young man, and that he had mentioned it to one of the doctors. The doctor's words to Taid were: "Some men shouldn't drink alcohol at all, as it affects their senses and they really don't know or care what they do after it. Now, unfortunately, is one of those men."

How on earth all the family lived in that little cottage I don't know. As you went in you walked straight into the family room, with a small window facing the road and a big black-lead grate where Nain Thomas used to do most of her cooking. There was a bedroom on the right as you went in, only big enough for a single bed and a cupboard, again with a small window facing the road. Up some very wobbly stairs there was another bedroom which they called y siambr – the chamber. This was also tiny. At the bottom of the garden stood the toilet, in the shed which people called y ty bach. Auntie Gladys lived in 1 Pant Carw for a while in the 1990's after Uncle Ned died and she swears there was a ghost there. Out of interest, 1 Pant Carw was on the market for £90,000 in 2004 and it's much the same size now as it was then, apart from the bathroom. The housing market has gone mad!

Dad was born with a physical disability. It didn't affect anything he did, but as he grew from a baby to a little boy it became more noticeable. He was born with his head leaning to one side. There was a sinew in his neck that needed an operation. Children are cruel aren't they, and the other kids used to call him Now pen cam, which means roughly "Now bent head." Poor Dad, only knee high to a grasshopper, would run into the house, crying his eyes out. His mother would bolt outside, shaking her fist at his tormentors. "I had to keep on and on at them b****y doctors before they'd do something for Now," Nain Thomas used to say. If something wasn't considered serious in those days it could wait indefinitely. His mother, being a very determined woman, wouldn't let them put it on the back boiler.

Dad's first day at school was on January 7th 1931 That would have made him about 7 years old! On the admission records he was down as Owie Thomas and lived at the Green Bungalow. In 1935 he went to Pant y Rhedyn School. School children in the early part of the twentieth century weren't encouraged to speak Welsh. In fact there were only one or two Welsh lessons a week, the rest of the time you were told to speak English. "As most of us spoke only Welsh at home," said Dad, "it was quite a shock to have that strange language drummed into you."

When Dad was about six or seven years old he went missing for hours. All the family and neighbours searched for him. Who knew where Now was? "He would often wander on his own with no thought of the time, but this particular day the weather was bad," said Auntie Freda. The Green Bungalow was little more than a hut really, close to the railway line. It was situated at the bottom of one of the gardens of a terrace of houses, demolished to make way for the A55, east of the village (on the way to Pen Dalar). His mother (Grace Bach) was frantic. They had searched everywhere they could think of. Then someone happened to look out to sea, and there was a little spot in the distance – Dad had set off on a great adventure. He soon got into trouble with the current and tide, but he didn't panic and he stayed aboard his little home-made boat. Henry Jorss went out that day in one of his boats and was only just in time. "Now would never have got back to the beach on his own, he's a very lucky little boy," said Henry Jorss. Turning to Dad, he said: "Don't you ever do that again." My dear Dad had spent the morning making himself a small coracle, made of anything he could lay his hands on. From a very young age, Dad was good at building things. Later, Dad said to his mother: "I only wanted to go sailing, Mam."

Auntie Freda said that Henry Jorss was a man who ran a boat-hire business on the beach in the early part of the twentieth century. "He was a great personality," she said. He was also in charge of the bathing huts (bathing machines) which were on wheels so that they could be wheeled to the edge of the water for the sake of modesty. In those days people were far more bashful than they are today. In the winter, the bathing machines were all staked up close to each other, near where Victoria Gardens are today. Henry Jorss used to pay the younger boys a few pennies to wheel the bathing machines to the sands, and hopefully they would wheel them back in before the tide came in. There were a few times when the bathing machines were to be seen floating as Henry struggled with them himself, the boys having forgotten to return!

In 1891 a new bylaw was introduced by the Urban Sanitary Authority (local board of Llanfair) regarding public bathing. There were lots of rules. Boys over the age of twelve had to have two clean towels and "a suitable pair of draws to prevent indecent exposure of the person." The rules stipulated: "A female may not approach within FIFTY YARDS of any place that a male above the age of twelve years may be set down for the purpose of bathing." I wonder how we'd fare if we had rules like that these days! While I'm on the topic of the beach, the Pavilion was built in the early part of the twentieth century at a cost of almost £700. Measuring 75 feet by 38 feet, it had a stage and used to give two or three concerts a week performed by travelling show people. It was owned by the council and designed by a firm from Manchester called Messrs Ginger, Lee and Co. When I was a girl we used to have our carnival dance there. When I was about eleven or twelve, and too young to go in to the dance, I knelt with the other kids on the wooden benches placed around the outside and spent the evening peeping in through the windows. It was wonderful to watch the tango and the waltz; all the dancers in their glad rags, skirts swinging brightly wherever we looked. The hokey cokey would get into full swing, with people throwing their arms and legs around as if they didn't belong to them. Music blared out over the beach. All these jollifications, as I remember, without a drop of alcohol in the building! It was a wonderful sight to see. At that time a man called Mr Lee Pickering ran it; he also owned the Victoria, the public house along the main road. My Dad, was quite friendly with Mr Pickering and did a lot of work for him. Incidentally, Mr Pickering's parents and brother ran the Pen y Bryn Hotel in the early part of the twentieth century. They also ran a charabanc business at that time from Pen y Bryn Hotel. A horse and cart taxi service ran from the Victoria Inn the late nineteenth and early twentieth centuries. Later on the family ran a white bus service between the Victoria Inn and Nant y Coed tea gardens, hence its name, bus wen – white bus. When I was a girl the Crosville Company ran a service between the beach and Ysgol Nant during the summer, the last bus up was 10pm but I had to be on the 9.15 bus. It was very handy, and we did miss it during the winter months.

When I was in school (Pant y Rhedyn) the headmaster Mr Lloyd Jones, who also taught Mam and Dad, told me that my father was a very pleasant lad in school and would do anything if asked, "but if you told him what to do you had no chance," said Mr Jones. That was my Dad to a T. He didn't learn at school, being rather a mischievous little boy who loved to build and make things with his hands. He was to tell Em later that he learned far more after leaving school than he ever did in it. "The school of life," he called it. I suppose that's true about most of us. Dad spent many a day walking and running with his dog in our lovely mountains or swimming in the sea, rather than go to school.

While I am on the subject of Pant Y Rhedyn School I want to tell you about a fire they had there in August in 1939. Dennis Garreg Wen (the painter), was a 14 year old boy on his way for a swim. He was riding his bike down past Maes Y Glyn when he saw a crowd gathering and looking towards the quarry. In the distance he saw flames jumping and leaping out of the windows of his school, up went black smoke swirling and twirling high until it disappeared into the clouds. Pant y Rhedyn was on fire, a sight not to be missed he thought, the swimming could wait for another day! He remembers cycling hell for leather along the sea front. Arriving to the school he promptly found a grandstand seat (on the wall opposite the school). The science room had gone up in flames! "Being the summer holidays the painters were in" said Dennis and they used the science room as a stock room for their paint. "This of course was not a good idea, as there were all sorts of other inflammables there, one thing led to another and before long the room was an inferno" he said. Up through the roof went the flames, the windows were shattering and glass was flying everywhere. They had a mobile water pump but had problems with water pressure. One of fireman Mr Ernie Richards (as it happens he was the local plumber) stood with a hose aimed at the flames and instead of a massive force out came a mere trickle of water. "We kids thought this was hilarious" said Dennis. However, despite these problems they eventually got the fire under control before too much damage was done to the school. "Only a matter of weeks before Mr Lewis our music

Panty Rhedyn School on fire 1939.

Water pump at Pant y Rhedyn fire.

teacher had taken our school choir to the BBC studio at Bangor and we had sung on the radio. For this the school were paid a fee" said Dennis. It was decided to use the money for a new piano. Dennis recalls the men carrying it into school, "they had a hell of a job it was so heavy" he said "I don't remember that we ever had a chance to use it before it went up in flames." It was with great excitement that the kids of the village watched part of their school go up in flames; an extended school holiday was surely on the cards! But this was not to be, the woodwork room was turned into temporary classes and was later on used for the evacuees.

George Roberts (Gof) 1980's.

Chatting to George Gof, I happened to mention that among all the class pictures I have there is only one showing my Dad. George answered with a grin, "I don't want to be cheeky, but old Now was never in school to have his photo taken!" That sums up Dad's childhood in a nutshell.

While I was talking to George he told me that the smithy and Ty Refail next door were built in 1848. Sion Roberts, George's grandfather, bought them in the early 1900's. Wmffra his son worked as a smith also, followed by George, who worked there until he retired in the 1990's. George's father Wmffra was walking home from the smithy one evening in the 1920's, when he met up with one of the locals who was partial to a drop of beer and was staggering slightly. The man was known to be good with words and looked up at the full moon and said:

O leuad wen, o leuad dlos,
Wyt ti'n llawn bob mis –
A fi yn llawn bob nos.

(O pale lovely moon, you are full every month – and I am full every night!)

School days of the brothers; Now - bottom row first right and Ned Thomas third from the right.

One of my Dad's favourite school stories was about a conflict between him and his brothers regarding which of them went to school on any particular day. There was only one pair of decent shoes between them, so the boys used to argue as to which one of them could stay at home. "The loser either went to school with shoes that were far too small, or had to stuff paper in the toes to keep them on," said Dad. "Either way, it was a long, uncomfortable day for one of us and at the end of it we would limp home and hope that the next day we would be the winner. In the winter months, if the weather was very cold, we would sometimes have to stay at home because we had no warm clothing. There were lots of us kids in the same boat and it was quite common then to lose a few days school for the lack of warm clothing," he said. "Breakfast for us was bread and dripping or a bowl of porridge, and if we were very lucky half an egg each, with a slice of dry bread. Very often we would go to bed with hunger pangs in our bellies." Dad was a good one for these stories – I wish I could tell them like he did. Their main diet in those days was *Tatws Llaeth* – potatoes with buttermilk; *Brwas Menyn* – bread soaked in hot water with a knob of butter or margarine, and salt and pepper; and of course that old favourite Mair yr Iar – Mary the Hen. Lob scouse was on the menu very often, with a bit of scrag end (lamb) added to give flavour. At Christmas, if they were lucky, Nain would go and buy a couple of old boilers from Auntie Mary Tyddyn Angharad (Gerallt's mother). Each child would hang a stocking on the mantelpiece. "Morning came," said Dad, "we were all very excited and couldn't wait to empty our Christmas stocking. A few nuts, an orange, an apple, a few sweets, perhaps one of us would have a home-made catapult or a game of ludo. Not much you might say, but it was such a treat that we were all content and happy."

The Fair came on October 1st, my father's birthday. "We would have a smashing day," said Dad. "A day off school and my birthday, so I would always have a copper or two to spend," he said. "All us kids would get together in Llanfair - shouting, playing the fool and having a good time teasing the girls; come rain or shine we would make for the village, as people had done for many decades. There were stalls selling everything you could think of down both sides of the village. The stall holders would be shouting and encouraging us to go and look at their goods. We didn't have much money, but what we did have we shared, a couple of pennies was a lot of money in those days Margiad," said Dad. "We would run up and down the street, up to all sorts of mischief and being chased in and out of the stalls, pinching a stick of Welsh rock where we could. This would go on until late evening. The chippy in the village did well." A circus came to town – what a lot of excitement that was. The fields in Pen y Bryn were the venue (before any houses were built) and sometimes the church field was used for this great event. Everything was so bright and colourful. There were elephants all dressed up in their finery. Elephants, as we all know, love the water, and they would be led down to the beach in single file. Trunk to tail they strolled through the village: "a sight to behold," said Huw Lloyd. There was even a black bear which had a wide leather collar and a large chain on which he was led around. He did all sorts of tricks and delighted the audience. There was one occasion, however, when this great big bear escaped from his master and ran riot, tearing his way around; in and out of the people he ran – people were screaming and shouting, pushing each other to get away from this wild animal. The bear made a hell of a mess before he was finally recaptured. Thankfully, no-one was seriously hurt.

One sultry summer's day my Dad and his friends went up to the old golf links to trap rabbits and hares. "Now was no more than 10 or 11 years old," said Auntie Freda. Off they went with their dogs at their heels. They were all very excited; they had a few jam butties with them, and the little stream running gently down past the old golf links saved them from having to carry water. The lads were having a good time, hiding from each other in and out of the rhododendron bushes up and down the hills. All of a sudden there was a scream. Someone shouted: Help! The boys ran towards the scream. There was my Dad with his arm sticking out in front of him, and hanging onto one of his fingers was a rat. Dad had put his dog down a hole to chase what he thought was a rabbit; the dog came back without a rabbit, so Dad put his hand deep into the hole and had the shock of his life – the rat had bitten him so hard that the other lads had great difficulty removing it.

Some time after he left school, Dad went to work for Mr Pugh of Tyddyn Drain, a building contractor in the village at the time. He worked for Mr Pugh for about a year, until he was old enough to join the Navy. Early in 1943, aged nineteen, Dad joined the Merchant Navy and completed one or two voyages on board the cargo vessel *Ville De Tamatave* as a fireman stoker. The vessel had belonged to the Vichy French. In June 1941 the British Light Cruiser *HMS Dunedin* captured the *Tamatave* and she was taken over by the Ministry of War Transport (MOWT). On January 24th 1943 the *Tamatave* went down with all hands whilst sailing from Liverpool to New York. Dad told Em a story once about a ship he should have been on but for some reason wasn't – a ship that went down with no survivors; this was the ship he was talking about, probably. After a few months he joined the Royal Navy, although he was still a merchant seaman, operating under Royal Navy rules: they were known as Royal Navy Ancillary Personnel. From November 9th 1943 he served aboard *HMS Mersey*. This was not a seagoing ship but an old red brick hospital in Liverpool which was used as a Depot Ship for RNAP. It seems that *HMS Mersey* was used as a depot for training in gunnery etc., to prepare the seamen for service on armed merchant cruisers: these could be any type of vessel, from small fishing boats to large liners. I can't seem to find any more information on Dad in the Royal Navy, but I have found a researcher who is going to check the records at the Public Records Office at Kew for me – so I live in hope! Having now exhausted all avenues, there is nothing more I can do regarding Dad in

Owen Water Thomas (Dad), Vancouver 1944.

the RN. It would seem that unless I find a service number for him (which is highly unlikely now), this is the end of the road. I have spoken to Eddie (Polo) Roberts from Penmaenmawr. He was in Vancouver at the same time as Dad and he remembers that my father was a bit of a bad lad who liked fighting after a bellyful of beer. Dad and a Cockney friend had been out on the town one night. On the way back to their ship they'd got into some trouble and it ended up in a skirmish. Dad and his mate were thrown into the brig for a couple of days to cool down.

Dad told me that he jumped ship when he was in Halifax, Nova Scotia. He was caught, but I don't remember what happened to him. There were a couple of occasions in the North Atlantic when he was torpedoed and spent many hours in the cold water; it was so silly of me not to have asked more questions! Dad had a couple of tattoos on his arms. One showed him kneeling at the grave of his taid John Water and the other had the name *Vera* on it. We grew up asking Dad about this name. I remember him saying she was his first wife from Canada: "Not a patch on your Mam," he would say laughingly, but nothing else was ever said about her. As I got older I picked up information from here and there. On April 15th 1944 in Vancouver, my father married his first wife Vera Ross Mcluskie. He was a leading stoker in the Royal Navy, she was a sales girl aged 22 who worked in a shop and lived in Vancouver. Her father was a psychiatric nurse; both her parents were born in Scotland. I have a copy of the marriage certificate so I have all the details, but it's very hard to get more information. Auntie Freda arranged the divorce for Dad but didn't keep the papers. She kept a photo of the wedding, and a while after Dad died she told me she had it. I said: "Cut the bride out and I will have it." She cut it up and brought me the bit showing Dad. I didn't want to see the bride at first, I suppose out of loyalty to my dear Mam. Years later, Auntie Freda said she still had a photo of the wedding and asked me if I wanted it. By this time our daughters were old enough, so I asked Auntie Freda to bring it with her the next time she came. It was a white wedding and Dad looked so handsome in his Royal Navy uniform. It does seem funny that Dad had had another life, half way across the world, which he never spoke about. Eddie (Polo) was at the wedding, but he doesn't remember much about it. "I do remember that Now didn't stay long with Vera as he was transferred to Victoria Island," said Eddie. Dad was in *His Majesty's Canadian Ship Naden*, the name given to a navy base in Esquimalt, British Columbia, Canada.

"Do you know if there were any children?" I asked Eddie. He hesitated, so I said there was a whisper that perhaps there was a child. "Well," said Eddie, "it's a long time ago but I think she was expecting a baby; I'm not sure what she had." This wasn't a shock to me because over the years I'd heard people insinuate that there was a child in Canada. My parents never breathed a word about it, which is really strange; Mam and I were so close. She was my best friend. Mam must have felt really strongly about it, not to have mentioned it to me. Having said all that, I never asked (see Note 17).

In the early 1940's my Mam, Megan, got married for the first time to Harry Owen. Auntie Alma (Mam's sister) remembers the wedding reception in Garizim Terrace (*Lawr Tai*). "The table was covered with all sorts of food, we had never seen so much. Food was, of course, on rations, and we kids thought our birthdays and Christmas had come, all rolled into one. I think people in those days would all muck in and help each other far more than we do today," said Auntie Alma. Anyway, Harry was on leave from the Army at the time and returned to active duty soon afterwards. Things didn't work out for them and they were eventually divorced. During those years I suppose people did things they would never do normally. Out of interest, food rationing didn't end until 1954.

During those years Mam worked for Radcliff Engineers in the Hotpoint building in Llandudno Junction (demolished now). According to her friend Dilys Eames, Mam had a strong voice and used to sing Vera Lynn's popular songs in the factory during dinner hour. It seems that Dad came home on leave around Christmas 1944. That is where my Mam came into the picture, although they'd grown up together. The next couple of years are a bit vague. I do know that Mam was working in the Llanfairfechan Hotel as a cleaner, and then she got promoted to barmaid. Auntie Alma told me on one occasion that Mam had had scarlet fever while she worked at the hotel and was really ill. She was so sick she couldn't be moved and had to stay there for a week or two. I'm sure that her mother and father (Nain and Taid Gwyn as I will refer to them) were absolutely mortified that Mam worked as a barmaid. You couldn't find two families more different than Mam and Dad's families. Mam's family were strong chapel people and lived so differently from Dad's family, but where there's a will there's a way, as they say, and Mam and Dad found a way to be together. The war ended and Dad came home for good; life was beginning to get back to some sort of normality. Dad went back to work for Mr Nathaniel Ames Pugh for a further two years and completed his time as a builder, slater and tiler. What a good reference Mr Pugh gave Dad on January 8th 1947: "Never have I had a man more willing to work," he wrote. Dad thought a lot of Mr Pugh, indeed I still have the reference. Dad used to say that Mr Pugh's motto was: "You can always tell a good worker by his tools – keep them clean and tidy after you, son." One more bit of advice Mr Pugh gave Dad: "Remember, don't work for your family – you will never get rich."

Recently I went to see Mrs Olwen Williams (Mr Pugh's daughter): she is 95 years old and like a spring chicken. We spent a pleasant couple of hours chatting and I'm sure that Mrs Williams enjoyed reminiscing about the old days. She told me that Arthur Morgan had also been an apprentice to Mr Pugh. "The only two boys my father took," said Olwen. "He was rather a quiet, serious man, my father and would never have his photo taken – he wouldn't even give me away on my wedding day," she said laughingly. She did manage to find me a photo of him, so I was lucky.

I was born on March 21st 1946. The first day of Spring – a lovely hot day, my Dad used to tell me. He was in his shirt sleeves digging in the garden at 3 Pen Bryn when he was told that Mam had had a little girl in St David's Hospital (now demolished), Bangor. At the time of my birth Mam and Dad weren't married and Mam lived in Lawr Tai with my Nain and Taid Gwyn. It must have been a real scandal in the village, although I suppose there were quite a lot of similar things going on during and soon after the war. How Nain and Taid Gwyn coped with the worry of it all, I will never know. I was the first grandchild for my maternal Nain and Taid so I do know that they thought I was wonderful. Taid Gwyn went out and bought me a pram. Nain Gwyn used to say: "When you were born, del, I waited till the nurse left the ward and picked you up, you were the most beautiful baby I had ever seen; you had lovely dark smooth skin and you were such a good baby. I could have eaten you!" I think maybe my Nain was just a little bit biased. After I was born Dad stopped drinking for a few months, I'm told, but of course he went back to it eventually. "Your Dad would walk around the room with you in his arms for hours just looking at you and talking to you, he was so proud of you," said Nain Gwyn.

During the next year Mam lived with Nain Thomas and the clan at 3 Pen y Bryn. Times were hard. Gwynfor (Mam's brother), who would have been about ten at the time, remembers going to see Mam, and Mam cutting him a fresh crust and plastering it with butter. "Hurry up, Gwyn, eat it before anyone sees how much butter I've put on it," said Mam – not that my Dad or his family were mean, far from it, but I suppose my mother, being young and in someone else's house, didn't always feel comfortable.

By the time my sister Valerie was born on March 23rd 1947 we were still living at 3 Pen y Bryn, and my parents were still not married. There was only a year and two days between Val and I. The four of us were living in Nain Thomas's by now – poor Mam! Nain and Taid Thomas and the family thought the world of my mother and were pleased that their son had "such a good girl." I used to say to my dear mother: "You must have been mad, Mam bach." "What choice is there when you love someone Mag. There have been lots more good times than bad, del," she would answer. I wonder sometimes if Mam would have made the same choice if she'd known what kind of a life was in front of her. I think she would have. My Dad and his brothers were all fresh out of the forces by then and they were up to all sorts of tricks. The house was like a bedlam, and things went from bad to worse for us. So Mam took Val and me to Nain and Taid Gwyn's to live; by now they lived at 25 Pen y Bryn. That was when my mother's troubles really started – we were far too close to Nain Thomas's house and my Dad.

Dad wouldn't leave us alone and he made a complete nuisance of himself at Nain and Taid Gwyn's. He used to go there after too much beer and cause havoc outside their house: shouting, kicking and throwing pebbles at the windows until someone answered. On one of those occasions Dad had pushed the door and walked in. Uncle Harry (one of Mam's brothers) was sat in an easy chair and told Dad in no uncertain terms "to get out and leave his sister and the children alone." Uncle Harry was like a match, he flared up when he was riled – but he was only slightly built and no match for my father. Holding up his fists, my Dad said: "Come outside and we'll sort this out now, mate." Having jumped up, poor Uncle Harry was quickly pushed back down by my Nain Gwyn and Mam, who promptly sat on him. Nain and Taid were nervous wrecks with it all. After a few pints Dad really didn't care as long as he had his own way. Mam didn't know which way to turn. Where could she go, with two little babies and no money? She couldn't stay in her parents' house; it was making them and the rest of the family afraid to sit in their own home. Can you imagine being too scared to answer your own front door? I have known what it's like to be afraid to answer the door, and believe me, it's not very pleasant. In those days there was no place to go, so Mam decided in her wisdom to admit herself with her two little babies to Dolwaen, the workhouse in Conwy. In 1930 they abolished the word workhouse and the term public assistance institute was used instead. After the workhouse was closed the building was used as a hospital for the elderly for many years. Sadly, it has been knocked down, and new houses have been built there recently.

Em and I visited Conwy Archives Services at Llandudno and found a piece in a newspaper headlined *Scene at Public Institution: Man Violent in Drink*. It really upset me to think of my lovely, caring young mother in such a position all those years ago, my sister Val only five months old and me only seventeen months. I know, of course, what kind of man my Dad was and what alcohol did to him. I saw it all at first hand, but even after reading that piece I could still feel sorry for him, such a foolish young man. Why did he drink as he did? I have asked myself that question many hundreds of times over the years and still I have no answer. Mam's words were: "Dad is more to be pitied than anything else, del."

On August 2nd 1947 my dear mother and her two little babies were in the Public Assistance Institution. I feel so saddened by all this. I feel I should have been there to help her – so silly of me, because I *was* there, but I was a seventeen month old baby. I have tears running down my cheeks thinking about my Mam, my Sister and my Dad. I have spent all my life trying to make life easier for my family; we were so close, even with all our problems (or maybe because of them). I have been so lucky to have had such a good husband to help me through it. This is what the *North Wales Weekly News* reported on the incident.

Scene at Public Institution. Man violent in drink assaulted police

"Your conduct was abominable and can't be overlooked. You are a danger to the communities when you are drunk. The police and the public have to be protected. If you can't control yourself we shall have to control you." The above remarks were made by Mr G H Edwards sitting with the Mayor (Ald. A. I. Parry) at a special court at Conway on Tuesday to Owen Water Thomas, (23) of 3 Pen y Bryn Llanfairfechan, who was charged with two offences of assaulting the police and also of being drunk and disorderly. Thomas was sent to prison for 12 months.

Mr J E Hallmark prosecuting said that about 9.30pm on August 2nd the defendant called at the Dolwaen Public Institution and demanded to see a young woman who had been admitted earlier with her two children. He was very drunk and on being refused, became very abusive and violent and the police had to be called.

Struck Sergeant

Sgt. C M Griffiths said that at 10.5pm in response to a telephone call he went to Dolwaen with Constable 48 Ellis. The defendant, who was sitting in the hall, refused to leave and was using foul language. All attempts to reason with him were of no avail and he had to be forcibly ejected. He became extremely violent and in the melee the Sergeant was struck a severe blow on the left eye and had to receive medical attention.

Constable Ellis said the defendant, who was raving mad, kicked him in the back and he fell on his face. Mr R P Lewis said: "In my 24 years as a master of a Public Assistance Institute I have never heard such foul language." Thomas, when the woman he demanded to see would not see him, refused to leave and said: "I'll see her even if I have to murder someone."

Thomas, who pleaded not guilty to the charges, said he was suffering from ill health. He did not remember anything of the incident. He had called at the institution to see a young woman whom he was going to marry when she obtained her divorce.

Dad was taken to the cells at Conwy after the incident and locked up for the night. This sounds terrible, I know and yes, it was terrible, but you must remember that my Dad was losing his beloved Meg and his little girls, whom he adored. His own fault, you might say, and there's no excuse for behaving that way and I agree with you, but my father was a law unto himself and after beer the man was not for turning! No amount of talking would dissuade Dad from wanting to see Mam.

Now and Megan Thomas (Mam and Dad) on their wedding day, 1948, with Auntie Hannah left and Auntie Annie Waters.

Years later Dad was to tell Em that he was afraid of getting a hiding off the coppers. "I told them that if one of them came near me I would make sure they would go home without an ear or a limb," he said. "In those days it was nothing for the police to give you a hell of a hiding", said Dad. Auntie Alma seems to think that Dad did his time in Liverpool Jail. One might suppose that Mam would enjoy a few months peace after all that but no, all she could do was worry about him. Once again her father, my dear Taid Gwyn, came to the rescue and gave her the fare to go and see Dad in jail. Dad served about eight months. On April 14th 1948, exactly a week after my Dad's divorce was made final; my beloved parents were married at Bangor Registry Office with Auntie Hanna and Auntie Annie Waters as their witnesses. There was a lot of heartache as well as happiness in store for my dear mother and father. In November 1948 my father was in fresh trouble and once again he found himself in front of a magistrates' court, this time in Bala. Dad was 25 years old and had been married for only seven months when he was accused of attacking a Mr J T Theodore at the Bull Hotel. He was also accused of being drunk and unruly. Sergeant Morris and Mr Theodore both gave evidence. It was stated that my father had many convictions against him and that he had been in jail before. Dad was fined £1 for being drunk and unruly and was sent to prison for a month for attacking Mr Theodore.

In 1949 Llanfair's population was around 3000 (See Note 18). In October of that year a new policeman came to Llanfairfechan. He lived at Sunnyside, a house in Upper

Mill Road. By a strange coincidence, our daughter Karen bought the house over forty years later. JEJ as I will refer to him, the new policeman, had been in the Army and had been a prisoner of war in Poland. He has written quite a number of books, some of them autobiographical. He has written about his time in Llanfairfechan. In 1987 I read a short story in *Y Cymro* about a policeman in Llanfairfechan who'd been in a fight with someone with the initials NT in 1950. I'd heard the story of this fight, though the version I'd heard was rather different, I must admit. Someone pointed out the story to Uncle Ned, and he in turn came to me saying: "It was your Dad Now, and I can tell you now that your Dad was the winner that night on the bridge."

One Christmas I read the story out aloud to my family as we sat around the fire in our home, Woodlands. It was very upsetting to read that my Dad, so many years ago, had had such a hiding off anyone, let alone a policeman. JEJ had written so accurately about my Dad that I could picture him in front of me - his actions, the clothes he wore, the way he spoke. I felt as if I was there, watching the fight. How clever to have a talent for making a story comes alive, as JEJ does. Here was my dear father coming back once again to haunt me, and him dead all of seven years. Anyway, I wasn't really interested in who the winner was. But I was upset, so I decided to write to JEJ. I didn't want to cause any trouble, just to let JEJ know that my Dad had a family who cared for him and that I wasn't happy about his story. JEJ wrote back immediately, apologizing that his story had upset me, and saying that he was unaware that my Dad had any family at all. JEJ went on to tell me that he and my Dad had both been rather headstrong young men and inclined to be quick on the draw. My father was, in JEJ's words: "A champion and indeed the idol of the young men of the village and it was they, to a great extent, who influenced him in a lot of the things he did." JEJ went on to write: "The confrontation on the village bridge all those years ago was inevitable, but it was I that was at fault, as I threw the first punch; I could not resist a challenge either." I am sure that my father didn't need any encouragement from anyone. He was a daredevil and was always up to some trouble or other after too much beer. JEJ and I have been in correspondence with each other since that first letter, indeed Em and I paid him a visit at his home a couple of years ago. JEJ story about the fight on the bridge was a little different from the version I had heard over the years, but these stories do get rather distorted with time don't they?

Dad was indeed a young, carefree, happy-go-lucky man who didn't worry about tomorrow. He lived all his life hand in hand with a pint of beer and a cigarette; when he'd had a few pints he loved a cigar. He was very high spirited and after a few beers he would sometimes get rather aggressive. I suppose I would call him a troublemaker, had I known him in those days - not a man you'd want your daughter involved with, but that's life.

There was a big fight on the village bridge (*Bont Pentra*) near the Llanfair Arms one Saturday night, all those years ago. My Dad had been out drinking most of the day with his brothers. They were roofers mainly, but could turn their hands to anything. My Dad was as strong as a horse; Gwyn (Mam's brother) remembers seeing Dad walking on a building site carrying a hundredweight bag of cement under each arm with no problem at all. If it wasn't for the drink, I'm sure the Thomas brothers would have been rich men. Such a waste! The brothers were excellent workers. In the days after the war they were highly sought after; there were lots of buildings going up and the Thomas brothers roofed many of them, for instance the Coed Mawr Estate in Bangor, and estates in Bethesda and Caernarfon.

One very hot Saturday afternoon in 1950, having worked hard all morning, Dad made his way to the pub and that is where he stayed until closing time (3pm). There was no money left for wages. Dad was a very generous man and would spend money like water in the pub, buying drinks for all he knew and some he didn't. When he was broke he would try and borrow a few pounds off whoever he could, and I'm afraid he didn't always pay it back. There was no consideration that there wouldn't be any money to take home to his wife and children. He often said to me, "Margiad fach, you can always get the price of a pint, but no-one will give you the price of a loaf." That day Mam was at home waiting for his wages, hoping to catch the shops before they closed. Dad walked in at around 4pm, the worse for drink and with no money. My dear Mother had more sense than to shout about money when Dad was drunk. The pubs in those days opened from 11am to 3pm and from 5.30pm to 10pm. It depended on how much money Dad had left as to what mood he was in. The pubs were closed all day Sunday; that was my Mam's favourite day – a day for the family.

When he came home from the pub in the afternoon my poor Mother would have tried to humour him and get him to go on the bed for an hour or two so that he would sober up a little. There was always food on the table when Dad came home. After eating his tea he would start worrying where he would get money from to go out that night. He could be very demanding "when he hadn't had quite enough to drink" as Mam put it. If she had any money, sometimes Mam would give him two shillings (10 pence), although she was a dab hand at hiding money (her favourite hiding place was under the carpet or lino). Depending again on what mood Dad was in, she would say: "Anything for a quiet life."

Mr Roland Jones (a member of the tailor family) and his wife Auntie Louie were neighbours of ours for many years and very kind to us. Val and I would go to their house to ask if we could borrow a shilling (5p) for Mam. Sometimes it was for the electric meter. They never refused us and they always got it back before we'd ask again. My dear Mam was independent and would starve rather than ask anyone for a penny, but needs must, and sometimes Dad would want what he called "entrance money" for the pub. Leading up to the fight, Dad went out to the pub in the evening, after boozing all day. Dad would usually make it to the pub for opening time. The young men of the village had been edging him on for many weeks about the new PC in the village, "a real tough guy" they said. It seems that Dad had reached boiling point that Saturday night. When he was a young man he could never resist a challenge; other people would make the bullets and my daft Dad would fire them. The villagers were all aware that Dad had been in prison for being drunk and disorderly and for assaulting a couple of policemen, so it was nothing new for him to take on another one. Over the years, Dad had many fights and wouldn't think twice about using his feet. After the pubs closed, confident and arrogant, and drunk too, Dad walked up the village with his father and a few friends and relatives. The village was packed, as it was on most Saturday nights. Mr Burns the chippy across the road from the Police Station was full and doing a roaring trade, but not for long. Mr Burns used to sell fish which he'd caught with his own line on the beach. The locals were all outside, waiting for a grandstand view of the long-awaited confrontation. It was whispered that Now Thomas was on the look-out for Constable JEJ. It didn't take long for word to get around, so even people who weren't usually out at 10.30pm made sure they didn't miss anything. Most, of course, were there to cheer my Dad on, but inevitably some people hoped he would get a good hiding. There were many, many of my family there waiting, watching and hoping for a good show. I'm sure they weren't disappointed! My poor, silly father once again in trouble. JEJ was one of three policemen in the village at that time and had boxed in the Army. Dad was quite tall, very muscular and as strong as an ox. When he'd been drinking he had no fear at all. He was as stubborn as a mule and game for anything. There was one problem, however, he'd been drinking and his coordination wasn't as good as it might have been. The place to be for young men in those days was on the village bridge. That is where JEJ stood. My Dad, being Dad, goaded him into a fight; both men had fought in the war and fancied themselves. Even a policeman, at the end of the day, is only a man. According to various tales about this fight, it wasn't one to be missed. I have seen my Dad fight a few times over the years and one thing I can tell you is that he threw a good punch. He wouldn't give up until he was well and truly beaten, or until his opponent was on the floor. In this fight on the bridge he fought like a tiger, said Uncle Ned. He wouldn't give in – he even tried to throw the policeman over the side of the bridge. Fists were flying and the policeman was connecting more often than Dad. My father's face was a hell of a mess, with blood everywhere. He couldn't open his eyes, but still he wouldn't give in. He kept going back for more of the same. The crowd by this time was going wild, shouting and screaming, betting on the outcome. "Your Dad threw a right hook with the strength of a madman, just hoping it would connect, and down went the policeman," said Uncle Ned. That was his version of events. After the fight was over another policeman PC 99, affectionately known as Champion, took Dad to the Police Station with the help of his father, Taid Thomas. Mrs Jones (PC 99's wife) was there ready with a bowl of water and some towels to bathe Dad's face. *Well Now bach, rwyt ti byth yn dysgu: am lanast ar dy wyneb di* –what a mess: will you never learn? Said Mrs Jones, who was a quiet, gentle lady and would do you a good turn if she could. PC 99 and his family lived in the Police Station house for many years. It was decided that the only charge that would be brought against Dad was of being drunk and disorderly. One of the reasons, probably, was that the policeman may have thrown the first punch and this was witnessed by most of the community. Dad pleaded guilty and was fined ten shillings (50p), which probably took Mam ten weeks to pay at a shilling a week. As I recall there were many fines to pay over the years.

Minutes of the court case in 1950, copied from J E J's book

May it please your Worship? This is a case of two spirited young men meeting headlong on a hot summer's evening, and that evening, your Worship, was a Saturday evening which, I am sure your Worship agrees, is not without significance. One of the young men a Police Constable recently demobilized from the army after serving throughout the war with considerable distinction. Your Worship will observe that the first ribbon on his chest is that of the Distinguished Conduct Medal. Needless to say, your Worship, such a young man is liable to act positively and decisively in any given situation.

The second young man is a working man, one who is known to be a very hard worker. He also served his country during the war in the Merchant Navy and braved many dangers on the high seas. He is known to be a young man of spirit, trained to react physically and instantly to the almost daily perils which he faced while serving in the Merchant Navy. Well your Worship, last Saturday was a very hot day. The defendant, who had been working hard all day, relaxed with his friends in the evening and enjoyed a few glasses of beer and there is nothing wrong with that. It may well be that, with the heat of the day and the hard work, the defendant had a glass or two more than usual, or it might have been that due to the sultriness of the weather, the drink had a greater effect on him. Be that as it may, suffice to say that by closing time he was a little the worse for drink, as the saying goes. However he caused no trouble to anyone and went towards home. On the way he came across the young Constable. These two young men came face to face, your Worship. Words were exchanged; a warning was given which was not immediately heeded. Not perhaps surprising, considering the circumstances. Further words were exchanged. There were several people in the vicinity and that had an adverse effect on the situation, making it very difficult for either of these spirited young men to give in to each other. Neither was prepared to lose face. This resulted in the young Constable being more determined and in the defendant being more obdurate. The result was inevitable. An ultimatum was given and rejected. Whereupon the Constable decided that he had to arrest the defendant. This he did and the result, your Worship, is that the defendant stands before you this morning having pleaded guilty to being "drunk and disorderly". That concludes the case your Worship.

On March 25th 1950, at 10.34am, Dad sent Mam a telegram from Birkenhead where he was working. The telegram read: *Priority Mrs M Thomas. Come first train today without fail, will send wire. Nowie*. Mam received the telegram at 11.20am. She went to the Co-op and bought Val and me a new coat, and a pair of shoes each. Then she made for the railway station, to catch the first train she could, having first sent Dad a reply by telegram. Dad was at the station to meet us with, guess what? Yes! A new coat and a pair of shoes for both of us. I have lots of letters which Dad wrote to Mam during the years he worked away. It is such a pleasure to read them and to have an insight into their lives together all those years ago. We lived first at 5 Tan y Bonc, a little row of six (two up, two down) terrace cottages at the very top of the village. Directly behind the cottages was a big bank, leading on to Tyddyn Angharad fields, making the back of the houses very dark and damp. Numbers 1 and 6 were the only cottages that could use the back door. In 1950 only 46 per cent of the British population had bathrooms. The view from our bedroom was really something special, although we didn't appreciate it at the time. To open your curtains first thing in the morning was a real treat. Whatever the season, there was always something new to see on Garreg Fawr, on Terrace Walk – or Ben Ochor as we called it – or down Valley Road. You could even see over to Beaumaris. It really is what picture postcards are made of, and all this from our little bedroom window. Tan y Bonc was the centre of my world when I was growing up. It was quiet, and seemed like miles and miles from the village. We were practically a law unto ourselves living up there. It was a long walk for us from the village, especially for my Mam with all those heavy bags of food she had to carry. Sometimes she would be lucky and Mrs Avis Bellis would give her a lift home after work. Dad always found his way home, even after a few too many. Many a night Dad slept it off at the bottom of the little bank just in front of 6 Tan Bonc, only to wake up in the early hours and roll into the house half frozen. "One of these days, Now Bach, you will come home with your head under your arm," Mam would say.

There was no water inside the houses in those days, only cold water taps near the front door. There was a row of sheds, with toilets, about fifty or sixty yards away, and galvanized sheets made for a noisy roof when it rained. I remember how we would use sacks and old clothing to cover the cistern: anything to try and prevent it from freezing in winter. Our last trip at night was a walk to the *tŷ bach* - I was a coward and always pushed my sister Val in front of me.

In 1895 Tan Bonc cottages, as well as Tyddyn Angharad farm, were owned by Elias Williams, a farmer. Elias sold 2,3,4,5 and 6 to Mr John Williams, a coal merchant from Bethesda. Strangely, there was no mention of number 1. The rent for each cottage in 1925 was 4/- (20p) per week. For one tenant, Mrs M Owen, an exception was made and 3/- was charged, owing to her being a poor widow and on parish relief. At that time Mr Jacob Roberts (Em's Taid), a shepherd, and his family lived in number six. There were no written agreements of tenancy. Mr D Williams of Forest Avenue, Llanfairfechan, collected the rents weekly. The cottages were to change hands a few times over the next fifty years. In 1948 Uncle Hugh (Tyddyn Llwyfan farm) bought numbers 3 and 4 for the grand total of £120. With them went the "water closets". He also bought the rent arrears of the tenants at numbers 3 and 4, which amounted to £11. A couple of years later Uncle Hugh and his wife, Auntie Lizzie, were to buy number 6 as well.

I recall my daily walk to school in the 1950's. Come rain, hail or shine, Uncle Hugh (Tyddyn Llwyfan) in his little green Morris Eight van, Hugh Gerlan, Gerallt and Will Tyddyn Angharad, Will Camarnaint and Ellis Glanrafon (whom I seem to remember always had a roll-up stuck in the corner of his mouth), plus many more local farmers, would congregate every morning outside the Town Hall in their old coats and flat caps, string knotted around their waists. What on earth was the string for, I used to wonder. On their feet were muddy old boots or Wellingtons turned down at the tops. Even the farmers who had no milk to sell would look forward to their daily meetings. The milk churns would be dragged from the backs of very old vans and tractors, which had rattled their way down Valley Road and various other little lanes and tracks leading from the farms to the village. There was no worry about bald tyres, bad brakes, or any of the vehicles being roadworthy, as long as they had four wheels and an engine of sorts. The Ministry of Transport Test (MOT) did not come into force until 1960, when any vehicle over ten years old had to have an MOT. The heavy milk churns were lifted high onto a sort of table by the side of the Town Hall, especially made for the churns. Llan Dairy milk wagon would pick up all the churns and off the driver would go to some unknown destination.

The family of Tyddyn Angharad c. 1914 hay making.
Left to right: Richard Jones Gerallt's great-grandfather, Mary his mother, his grandparents Jane and John Jones and his uncle Henry Richard. Front row middle is his father Robert.

Among the farmers would be David Llanerch. Now David was always late with the milk. Having driven like a fool from Llanerch farm he would arrive with his brakes screeching, and jumping out of the van he would shout: "Where the heck is that wagon, don't tell me he was early again." The farmers would answer him laughingly: "Well David Bach, you've missed the boat again," and poor David would have to take the milk to Llan Dairy in Penmaenmawr. The farmers would put the world to rights, catch up on the latest village gossip, and discuss who had been fighting whom last night. It must have been a man who said "women talk a lot." The men would enjoy a roll-up, or a pipe. Perhaps they would discuss the latest headlines in the newspaper they'd just purchased from "John Dick" the newsagent across the road. Of course the biggest discussion of all would be about market prices. Having finished their morning ritual, off they would go in their different directions, ready for the hard day's work ahead of them.

Dad did quite a lot of work at Gerlan and Tyddyn Llwyfan, and every chance I got I went up with him. I loved it up there on the farms. I recall he did some concreting in the cowshed at Gerlan and as well as wages he always came home with a couple of turnips or a few pounds of spuds. He did some work for Uncle Hugh in Tyddyn Llwyfan and as usual I traipsed after him. For some reason Dad had to go through a field full of cows, and there in the middle was the old bull. There was no way I was going through that field, even with my Dad! I stood on a seat, looking over the wall, watching Dad and Uncle Hugh crossing towards the bull. I nearly had a fit and screamed for Dad to come from there, but to no avail – there was a job to be done. I can't have been more that 6 or 7, and I was afraid that the bull was going to attack my beloved Dad. I remember that fear as if it were yesterday.

We went for a walk to Tan Bonc recently and I decided to have a quick peep at the old toilets; would you believe it, they're still there, down a narrow and overgrown path.

In the summer of 1951 Dad was working at Gwrych Castle near Abergele. It was decided that we as a family could go there for a little holiday. What excitement, going to sleep in a castle with twenty odd bedrooms in it! Can you imagine what we felt like? Here I was; five or six years old, and I had never been on holiday. It was wonderful; Mam had washed and ironed our clothes, and they were like new. We were all packed and ready to go. The day dawned, the sun shone and we were off. I have no memory of how we got there. The thing I remember best was the massive grand marble staircase facing us when we entered; it had a thick red

Gwrych Castle

carpet on it. I felt like a fairy queen. The furniture was like none I had ever seen before – big, dark, heavy and very ugly I thought. My dear Mother was thrilled with it all and said:"Where are we sleeping, Now?" "Come on Meg, I'll show you the bedroom; it's huge, bigger than our entire little house put together," said Dad. He took us up these lovely stairs to a bedroom that we all had to share. It was eerie; one could just imagine the posh people in the "olden days" with their fancy dresses, sitting near a big warm fire with maids and servants running around after them. Once the door was closed I couldn't believe the size of the room. It had one huge brown bed in the middle and another smaller one by its side. On the floor a colourful carpet covered most of the floorboards. The window had heavy dark curtains that seemed to reach to the roof. There was

Randolph Turpin and Grace Bach in Gwrych Castle in 1951.

some massive furniture there. I thought why in the world would people need so much space to keep clothes? To finish the room there was a gigantic, ugly stone fireplace with some sort of a screen in front of it. All in all it was pretty scary, and surely there must be a ghost somewhere there – but that didn't matter because my big strong Dad was with us. I really don't remember how long we stayed there. One of the strongest memories I have of the occasion is that the long bedroom curtains didn't close properly and I wouldn't go to bed until Mam sorted something out. What or who could have peeped through those curtains is left only to a child's imagination! Eventually Dad went and found a safety pin. There we were in a lovely fairytale castle in the middle of nowhere, with a safety pin holding the curtains together.

That was the summer that Randolph (Randy) Turpin of Leamington Spa and Sugar Ray Robinson fought for the middleweight championship of the world. Randolph Turpin did some of his training at Gwrych Castle and held exhibitions there. My Dad met him. "A very nice man he was too, a gentleman," said Dad, who was later to do a little work for him at the Great Orme Hotel (now the summit complex) at Llandudno. My grandmother Grace Bach also worked there at this time and had her photo taken with the great man. Randolph Turpin beat Sugar Ray in Earls Court in front of 18,000 people on July 10th 1951. He was only 23 years old. Just three months later in New York City, Sugar Ray was to regain his title. Randolph Turpin took a terrible beating and the fight was stopped two minutes into the tenth round.

After a couple of years in 5 Tan Bonc we were lucky and were able to rent No 6 from Auntie Lizzie Tyddyn Llwyfan. Lucky, did I say? The sadness was that Jacob the shepherd and his wife Liza Zack – Nain and Taid next door– had both died by now, which was why we moved to No 6, their former home. This was the end house and much better for us because it had a toilet on the side of the house – a little shed with a corrugated iron roof and a green door. I remember well the door having a little chip of wood missing at the bottom. Inside, a kind of wooden box had been built around the toilet. No 6 was like a palace to us, with a back door and our own toilet next door. We couldn't always afford a toilet roll so our task as children was to cut any tissue paper, left from the bread, or newspapers into small squares. What a thought! We had a tap right outside our front window when we first moved in. As you walked in the front door the stairs were right ahead of you, with the door to the living room to your right. It was not a very large room; there was a big black lead grate in it that Mam used to cook on. "This oven is so good for making pastry in," she would say. We had a table under the window, some odd chairs around it, and a couple of easy chairs. On the wall between the back kitchen and the living room was a sideboard. Floor covering was usually lino in those days, and a mat in front of the fire which we had spent hours making out of old clothing (*mat racs*). That was our living room, parlour, dining room and play-room, but we were so happy despite all our troubles. The back kitchen was very small; about four to five feet wide, by maybe twelve feet long. There was no water at first, until Dad added a cold water tap and slop stand. A second hand mangle was bought; it cost about £2 and it had big wooden rollers. It folded down to a kind of table and Dad stuck some brown Formica on it. I can hear my dear Mam now – she thought she was the bee's knees, having a second hand mangle: "Mag, come and help me with these sheets, del." I had my fingers caught in that cruel mangle many a time. The flannelette sheets in winter, or cotton in summer, were really heavy and of course Mam had washed them by hand in the sink. Dad's jeans were a nightmare to get clean. Mam would use the metal scrubbing board and scrub till her knuckles literally bled. Under the stairs near the back door was where we kept the coal. When it rained we would quite often have a flood in the back kitchen, because of the bank behind the house. Upstairs there was Mam and Dad's bedroom, the back one, with the stairs leading straight into the room and space only for a bed and a small chest of drawers which was really quite sufficient for the amount of clothes they had. Later on after Dad had put hot water in the house there was a tank in their room that helped keep the bedrooms warm. It had a window looking onto the bank behind, so close that it was always dark there, and needed the light on during the day. We girls reached our bedroom by going through their bedroom; we had a double bed and a chest of drawers that we shared. The window was in the middle of the wall; Val and I would sit on either side of the windowsill waiting with great excitement for our Dad to come home. He would give a whistle from down the road and we would run like the wind into his arms for a swing. He'd lift one of us on his shoulders and take the other in his arms. At last, he was home!

In the winter the bedroom window would freeze up and I don't mean from the outside. There would be so much ice on the inside of the window that you couldn't see through it; the lovely starry patterns made by the ice on the glass were far nicer than anything I could draw. Our extra 'blankets' in winter were a couple of old heavy Army overcoats kept especially for the job. Everyone was my Auntie and Uncle and we had three or four sets of 'grandparents' - Nain and Taid next door (before they died); Nain and Taid Pandy (honorary grandparents), and of course, our own two sets. It was so special, living and growing up in Tan y Bonc. I loved the place, loved the neighbours, and loved my life. Most of all I loved my parents and my sister Val, even though we did more arguing than anything else. We were indeed privileged to have grown up in such a place and at such a time.

Here is a well know Welsh verse that Mam and Dad used to sing to us: I have just taught it to our little granddaughter Megan.

Gee ceffyl bach yn cario ni'n dau,
Dros y mynydd i hela cnau,
Dwr yn yr afon a'r cerrig yn slic -
Cwympon ni'n dau, well dyna chi dric.

It tells of a horse taking us two up the mountain to collect nuts. There was water in the stream and the stones were slippery - so down we tumbled, into the water.

Em's Auntie Lizzie, as I have said, owned No 6; Val and I would go and pay the rent every two weeks. Up we'd go to Tyddyn Llwyfan farm; we'd always get a welcome in the massive farmhouse kitchen, with its stone slabs on the floor; it was always so clean, despite the men coming and going all day. Auntie Lizzie would inevitably have something for us to eat; a hot Welsh cake or a piece of her special fruit pie. The kitchen always smelt of something mouthwatering and we could not wait to get our little teeth into whatever there was on offer that day.

Our rent was twelve shillings (60p) a week so we'd pay her one pound four shillings and she would give us two shillings each back. When the rents in the area went up Auntie Lizzie told Mam that she wouldn't put our rent up but she would no longer give us two shillings each back. How was that for kind!

John, Auntie Lizzie's son, tells a story about a bull in Tyddyn Llwyfan. The night was quiet with not a breath of a breeze, since the farm nestles just under Dinas, and the only noise was an occasional sheep braying as it made itself more comfortable in one of the fields around the little farm. One of the sheepdogs barked lazily. The family was all fast asleep, said John. "It was just before dawn, when all of a sudden there was a hell of a bang downstairs. I jumped out of bed, not really knowing what I'd heard, and as I came out of my room I saw my father Hugh running to the top of the stairs. What a sight! He was in his long johns. Dad was looking down the stairs and shouting *myn diawl, mae'r tarw yn y tŷ* - by heck, the bull's in the house!" Soon, Uncle Hugh was half way down the stairs, kicking and waving his arms, screaming his head off at the bull and trying to get him out of the house. John went to help and they eventually got the bull away from the stairs and out through the front parlour. The old bull had broken down a side door leading into the parlour and smashed some of Auntie Lizzie's best dishes. A bull in a china shop comes to mind! "The bull was not for turning and it was in a hell of a temper by now," said John. "After some more kicking and shouting, and using our walking sticks, we managed to get him into the stable." Uncle Hugh was in as much of a temper as the bull by now and was seeing red! They got the stable door closed; the only problem was that Uncle Hugh was on the wrong side of it. The bull turned on him and he had to scramble up the stable wall, just managing to get up to a feeder that held straw. With his legs dangling, kicking away in his long johns and Wellingtons, trying to keep away from the mad bull, he managed to reach a trap door and pulled himself out of harm's way. "A sight for sore eyes," said John.

Here's a poem that John's nephew Geraint Hughes wrote a long time ago.

Days on the Farm

Many a long summer,
Occasionally lingering until autumn
On Tyn Llwyfan farm,
My boyhood years I would spend.
Bringing recollections of an age
Now past.
Memories of men, workers of the earth,
Who toiled from dawn till dusk;
Who smelled of sheep and sweat,
and nature's husks,
And of women who prepared
Food, cooked on an open fire
With home made ginger beer
Fermenting until clear.

September was the harvest month
When men from near and far
Would come
To scythe the hay
And have their say,
A dozen or more.
Old John, an ancient man,
Married an English woman
The name of Mabel;
And when seated at the table
His tea he would slurp from his saucer.
But not before a good blow
To ensure he was able
To consume the tea's glow
Without being too slow.
There too would be faithful Gerallt,
A man of few words;
And the man from Pandy
And others – all very handy.
At noon the meal was served,
The men consuming huge portions
Well deserved;
And talking in Welsh
The old mother tongue,
As indeed many others have done
In centuries past.
As a boy I sat amongst
These men of old
Not knowing one day their tale
Would be told.

And now I know their kind
Are no more.
A farming tradition;
A way of life forever hidden
In memories.
But in my soul I feel their presence
And their prevailing essence
Existing in another world.

One day the old bull was grazing in the field behind Tyddyn Llwyfan farmhouse. It was known to be dangerous and unpredictable, so it had a metal shield over its eyes to prevent it from charging. On this occasion it didn't work! For some unknown reason it charged at the fence, and in doing so fell down the bank behind the house. It was able to stand up and walk along the back of the house. Then it came to a sudden stop. There in front of it was a huge tree stump. It could go no further; there wasn't enough room to turn around. The poor beast was well and truly stuck, and was it mad! Despite the best efforts of the neighbouring farmers, working with a tractor, nothing could shift the tree stump, and certainly no-one could shift the raging bull. It was decided to call on John Bach (Hugh's brother), who lived down the road. John worked in the quarry and was able to get his hands on some gunpowder. In their wisdom, they were going to blow up the tree stump: a very delicate operation, since they didn't want to harm the old bull, which by this time was getting more and more agitated. The men decided it would be best if they waited until it was late at night to do the blasting; hopefully all the neighbours would be asleep, and wouldn't hear the blast. The time crept slowly by and the old bull was getting more and more exhausted, struggling and kicking and making all sorts of funny noises. He was not a happy bull! At last it was midnight; the time had come to put the powder in the tree stump. Having managed to coax the bull as far away from the stump as possible John Bach went about the job of laying the powder. Hopefully, he knew what he was doing and wouldn't blow the house and the old bull to smithereens. There were other farmers there, helping and watching with great anticipation, hoping that things would go well – but if things went wrong, they wanted to be there to see it! The explosion was very loud, with dirt, splinters of rock and bits of the tree stump flying everywhere. The old bull went berserk, said one of the men who was watching that night. All went well, and with a lot of persuasion and some poking they managed to get the tired old bull into a field. The farmers didn't get much sleep that night.

In the meantime, across the valley at Hengae, Elwyn (Nant) – otherwise known as Butch – woke up to "a hell of a bang." He shot downstairs, not even stopping to put on his trousers. In the pitch dark he ran out to the shed, thinking that the bang was his home-made beer erupting. It had been fermenting nicely when he'd checked it a few hours earlier. With great relief, he found all his bottles intact. Elwyn spent the rest of the night scratching his head, wondering what the explosion was. Next morning the men were all at work in the quarry, having a cuppa, when Elwyn asked John: "Did you hear a loud bang in the night?"

"You must have dreamt it," said John as he turned away, chuckling to himself.

After living at No 6 for a while Dad put in hot water, and out went the big black lead range; hundreds of cockroaches and centipedes scuttled from behind it. In went a beautiful second hand tiled grate with a tiled stool each side and a back boiler to heat the water. "Don't sit on those cold tiles del," Mam used to say, "they will give you piles." We were very posh now; hot water in the house – what a treat. Bath nights meant a galvanized bath in front of the fire on Sunday nights, or as we got older we'd have the bath in the back kitchen. I would get in first and Val would use my water afterwards. Then we would spend some time listening to a play on the radio or doing the News of the World crossword; Dad and I really enjoyed that. Then up to bed for the two of us; I can still smell those lovely clean cotton nightdresses, the crisp white cotton sheets, beautifully ironed. Our sheets were changed once a fortnight. In the early days we used to have an old fashioned iron made from black cast iron, which Mam put on the glowing fire to heat – no electric iron or ironing board for us then; it was the table, with an old sheet as a base for the ironing. I never saw an ironing board in my mother's house. Later on we had a new electric cooker; there was no gas up there, and there still isn't. We would put one shilling (five pence) in the electric meter; quite often we had no money so Dad always had a piece of lead, cut the same size as a small shilling, and we popped that in the meter. The electric man would empty the meter every quarter and in the midst of our rebate would be the dud lead shillings; the electric man was more often than not very nice about it. Mam would tell Dad there was less money in the meter than there was. I'm sure that Dad always knew when Mam was telling him one of her little white lies.

I remember when Dad bought an incubator for hatching eggs. We managed to get it in the back kitchen and we'd sit up as late as we could in the hope of seeing the eggs hatch. It was so wonderful to watch the chicks crack the egg, their little beaks struggling with the shell. All of a sudden there were these little scraggly things which turned into lovely little balls of yellow fluff, going tweet tweet, which fitted into the palms of our hands. By this time Dad had built a big brick shed at the bottom of the garden and kept chickens. "We're going to make a lot of money," he said. Some hope! We kept a few pigs, ducks and geese as well as chickens. Not all at the same time, I might add. There was never a dull moment in our house.

Our favourite dog was a greyhound named Fly. We'd go coursing hares and rabbits with her, and she put many a rabbit on our table. Then we had Tish our cat – she was just like a little baby. We'd chew some bread and butter and there she'd be, waiting for some food straight from our mouths. She would follow us down to a certain spot on Valley Road and then turn back; when we came home she'd be waiting in the same spot for us. Heaven knows how she knew when we'd be back. One day Mam was folding some wet clothes up on a long wooden slatted hanger that used to hang over our fireplace. She stood on a chair to do this job, and as she came down she felt something under the heel of her shoe. There was poor Tish, lying dead on the floor, with blood everywhere. It happened in a moment and I have never forgotten it. My dear soft-hearted Mam sat there and cried her eyes out. We buried Tish in the garden and Mam was upset for days.

We had quite a large garden at the side of the house, backing onto Tyddyn Angharad's fields. When we had our first telly in about 1956 we had to put the aerial on a tree high up on the bank behind our house in order to get a good reception on ITV. In those days the signal came from Winter Hill near Manchester. It was a black and white TV which we hired on a weekly basis from the Co-op first and later on Curries. It was no problem getting permission from the farmer. It was Gerallt's parents who owned Tyddyn Angharad. Dad and I would be like two monkeys up the tree, waiting for Mam or Val to yell up to us, "turn it a little to the right, a little to the left, now hold it." We could never get it dead on, it depended a lot on the weather as to what kind of picture we got. After Dad built the shed at the bottom of the garden we kept a couple of hundred chickens in it. We had some Rhode Island Reds, some bantams, and others which I can't remember. Dad would put some Stokholm Tar on any sores they might have, to deter the other hens from pecking them. It was hard work, but Val and I enjoyed searching for the eggs amongst the straw. We had a couple of geese which we were scared of. We were fattening them up for Christmas but when the festive season came we couldn't eat them, so I think Dad sold one to Mr Lee Pickering (who owned the Victoria Inn) and the other to a gentleman named Mr Culpin - he owned a factory that made blankets in Yorkshire and used to come to Llanfair to stay sometimes. Mam used to clean for Dr G Bellis and his wife, and one day, when she came home from work, there was a surprise in store for her. We had to pass the chicken shed when we went into the house. Mam thought it was very quiet in the shed; there wasn't a peep from the hens. When she opened the door all the chickens had gone. Dad had sold the lot, to start yet another scatterbrain scheme. For a while after that Val and I spent happy hours playing "little house" in the shed with our friends. Dad was to convert it into some sort of workshop; he always had a new project on the go. I think I must be like him.

When Dad had been drinking in the afternoon my Mam used to try anything to get him to bed, and after being told the wrong time he would be fooled into going up for a couple of hours sleep. We would have to be so quiet, making sure not to wake him, since it was a tiny little house. What a life, having to keep two kids quiet in those circumstances. Dad would sometimes wake up, asking for the time, and Mam would tell him a bare-faced lie so as to keep him in bed longer. "A white lie, God will forgive me," Mam would say. It has been known for Mam to go to bed at eight thirty in the evening, having turned the clock forward so that Dad thought it was ten thirty. In those far-off days we only had one clock in the house. Mam would wind it up last thing at night, set the alarm for morning, and off she'd go up the stairs with the clock in one hand and her ciggs and matches in the other. Mam would even turn the clock back, sometimes, so that Dad would miss his bus to Pen and give him less time in the pub. We never told Dad the truth about the clock; he would never have trusted us again although I am sure that sometimes he had his suspisions.

Dad wasn't afraid of doing some housework. He was far better at sewing than my Mam and a very good cook. I was very heavy on shoes when I was a girl, and one day Dad threatened to buy me some hobnail boots. "Ha ha - I'm a girl and I can't wear hobnails," said I. One morning, to my horror, when I was getting ready for school, I discovered that Dad had put some hobnails in my leather-soled shoes overnight. I couldn't believe it, but I was forced to go to school wearing them. Our shoes were always so shiny you could see your face in them (Navy training, said Dad). There was an up side to my hobnail boots - I had some good slides on those shoes; my friends used to drag me around the school yard.

Here's a little story about the kids in Nant y Pandy during the last century.

The children of Nant y Pandy were neglected as far as a Sunday school was concerned so it was decided by the elders of Horeb chapel to do something about it. At the top of Valley Road there was a *Cwt Powdwr* - a little powder hut which had been used to store gunpowder for the quarry. That is where Nant Sunday school was started. Over a hundred people went to Nant Sunday School in those days. After a few years it was decided that the little hut was far too small for the congregation and once again Horeb's elders stepped in. The new Ysgol Nant was built in 1887 at a total cost of £222/14/3. Such a small sum, but in those days it was a huge amount of money. Mr William Williams (Camarnaint) and Mr R B Roberts (the Chemists) took care of the Sunday school. It seems that the first winter in Nant was a great success and Mr R B Roberts was asked if he would continue to take care of the venture. Mr Roberts (the Chemists) used to walk up from the village on Sunday afternoons and all the children from Nant y Pandy would be waiting for him on the bridge; up they would go for their hour of prayers and, of course, those all-important few sweets. In those days the name they used for Nant was "The Ragged Sunday School" because the people and little children who went there were very poor - so their 'Sunday best' was their *only* clothing. I well remember going to Ysgol Nant, from 2pm to 3pm every Sunday. All the children sat in the main room for the prayers and a hymn, and one of the kids used to go up front to recite something from the Bible. I always said the same adnod (verse): *Gwyn y byd y rhai pur o galon, canys hwy a welant Dduw* - Blessed are the pure in heart, for they shall see God (Matthew chapter five, verse eight). After a couple of hymns and a prayer or two we kids went down to what we called the cellar. It was a lovely room with lots of sunshine in the summer, and with a nice lawned area outside on which we could sit to play or do our work. I can see it now, the sun shining down on us as we made daisy chains on the short grass. Auntie Nell 'Shop' was in charge of the little children and would always bring some sweets from her shop in Valley Road. We sat at our desks to do our writing and had small brightly-coloured plastic letters to teach us to spell; when I got older Mr Idwal Thomas was my teacher. There would be a group of us children sitting in a corner of the room discussing the scriptures. After the discussion, Mr Thomas always brought out some Cadbury's chocolate to share. Oh! What a treat it was. Where indeed have those days gone? After finishing Sunday school we gathered at a table bench at one end of the main room, to hand in our Christmas Club money. Mam wouldn't always have money to save but I do remember one occasion when I was about nine or ten. I skipped Sunday school and went to play, but what should I do with the Christmas Club money? What would I say to Mam? What I did was to hide the club card and the money in the hedge across the road from Ysgol Nant (it's probably still there) and went home. "Mam," I said, "I've lost all the money and the club card. I've looked everywhere for it." Mam was very cross. Off we went to look for it, but of course I couldn't betray myself by leading her to the hedge, even if I'd known where I'd put it. Eventually I had to tell her the truth. What a telling off I had. There was my dear Mam, struggling to save a few shillings for Christmas, and I had to do that.

Ysgol Nant Sunday school trip to Aber in 1915.

Every summer Ysgol Nant would organize a sports day in Tyn Llwyfan fields. The children of Bont Newydd orphanage in Caernarfon would come for their annual holiday to Benarth in Park Crescent, Llanfair, and they would join us for a day of sport and a party afterwards. It was a great day - we would have a sack race, egg and spoon race, three-legged race and many other sports. The strange thing is, I can't remember it ever raining on sports day. It does seem as if our summers were longer and hotter in those days.

One of our other treats at Ysgol Nant was the annual summer Sunday school trip. It was something that we kids really looked forward to. It was usually a trip to Marine Lake in sunny Rhyl.

Val and me on Ysgol Nant's Sunday School trip to Rhyl in 1951.

Oh, what excitement; we had a new dress especially for the day. If Mam could afford it we would have a new bag and purse each as well. Having been around the family, we always had a few shillings to spend. Dad never came on these trips, but he always made sure we had enough money to go. The day dawned and we couldn't wait. Mam would make a picnic with loads of sandwiches, some cakes and a bottle of home-made lemonade, or if we were very lucky we'd have a bottle of fizzy Corona lemonade. We were up and ready to go long before time; Val and I would be quarrelling before we even left the house. Down we'd go to the village with Auntie Blod (1 Tan Bonc) and the kids. At last, it was time to board the charabanc; we'd all race for the back seat. Settling down in our seats, we'd open our purses and count our money for the hundredth time. Off we went to Rhyl, a day of fun and laughter ahead of us. We rode on the carousel, the ghost train (how I loved being scared to death), and the boat on Marine Lake. We stuffed ourselves with all sorts of junk food. Oh, but life was smashing! Then it was time to get back to the bus, our lovely new dresses dirty and grubby. No money left, and we were all tired. Never mind, we'd bought a little souvenir for Dad and our Nains and Taids. We were ready to go home. I'd have stuffed down so much rubbish I'd feel sick all the way back.

Dad used to make buttermilk. I think we used sour milk. You'd shake the container for what seemed like hours; eventually the milk would separate and you were left with butterfat and the *llaeth enwyn*. Mam, Val and I would eat the butterfat but we'd never touch the *llaeth enwyn*. It was horrible. My Dad loved *tatws llaeth* (hot potatoes mashed with the cold *llaeth enwyn*, with plenty of salt and pepper). To the day he died he enjoyed *tatws llaeth*.

There was nothing I liked better than to go collecting logs with Dad when I was a girl. I suppose it's what Dad had done as a child and these things carry down, don't they? I'm sure that if I asked our grandchildren to go and help me collect some logs they'd think I was going mad. My sister Val and I spent many hours up Llyn Nant, Three Streams, and the woods around that area, sawing, cutting and carrying. It helped to stretch out the coal and sometimes it was all we had to burn. In those days you could cut trees and branches almost where you liked.

While I'm on the subject of Llyn Nant I would like to mention a tree on the way up to the pond. It had a soft bark but I have no idea what it was called. We used to go there as kids, after Sunday school with a picnic; Dad and his brothers used to practise their punches on it, and have some fun larking about with a punch bag and with each other. At one time a little café was opened by the side of the pond by Mr Jones, Nant y Coed the foundations are still there today.

I myself remember Nant y Coed as a little tea garden on the way up to Three Streams, a whitewashed house in the middle of all sorts of fruit trees blooming with vibrant colours. I can remember the pleasant smell of wood burning in the fireplace, the white smoke curling up gently, high over the trees from the black chimney pots; the well-tended gardens, a few tables scattered around with glowing white cloths on them and cups of tea, home-made lemonade and fresh home-made scones baked the same day. Swings, see-saws for us kids, and trees to climb (if you didn't get caught). Mr and Mrs Jones (Auntie Kate) lived there with their sons, seven of whom fought in the Second World War. We would call there on the way down from picking bilberries, dead tired. Mam and Dad would enjoy a cup of tea while Mrs Jones fed my sister Val and me.

In 1925 Nant y Coed's tenant was Mr Nightingale, and he decided it would be a good thing to have a brass band playing on a Sunday. "Not only for my business, but also it would be good for the poor people that could not afford a wireless to listen to some music," said Mr Nightingale, who was also the band leader. There were some objections from the churches and chapels. "It is not right to have it on the Sabbath," they said. Despite the objections it was allowed to go ahead.

Here is a poem, written by a visitor in 1945, which tells you about Nant y Coed, far better than I ever could.

Nant y Coed

In a setting as perfect as any could be
There nestles a cottage twixt mountain and sea;
A stream flows near by over moss-coated stones,
The home is completed by kind mother Jones

The path leading to this house near the stream
Winds on like a ribbon to end in a dream;
Once there, far removed, from the smoke of town,
One captures a jewel in nature's green crown.

Surrounded by roses, hydrangeas and trees,
This white-washed old homestead is sheltered from breeze;
Within its four walls where the brasses all gleam,
One had to bend low 'neath an old wooden beam.

And here at this cottage - which can't help but please,
A notice enticing says "Afternoon Teas";
How could one resist such a charming old spot?
"Good-bye" Mrs Jones and here's "thanks a lot".

Nant y Coed.

One night, when I was about thirteen years old, I'd gone to bed; I think Val was in hospital at the time. Mam, as usual, waited up till Dad came home. This particular night Dad had come home the worse for wear and went to sleep in a chair. So after making sure the fire was low enough, Mam went to bed and left him sleeping. A while later Dad must have woken up because he was cold. The first thing Dad did after waking up was light a cigarette, and this time was no different: he must have finished his smoke, and then gone up to bed. In the early hours of the morning I felt someone shaking me. "Mag, hurry up, the chairs on fire, come and help me," said Mam. Woken up by the smoke, Mam had already been downstairs to see what was burning, and had found that the easy chair was smouldering away in our living room. We both rushed downstairs in our nightdresses through the thick smoke, coughing and spluttering, and shaking like a leaf. We managed to carry the smouldering chair to the garden, our eyes running and burning. We went back in, opened all the windows, and went back to bed. There wasn't much more sleep for us that night! Next morning, all that was left of the chair was a few springs and screws. We were so lucky that my dear Mam had woken up. Dad slept through it all. He wasn't safe with a cigarette after a few pints and must have dropped the lighted stump into the chair.

During the war quite a few planes came down in the mountains above Llanfairfechan. In January 1944 a Consolidated B-24 Liberator bomber, *Bachelors Baby* (so named because all her crew were bachelors), crashed into Moelfre. It was a particularly wet and misty day, with very low cloud. Aboard the plane were ten American airmen and their mascot, a little black and white fox terrier named Booster. Seven survived the initial impact but two died later at the C&A Hospital in Bangor. Booster was among the dead. High above Llanfairfechan, in those lonely hills, there's a slate plaque with the names of the men – and dog – that lost their lives on that flight.

In September 1944 a De Havilland Mosquito came down in the dead of night and crashed into the east side of Drum, a mountain behind Aber Lake. The plane was built mainly of plywood, to keep it as light as possible. There were no survivors.

In the early 1950's Dad and his brothers used to go up the mountains looking for the wrecks of these planes. In 1972 a new Act came out, for the protection of wrecks. They became the property of the RAF, and removing any part of a wreck carried a heavy penalty. Anyway, one day the brothers had no money for wages for their wives. They decided to go up the mountains in an old jeep in search of a wreck. They came across what was left of a wreck and loaded what they could of the aluminium onto the jeep. Tying the cockpit to the back, they set off for home. What a time they had, getting back down to Aber where Uncle Bob lived. The mountain tracks, as you can imagine, were so uneven that every few yards something worked its way loose and fell off the jeep. Worse was to come - the jeep broke down when they still had a few miles to go. The brothers were all quite good at fixing cars, so after a temporary job repairing the jeep it was ready to go again. What a sight it must have been - three or four men driving an old jeep full of aluminium, and dragging a rusty old cockpit down the mountainside. Having reached Uncle Bob's house in Aber the men started to break everything up. It was too late to take the metal to a scrapyard they used in Conwy so they decided to wait until the next day. When they eventually arrived there they took some copper, iron and tin as well as the aluminum. If you kept the different metals separate you got more money. Somehow or other Dad managed to get his hands on the money and off he went to the pub - and that's where they found him, many hours later. He had spent his brothers' share. Now it was payback time; the brothers gave Dad a good hiding outside the Llanfair Arms, where he'd been drinking most of the day. They threw him into the back of the jeep and drove him up to Drum. On reaching the top of the mountain they took off his shoes and socks and left him to walk the five miles back to Llanfair over the rough mountain track in his bare feet.

Dafo, one of Uncle Bob's boys, told me: "I remember how much fun we kids had, playing in the back garden with that old cockpit."

I myself went with Dad up Drum to collect aluminium. I think that in those days there was some sort of radar or weather station on the summit of Drum. The weather turned really bad, quickly, as it can up there. We could see only a couple of yards in front of us; the mist had come down, it was raining and the wind was blowing so hard we could hardly stand. Our clothes were soaking wet and sticking to our bodies. We had no waterproofs. Dad kept hold of my hand so tight it hurt. "Come on del," he said, "we'll have to look for some shelter." Dad knew the mountains like the back of his hand, but in those conditions we were in great danger. Luckily, we reached the summit and found the hut quite quickly. A man answered our knock, saying: "What a day you chose for a walk, you'll have to stay a while until the fog lifts; I'll make you a cup of tea." *Diolch i Dduw* said Dad - thank God!

Dad used to collect old electric wiring from anywhere he could; lots of houses were being re-wired in the late 1950's. Perhaps he collected the wiring from a job he'd been working on, or someone had thrown it out. It would pile up and when there was enough of it we'd make a fire in the garden and burn all the plastic coating off it; the smoke from it was really black and there was a terrible smell of burn-

Village School 1957. Back row left to right: Lloyd, David, Tommy, Capper, John, ?, Donalld and Emyr. Second row: Mr. Thomas (headmaster), Bobby, June, Beryl, Helen, Susan, Falmai, Heulwen, Iona, Bobby, Teacher? Third row: Gwenan, Iona, Margaret (me), Janet, Dorothy, Joan, Christine, Sylvia, Lillian, Ceris. Front row: Richard, Graham, Winford and Michael.

ing plastic in the air. Afterwards we were left with copper wire, which was worth a few quid. Dad and I would go by bus to Raymond's scrapyard on Morfa Conwy to sell it; sometimes it was worth practically a week's wages for Mam.

I loved going to school. It was a long walk from Tan Bonc, about a mile and a bit I should think. In those days the grassy area on the river side of the road was effectively a field, with a wall going all the way up from Pandy Bridge to Tan Bonc. Will Parry kept his chickens there. It was about four feet high; although I used to think it was a lot higher. When it was dark I used to be afraid in case someone jumped out and scared me, so I'd run most of the way from Pandy bridge home. In a couple of places there was a break in the wall, with a water trough and an iron animal-shaped head a little higher than the trough. "The water used to gush out of the animal's mouth in the olden days," said Dad. This was used as a communal water supply for the people of Nant Pandy, before water was piped to the houses. There was a dam in the river near Tan Bonc, allowing water to be turned into these troughs. The times I've tried to conquer that river while it was roaring and jumping down towards the sea, only to find myself going home soaking wet! We were so lucky to have these magnificent places on our doorstep, and we made the most of them.

Another thing that used to scare me on my long walk to and from school was the geese from Pandy farm. There must have been around six or seven of them. I would be walking past the opening to Pandy, and all of a sudden these terribly dangerous birds would appear, as if by magic. Their wings would open and they'd all seem to be running or flying towards me. I was scared to death. Sometimes it would take what seemed like hours to pass them. Occasionally Taid Pandy would be there with a kind word to give me confidence and I'd pretend to be brave, when really I was shaking in my shoes!

Uncle Evan and Auntie Blod lived at No 1 with their children Ivor, Brian, Pat and Gwenda. Uncle Evan was a builder and worked for Owie (Queens) who had a builder's yard in Pig Street. Uncle Evan had made many alterations to No 1; being an end house, it was much bigger than the other five. The yard was concreted, so sometimes – when Uncle Evan was at work– we were able to play tennis there. Auntie Blod and my Mam remained best friends even after we moved to the village to live. Indeed Auntie Blod was a regular visitor to Mam's house until the day Mam died, always with a small gift for her. While our girls were growing up she always made sure there was a Christmas present for them.

Village School 1952. Back row left to right: Robert (Fredric), ?, ?, ?, ?, ?, ?, Val (my sister), Joan Thomas, ?, ?. Middle row: ?, ?, Pauline Dunkley, Annwen P, ?, ?, ?, ?, ?, ?. Front row: Robert, Winford Owen, ?, ?, ?, Gareth, Gwyn, Lesley Evans, Trevor Owen.

The farmers of Llanfairfechan have added much to the richness of the village. Early in the twentieth century there was an old farmer named Henry living in Hengae Farm. Henry was known to over-indulge in the demon drink and every Saturday night, without fail, he could be seen enjoying a pint or two or three or four or even more in the Virginia Inn. When he was short of a bob or two he would pay a visit to the hen house with a sack – the hens screeching and flapping, feathers flying everywhere. Those poor chickens were all trying to escape; eventually one poor hen lost the fight and was popped inside the dreaded sack. With the chicken safely in the sack on old Henry's back, off he went down the track for his usual pint, the poor chicken to be payment for his beer that evening and probably Sunday lunch for the innkeeper the following day. This went on for many weeks; his hen house was getting quieter and his chickens were getting fewer and fewer. On the way down to the pub one evening he met up with a neighbour who asked him: "What will your wife say when she finds out how many hens you've been taking Henry?"

"Don't worry," said old Henry laughing, "she can't count."

In Hengae Cottages in the mid 1950's lived John Hughes and his wife Auntie Grace with their six children. I was friendly with their daughter Lydia and used to play quite a lot up there. On one occasion we had fallen out and Lydia followed me home, shouting: "I am not friends with you, you wait until I get you." Running all the way home down the fields, slipping a few times, and getting mud all over my clothes, what did I care? I just wanted to escape. I had a stitch in my side and of course I wouldn't let her see I was scared – she was a couple of years older than me. I finally got home and ran into the house. As soon as I got in Mam said: "Go and get some water in will you, del." (The tap was outside). Who was near our gate, waiting for me, but Lydia. "You go back to your own house, you bitch," I shouted. My Mother heard me and was out of the house like a flash. "Don't you dare let me hear you use language like that again, Margaret, you go and tell that little girl you're sorry this minute," said Mam, and of course I had to apologize. I was telling Lydia about this story only last week and we had a good laugh but she didn't remember it!

Val and I would never dare use swear words in front of our parents. Dad's motto was "don't do as I do but do as I say." The worse word we ever used to call each other was *pig*. Up to the day my parents died I never used a swear word in front of them; not because I didn't swear – I suppose it was the way we were brought up. On the subject of bad language, even in drink I never heard Dad use really bad language in front of us. While I'm on the subject of naughty children, there's another little tale to tell. High up over the mantelpiece in our house was the dreaded *gwialen fedw* – a birch rod which Val and I had helped make. All my parents had to do was look at it and we'd behave. There was only one occasion I ever remember having it across my legs. I can't remember why, but I must have been a really naughty girl for my parents to use it. I will never forget the sting and the marks it left behind.

The kids of the area had such fun playing in the wilds! We'd run like mad if Mr Thomas (Bob Bach, a farmer) saw us making fires, when we could get some matches from somewhere. Up Garreg Fawr we'd go, setting fire to the gorse. After kicking a small hole in the bottom of the bush and then putting a lighted match to it, what a fire it would make, the flames and sparks jumping high into the sky, with us kids behaving like a load of screaming wild Indians. The smoke would stream from the fire, curling and swirling in the wind, with the bravest of us kids jumping and running through it. How our clothes would stink after, what a job we'd have, explaining the smell on our clothes when we reached home. We'd spend hours in Pen y Bryn Park making small fires and playing kiss chase with the boys. There was a long stringy kind of weed that hung from the trees there. What it was called I have no idea; our name for it was Tarzan Rope. We would gather around a camp-fire to smoke it – what a daft thing to do! There was a gamekeeper named Hector who'd always be on the lookout for kids trespassing in the park. He was a giant of a man as I recall and we were all terrified of him. It didn't stop us going there though! If you were caught, watch out!

Val and I would go with Dad along the road to Llyn Nant and we'd collect watercress which grew wild – Dad's favourite for making sandwiches. "So good for you, lots of iron in it," he'd say. Llyn Nant, at the bottom of Dinas, was full of tadpoles, newts and frogs. Yuk! If there's one thing I dislike it's a frog; you never know where it'll jump! The woods leading up to Llyn Nant were enchanting to us kids, with the trees making all sorts of creepy shadows everywhere, the river flowing gently down, or sometimes raging, with white water rushing over the mossy stones. We used to love playing in the river, the boys lying on their bellies, tickling the fish. When they did finally catch one it was so small that they'd throw it back in the water.

On Mother's Day I'd go and pick some of the primroses and violets that grew between the trees. They made a lovely bouquet, the yellow and violet making a wonderful contrast; Mam used to make such a fuss of them. Nothing was too good for my Mam! When the bluebells were in full bloom the banks above the track were a sight to behold. It looked as if someone had laid a bright blue carpet in between the trees. It does seem that our kids miss such a lot these days; even if they wanted to we would be afraid to let them wander too far from home. In the autumn it was such fun taking a picnic up to Three Streams to collect hazelnuts. Nearly at the end of our walk up there was a huge stone which we would use as a slide. Of course there was always a run for the first slide on it. When we got there like squirrels we'd scramble up the trees, stuffing the nuts in our pockets, and ripping our clothes, but what did we care. None of us was happy until we'd filled every pocket. Cracking them open with our teeth, there would be a trail of hazelnut shells behind us all the way home. Mam would say the same thing every year: "Let's keep them for Christmas del." We never did!

Val, Mam and me in the mountain 1957.

Further up again was Camarnaint farm, where a school friend of mine, Falmai, used to live; we used to walk home from school together sometimes. Falmai remembers us both walking up Valley Road with my Dad between us. "He was a little the worse for wear," said Falmai, "so we each took an arm and helped him along." Sometimes her dad would come down in a van as far as Tan Bonc to meet her. It's a long walk up!

Falmai moved away but when John her husband retired they moved back to Llanfair; they now live in one of the small farms near the village. We were up at their home recently and Falmai was in the garden doing what farmers have done for generations, only on a smaller scale. She had grown all sorts of fruit and veg. "I was taught not to waste anything," said Falmai, giving me some cooking apples after making sure I'd use them. "I paid £1.30p for three cooking apples last week, what a price," I told John.

Back to my little tales. One day Dad decided it was time to get rid of a dog we had. I'm not sure if the dog was ill or not, but it had to go. How terrible - but it was the sort of thing that was done then. I remember that if anyone's cat had an unwelcome litter people would pop the kittens in a bucket of water, and that was the problem solved. One cold, wet winter's day, Dad decided to take the poor dog out for a walk. The dog wagged its tail excitedly as Dad put his coat on. Little did it know. Up they went, master and dog, along the wet muddy track, the rain lashing down between the trees leading up to Llyn Nant. Reaching the pool, Dad took a sack out of his pocket and a piece of string. He put a couple of large stones in the sack and then managed to get the wet, trusting dog inside it. He tied a knot in the top of the sack and threw it in the pool. That sounds so cruel doesn't it - and yes, it was cruel. Dad made his way home. He walked down that lonely track, in the pouring rain, thinking of the old dog. By the time he arrived back home he was soaked to the skin and very upset at what he'd done. By this time the rain was easing off a little. Dad settled down in his chair in front of the fire; he was chilled to the bone. I took my usual place on the floor, sitting between my beloved Dad's legs. We were all sitting comfortably, watching something on our new TV, when all of a sudden we heard a noise at the front door. Mam jumped up and went to open it. "Come to the door," said Mam, and we all jumped up to see what was going on. Lo and behold, there was the old dog looking like an over-sized drowned rat. Mam, Val and I were hysterical with laughter as Dad looked down disbelievingly at the dog. "How the hell did you escape from that sack?" said Dad. The poor old dog had chewed his way out of the sack and found his way home. Needless to say, the dog had a reprieve and we kept it.

Pay day in our house wasn't always what it should have been. When Dad was on the dole he would have to go and sign on every Wednesday. On Friday morning he would go and pick up his unemployment benefit. "Black Friday" Mam would call it. The dole office was a rented room in Castle Buildings, Station Road. When there was no school Val or I would go down with him to pick up Mam's living money - or we wouldn't see Dad again until late that night, minus the money. This would mean that any little money my Mam had managed to save was used to keep us for the following week, or my Nain and Taid Gwyn would help out.

In the late 1950's Dad worked on the new Conwy Bridge - he used to work in a diving bell. We would go and meet him on a Friday to do a little shopping in Conwy. There was a pub called the Blue Bell (still there I think); it had a beer garden and we'd spend an hour there with Mam and Dad before getting the bus home. Val and I used to love climbing on the walls and looking over to the river. On one occasion Dad took the train home and met an old Navy friend from Ireland. Mam didn't see him again for a few days - he landed up in Ireland with his mate!

Another of my memories of Dad, from the mid 1950's, is rather upsetting. He went out to play dominoes one evening – he used to play for the Mountain View and the Bron Eryri in Penmaenmawr. Dad had been banned from the pubs in Llanfair due to his behaviour after drink. He went for his usual bus from Llanfair at 5.45pm but by the time he got to Pen the team had left without him for some reason and Dad was most upset. He drank his fill of beer and then bought a bottle of whisky and drank it on the way home, which was unusual, as Dad was a beer drinker. Over the years I'd seen Dad drink excessively but I'd never seen him really ill afterwards. On this occasion we thought he was going to die – alcohol poisoning comes to mind! He was in bed for a week or so. I recall that there was a bank manager in Llanfair at the time called Mr Owen 'the bank', a real gentleman, who was very friendly with Dad. "Well Now Bach, what have you gone and done this time?" asked Mr Owen when he visited Dad, bringing him a packet of Woodbines. Many years after this incident Mam and Dad were trying for a council bungalow in Llwyn y Gog. Without the help of the bank manager's wife, Mrs Owen, who was a councillor, Mam wouldn't have been given a bungalow. Why, you ask? "Who wants Now Thomas living next door to them?" said some of the councillors. Mrs Owen's words were: "Why should Mrs Thomas suffer because of her husband?" Thanks to her my parents got the bungalow; my Mam was thrilled to bits as she had difficulty climbing stairs, owing to her failing health.

Living next door to them in Llwyn y Gog for many years were another local couple, Mr and Mrs Lesley Lewis, who were marvellous neighbours; I like to think that my parents were good neighbours too. The weekly rent for the Llwyn y Gog bungalow in 1970 was £4.25p. Mam used to pay an extra few shillings a week so that she would have a free week at Christmas. "Whatever else in life, always make sure you pay your rent, so that you'll never be without a roof over your head," Mam would say. In 1982, when Dad died, the rent for the bungalow was £19 per week – just a few figures which might interest you. Mam kept her rent books until she died.

In our house, when Val and I were girls, Dad would ask if we'd like some "turkey pie" and we'd jump with glee – it was yet another name for *Mair yr Iar* – Mary the Hen, which was bread with boiling water poured on it plus some salt and pepper. There were many happy meals in our house. I would burst into the house shouting: "What's for tea Mam?"

"Three runs around the table and a blue duck," Dad would answer. My parents were my whole world and our house was always filled with love and laughter, despite the hard times.

There were lots of happy times in our house; Dad would come home from some job or other with a pair of shoes in each pocket for Val and me and a present for Mam in his inside pocket – a string of 'pearls' one time, I remember!

Bonfire night was a night to look forward to; with a huge bonfire in our garden and the sparks flying so high we thought they would reach the clouds. We had a box of fireworks each; Dad would nail the catherine wheel to the washing line prop; round and round it went, with us kids screaming with glee. The *Jack Sponcars* would jump all over the place as we tried to dodge them. Mam washed potatoes to put in the embers of the fire. When they were cooked they were so hot and dirty we could hardly eat them, but what did we care. One year Dad was away working away on bonfire night. A couple of days before the big night a parcel arrived in the post; we were so excited we could hardly wait to open it. A box of fireworks each for Val and me! There was also a box of chocolates for Mam (Dad never bought us anything without something for Mam).

I particularly remember a birthday party when I was about eleven or twelve. Val and I had a friend up for tea – June Williams *nee* Fellows, a lifelong friend of ours. Anyway, we all sat around the table to enjoy sandwiches, some cake and of course jelly and blancmange. "Look," said my Dad pointing at the window, "there's an aeroplane falling from the sky." He said it so seriously. We kids, of course, immediately stopped eating to look out of the window. "Gotcha!" said Dad as he pinched a couple of butties off the plate.

There was a family of about six brothers living in Hengae cottages Auntie Alice their mother I remember was a typical strong Welsh kind-hearted lady. Hengae was about a half a mile further up than Tan Bonc. They were all about Dad's age. I remember well how friendly they used to be, even working a lot together. But on more than one occasion there was trouble between them and they would all end up doing what they enjoyed, using their fists on each other. Before long the men were all best of friends again. That was how it was in those days. Entertainment on a Saturday night after the pub was a good old-fashioned fist fight.

On another occasion Dad had just got home from the pub – it must have been around 10 pm in early spring. I was about twelve or thirteen years old. I remember the hedgerow and trees along the narrow path to our house had started budding. Dad had been telling Mam about an incident in the pub earlier, when Jo (as I shall call him) was causing trouble. Dad, having a reputation for being a troublemaker, was frequently challenged to "come outside." Being relatively sober this time, Dad declined the challenge and tried to speak calmly to Jo. It didn't work! "He took a swing at me Meg and I thought it best to come home," said Dad. "Wonders will never cease," said Mam. No sooner had Mam spoken than someone was banging on our door. Dad jumped to his feet. It was Jo, ready for the confrontation that should have happened at the pub. Jo lived lower down in the village and had staggered all the way up in pursuit of my father. Dad went out to speak to him and managed to persuade him that our house was not the place for a fight. Mam and I could hear their raised voices as they walked along our path to the road. Pulling our coats on, Mam and I ran after them. "Go home, come back in the morning," we heard Dad shout, but I'm afraid that Jo was far too worked up to listen to advice. By now the fists had started flying. Jo was like a madman, swearing and shouting, his fists punching the air, but not really connecting with Dad's face. Dad was ducking and diving, he was very nippy on his feet. He didn't want to hurt Jo, a sure sign that he wasn't very drunk! They went on like this for a few minutes, both men punching each other. A left hook from Jo caught Dad smack in the mouth. "OK Jo, that's enough - you're in for a hiding," said Dad through his thick lip. Dad had tried and failed to calm the situation, and was by this time very angry. A right hook to his nose sent Jo reeling, the blood was streaming and I was scared. What if something awful were to happen here? I thought it was time to do something about it. But what? I didn't know. I remember, like yesterday, getting between the fighting men. I was pulling at Dad's clothes, trying to get him from there, when all of a sudden - bang! I got a left hook for my trouble. For a second I felt dizzy, but I think I must have caught the tail end of a punch. As young as I was, I saw a way to stop the fighting and I pretended to fall over. Of course, the two men stopped fighting immediately. Dad was really upset and the man panicked, seeing me on the floor. Mam said: "Are you mad, Now? What in the world are you doing, fighting like this with our Mag here - look what you've done!" Dad picked me up and carried me back to the house - I was a lot lighter in those days! Mam fussed over me and even Jo stayed to see that I was OK. As I remember it, there was no grudge held between the two men.

One of my Mam's biggest fears was Dad killing someone while fighting. "So easy," Mam would say "to knock someone down and them knock their head on the pavement."

In about 1961 we moved from Tan Bonc to Britannia House in the village. The house is on the river bank. Uncle Harry (Mams brother) bought the house for us and my parents paid him rent. "Don't worry Harry, I'll do all the work and you needn't pay for anything," said Dad. Uncle Harry paid for most of the materials and my Dad worked hard on the house. There was a terrible mess there. The house was a mere shell, it had been empty for years. I remember standing on the ceiling beams and kicking down what remained of the lath and plaster ceilings. The dust was everywhere, and despite having rags over our faces it went up our noses, down our throats, into our hair; our eyes were burning and running, with so much lime in the dust. We were so black and dusty you wouldn't have recognized us. What a good time we had; I loved doing that kind of work. My dear Mam used to say I should have been a boy! We put in a new kitchen and bathroom. After a couple of months of hard work we moved in. At last, we had an inside toilet and a bathroom: it was lovely. I was fifteen and I had a bedroom of my own. We had a lovely kitchen and parlour - there was so much room, my dear Mam was over the moon!

Finding Vera

In the winter of 2004, after over two years of looking for Vera (Dad's first wife), I found her. I could hardly believe it. I had gone through the Vancouver phone directory and made fifty or sixty phone calls to various people with the same name, or having the same initial, as Vera but to no avail. I was, however, able to get information about her parents through some people who call themselves *—; they have been a great help to me. It is far easier to find information about the dead than the living. I had advertised in two Vancouver newspapers and written countless letters. One evening, whilst still going through the Vancouver directory, I rang a number in Burnaby, a suburb of Vancouver.

"Is that Mrs Holmes?" I asked.

"Yes," a voice answered.

"Is it Mrs Vera Holmes?" I asked.

"Yes," she said.

"Were you married to a sailor called Owen Water Thomas during the war?"

Shaking a little, the voice answered: "Yes I was - who are you?"

I nearly dropped the phone. What a shock. Here I was, speaking to Vera at last. "I'm sorry to bother you, I am Owen's daughter from his second marriage," I answered.

I'm not sure who had more of a shock, Vera or me. She hadn't heard anything about Dad for sixty years. "Good Lord," she said, "I was only thinking about him last week, wondering what had happened to him. How did you find me?" I explained that I was doing the family tree and that I was writing about my family. "How amazing! I can't believe that you've found me after all this time – wait until I tell my children," said Vera. We were both so excited; I felt as if I'd found a long lost member of my family. I wrote to Vera and thanked her for speaking to me. I also sent her a few photos of our family and a couple of my Dad. I asked her if she would mind trying to answer a few questions for me and jot them down on paper. After a suitable interval I phoned Vera again; she had received my letter and would try to answer some questions for me. She also had a couple of little snaps of Dad that her daughter was going to copy for me. How wonderful to see a photo of Dad in Canada, when he was 21 years old. "Margaret," said Vera, "I have remembered something else. Your Dad did tell me that there was a child back east, in Toronto I think. He was very honest with me and told me before we were married. I can't remember any names." Another shock! There is (or was) a child, a half brother or sister. Once again I don't know how I feel. I will have to find a starting point to look for this sibling; it won't be easy, with no name and no idea of the child's sex. I will endeavour to do my best.

Eventually I received a letter from Vera with a couple of photos of Dad aged twenty one, in Royal Navy uniform. Em said: "I can't believe it – after all these years, a photo of your Dad which we've never seen, from across the world. It has given me a strange feeling down my spine."

Vera wrote that she and Dad were married quickly. They knew each other for only four months before Dad was posted elsewhere. "I loved him so much," she said. I cannot begin to explain what I felt when she said this. I was upset, sad, I was goosepimply. I just felt so strange; I wished Mam and Dad were here to talk to me.

Vera said that Dad was known as 'Wally,' short for Water. What a name, I ask you! "He didn't want to be called Owen; he altered a room for us in my parent's house and that is where we lived for our short time together," said Vera. She continued: "He was very well liked by my friends and family here; he was very jolly and loved to sing." There were no children, which was a disappointment to us all. What a nice lady! I was so lucky that she took the time to speak to me. Vera said: "We had only been married a month when he was posted on a flat-bottom ship to New York. He was then shipped back here to Vancouver by train to go on another flat-bottom. He jumped ship in San Francisco and went to stay with my Aunt in Seattle. He then made his way back home here to me (Vancouver). He stayed a couple of days with me and gave himself up at the immigration building. He was sent to the detention barracks in Victoria Island, he was not locked up and was allowed to go into the city as and when he wanted to. When it was time for him to ship out for home I went to Victoria to meet him. He came back and stayed a few days with me in Van before my mother and I put him on a train to go across Canada and pick up his ship for home. He said he was going home to see his mother. That was the last I saw of him. This was in the winter of 1944. I received one letter from Wally, telling me how sorry he was. His sister wrote to me a little later telling me to get on with my life as he had met up with someone whom I now know to be your mother." She was sad to hear of his death and asked me if he had lived in Llanfairfechan all his life. She pronounced Llanfairfechan like a native of the village. I asked Vera if I could phone her again. She said she would be delighted to hear from me and thanked me for getting in touch. A few weeks later her daughter Debbie sent me an e-mail, saying how pleased she was that I had got in touch with her mother. "My mom was delighted to hear news of her first husband after sixty years," said Debbie. She said she would send me some photos of their family via e-mail.

In 1976 my sister Val was knocked down on the zebra crossing in Llanfair. She sustained a broken pelvis and was in hospital for a while. Val received £2,120 in compensation for the accident. The money was Val's but as usual the family had a share. Our daughters, I recall, had a new coat each and Em had a new radio. A twin tub washing machine was bought for Mam. Some money was put away for Val.

Dad wanted to go back to Canada for a visit, so he was given some money for the trip. Why did he go back to Canada? Who knows? Dad said it was nostalgia. I wonder whether he went in search of the child he'd never seen. I wonder what Mam really knew, and how she felt about it all; I should have asked them both. At this time Dad was working at Hotpoint in the Junction and was given leave of absence for the trip. His wage in Hotpoint in 1973 was £19.45 for a forty-hour week.

By now my Mam was really ill: she suffered from chronic bronchitis, asthma and emphysema, and most days she couldn't even get out of bed. How she suffered: never complaining, always laughing. Our GP called on Mam once a fortnight to see how she was.

My dear Dad flew to Vancouver on January 27th 1976. We didn't see him again for five months. He was to tell us later that those months away were the longest months of his life. Dad stayed in Vancouver for a few days, and then made his way to Toronto; again, I have no idea why. On February 2nd, only six days after Dad had left home, he was in Toronto, staying at the Skyline Hotel, when he was arrested for starting a fire in his room. There was nobody else involved and he wasn't injured.

A local policeman went to Mam's house (8 Llwyn y Gog) and told her that Dad had been arrested in Canada. He didn't know anything else. I remember going to the phone box in Bryn Rhedyn to phone the British Consulate in London for advice on what to do. I must say they were very helpful. Dad had always been one for smoking in bed, so I would have thought he had fallen asleep with a fag in his hand. That's my theory, anyway. Dad didn't speak much about it. He was taken to The Old Don Jail in Toronto where the hearing was scheduled for March 8th. Initially, Dad was unfit to plead. But by March 8th it would seem he was better and was to fit to plead. The Old Don Jail was also a remand centre for men awaiting trial. These men had not always been convicted of any crime, but sometimes spent years waiting for their trial there. Some prisoners suffered with mental health problems. "A huge jail," said Dad, "it must have held close on two thousand men. You couldn't even imagine what the conditions were like there Meg. The overcrowding was bloody awful. I had to share a cell with two other men when it wasn't even big enough for one of us really. We would take turns for showers and shaves; if you were lucky you would get a shower once or twice a week. I was not used to showers; a bath was what we had at home. I used to tell you girls, when you were little, that I would bathe once a year whether I needed to or not, and how the two of you would laugh. But I wasn't laughing now. I was to think of those words often while I was in that stinking hole of a place. It was infested with mice and cockroaches as big as your fist running around everywhere – not a place anyone should be."

The last execution in The Don was in 1962. In 1976 there were still men on death row. Capital punishment was abolished there that same year. Dad told Em years later that he wasn't too badly treated there – owing to him being a Welshman, he believed. How Dad got through that time in his life, without one of us there, I will never know. I remember Dr G Bellis telling Mam at the time: "Longing for the living is far worse than longing for the dead."

In a letter from Canada dated April 11th 1976, Dad told of the *hiraeth* (longing) he felt. "I wish to God I was back home with you all, don't worry about me Meg, I am OK. Make sure you get sorted with some money, as I said in the last letter I won't be home for some time." He continued: "Will you write to the prison doctor here to thank him for being so good with me Meg, he's a very nice man. There is nothing I need here, I get plenty of cigs." He went on to thank Mam for sending cigarettes, and urged us all to write as often as we could and to send photos of Lorraine and Karen in the garden. Both Mam and Dad liked flowers and their garden was always full of all sorts. "I live day to day and can't wait to come home; your letters are a great comfort to me." At the bottom of this letter he'd copied a poem he'd read while sitting in his cell.

The years creep slowly by Lorraine

The dew is on the grass again.

The sun's low down in the sky Lorraine

The frost gleams where the flowers have been.

A hundred months have passed Lorraine.

Since last I held your hand in mine.

And felt your pulse beat Lorraine

Though mine beat faster far than thine Lorraine.

Who wrote it, I wonder? I remember the day Mam received that letter. Em was taking us all to Uncle Harry's in Conwy - a real day out for Mam. We were all in the car and I started reading the poem. Talk about sad, we were all crying and thinking of poor Dad so far away. I don't remember what happened at Dad's hearing or how long a jail sentence he received.

On June 14th 1976 Dad was granted parole for "Voluntary Departure to Wales." If he returned to Canada before the termination of his parole, it would be revoked immediately. His parole expired on September 24th 1976. It would seem that Dad was let out of prison three months early. Two detectives put him on a plane - he was coming home. He arrived on June 24th. He was not at all well and looked dreadful. Mam wrote in her diary: "Now came home from Canada today. He doesn't look well, he's so thin and pale, and he's gone to bed dead tired. He has been travelling for over twenty-four hours. He was too tired to talk to us." Poor Dad could hardly speak. Not surprisingly, he was tired and traumatized after all he'd been through. It took Dad many weeks to recover. I remember sitting around the kitchen table with Mam and Dad, and seeing the anguish on his face as he told us of his time in jail. Eventually he was well enough to go back to work and he was given his job back in Hotpoint. He started back on October 23rd 1976, ten months after he'd embarked on his escapade.

During the last year of my dear Mother's life she kept a diary every day. She was mostly confined to her bed. A phone was put in on June 12th 1979. "It's smashing, I'm so glad we've got it - I wish Mam had one," she wrote. On July 11th in the same year Mam wrote in her diary: "I've given a ring to Mag today, the one Dolly (Bob's girl) gave me. I thought the world of it and I had a job to get it off so Mag got it off with Vaseline. It would not fit Val so she's a bit cross about it. I thought it best to get it off now while we could, if anything happens to me I know that the ring is off. I don't want it on my finger when I die. It would be a shame to leave it on when I get buried. Val calls me morbid but we have to face these things." Her whole life revolved around her family and it shows in her diary. On one occasion, just before she died, she was in hospital very ill and she sat up in bed and said: "Mag - please, please let me go quietly next time del." She'd had enough pain and suffering. The lump in my throat is as big as Garreg Fawr. I will never forget those words. I suppose I was selfish, I didn't worry about how much my dear Mother had suffered or indeed was still suffering, as long as I could still keep her with us. It was not to be. My Dad had been by her bedside throughout those five weeks - feeding her, taking her the "white ice cream" she loved, helping her, encouraging her, begging her to get better. I remember him saying after she died that she was sure she was going to her father. "I hope she got her wish," said Dad. On February 9th 1980 my dear Mother died aged 57. It was her mother's 80th birthday. Mam had been in hospital for five weeks. Dad, Val, Em and I were with her when she died.

One of my Mother's biggest worries in life was: "What will become of Dad and Val when I'm dead?" It was a worry no more to her.

What would we all do without my dear Mam? What a loss to our daughters Lorraine and Karen - to lose their beloved Nain. Not to hear that infectious laugh, or hear her call our names. Val was like a lost soul. "What will I do now Mag," she cried. Dad was devastated. "All our married life, through thick and thin your Mam has stuck by me," he said. "She never let me down and now she has gone and left me here on my own."

I remember standing in the bathroom in Woodlands and saying to Em: "I would like to go up and stand on Garreg Fawr, to shout and scream my head off." Of course I didn't. I had a husband and two daughters to care for, not to mention a broken-hearted father and sister. My poor Nain was 80 years old on the day she lost her beloved daughter. It was a great loss to Mam's siblings; they were so close as a family. They had always watched out for Meg, and gave her a helping hand when she needed it.

I woke up one morning, about a month after my beloved Mam died, and outside our bedroom window I heard the little birds singing in the trees; it was the first time since Mam died that I'd heard them. It was as if my Mother was saying to me: "Get on with life, Mag Bach." I went up to Dad's and said: "Dad, I have to carry on for the sake of Em and our girls."

"Margiad fach, your mother and I would expect no less of you," was his answer.

Dad was now living on his own. *Yr hen gwt* – the old hut, is what he called his bungalow; it became hateful to him after Mam died. It was only around the corner from us, and our girls would call in on him after school most days. I would see him every day and Em would take him for a pint sometimes. Dad wouldn't do much for himself once Mam died. I used to do his washing and cleaning. When we had a dinner one of the girls would take him a plate across or he'd come to us for it. I would handle his money and try to make it stretch for him, so that he was able to have a pint or two most nights. He liked the company. My Mam, I'm afraid, had spoiled him rotten.

I was in Dad's house doing a little tidying up for him a few months before he died. It was around three thirty in the afternoon when I looked out of the window and saw my dear silly Dad wobbling up the hill with his walking stick. I was cross with him for drinking in the day and said: "Don't tell me that I've got you to worry about for the rest of your life."

"I'm afraid so Margiad fach, the Bible says three score years and ten," he said. I think often about those words I spoke to my Dad in anger. Be careful of what you wish for, you might just get it. A matter of weeks after my Mam died Dad went up to his brother Will's house. It was a dark and cold winter's night, and of course it was after the pub. Somehow Dad sustained a broken hip. He was drunk, so it was a bit of a blur to him. He always said that someone had run him over that night, accidentally, but nevertheless hit him with a car and failed to stop. Another hurdle for him to get over.

He had been in Eryri Hospital in Caernarfon for only a short time when I had a phone call at work at the West Coast factory. *Tyrd i nol fi Margiad, mae pobol yn marw fan hyn* – come and get me, people are dying around me here and I can't stand it. Off I went to pick him up. I took him home and he managed, with a great deal of help from us. After a few weeks he was walking down to the Castle Hotel with his Zimmer frame. I can't help but laugh. I was furious when I found out that he'd walked down, but I had to admire his determination. Our girls loved their Taid and would spend many happy hours at his house, driving him mad. They would tease him unrelentingly and he would shout at them, hiding the grin on his face.

In November 1982 Dad phoned me from the Castle Hotel. Could I pick him up? He had a headache. I was furious with him. We had an unspoken pact, Dad and I. When he was drunk he was neither to call me nor come to our house. He didn't always adhere to this but it worked most times. This particular night, Dad wasn't drunk. He had such a bad headache he could hardly see. "I'm sick Margiad fach," he said. "Put your head out of the window," I answered as I drove him home. How cruel can you get! Having seen that he was really ill, I saw that he was comfortable and gave him a couple of pills for the pain. Dad had always suffered bad headaches. I had known him to take three or four tablets at a time, so I thought this was probably just another bad head. During the next few days his headache got gradually worse. We called our GP and Dad was sent to the hospital. As the ambulance men took him on the stretcher down the steps he said to Em: "If I thought I was going to Meg I wouldn't care." That was the last time Dad went down those steps.

They didn't know what the matter was with Dad. They even suggested that he had been taking too many paracetamols over a period of time. Still, they weren't sure. I stayed by his bedside for the first five days and wouldn't move from there. I would try and grab a couple of hours sleep in the day room; the staff at the C and A Hospital at Bangor was brilliant with me. Our daughters were really upset: Karen was sent home from school – full of worry, said her teacher. Lorraine couldn't concentrate on her school work at all. I was absolutely exhausted. I was light headed, doing and saying things I couldn't remember through lack of sleep. All I could think of was poor Dad. Em at last managed to persuade me to go home at night. I had to give in, and leave Dad in that hospital, on his own. "Remember," I said to the nurses, "any change at all and I want to know, whatever time, day or night." This went on for a couple of weeks, with Dad getting worse. On December 6th 1982 at around 5pm we were having tea when the phone went. As you can imagine, every phone call made us jumpy. Well, this was the one we had all been dreading. Dad was deteriorating – could we come quickly? The girls stayed at home, Em and I left hurriedly. We called to tell Uncle Ned that Dad was very ill. He said: "No del, I can't come and watch your Dad die. I prefer to remember him as he was." That was OK – we each have our own way of coping with death. We arrived at the hospital and sat with Dad for a short while, but he didn't know us. A few minutes later, Dad was dead. After the post mortem they said that clots on both sides of his brain had burst.

We sat with him for a while. I was hit by a flood of emotions. I was devastated and heart-broken, longing for my Dad yet relieved that he was no longer in pain. I was shocked that my Dad could die and leave us, yet glad that he'd gone at last to his beloved Meg. I also knew he'd no longer be a worry to me, and felt guilty for feeling like that. What I wouldn't give to hear his voice one more time. My beloved Dad – the giver of my life, gone forever out of my reach.

We buried him on December 10th 1982, just two years after Mam. St Mary's Church that day was packed. There were people there I had never seen before; people whom I thought would never have given my Dad the time of day were there to pay their last respects. The Rector paid tribute to Dad and said it was a long time since he'd seen the church so full; it was a tribute to Dad's memory to see so many people there. I am writing this through a haze of tears. It took the death of my Dad for me to realize how much he was thought of. There was a cup of tea and some sandwiches at our house after the funeral (I hate that word wake). Uncle Ned asked Em if it would be OK if he laid on a spread for Dad's drinking friends at the Castle Hotel. How could we refuse - Dad had spent a major part of his life in a pub. It seemed fitting, somehow, that his pals should raise their glasses to him there that day. I remember one man in particular, sitting in our home at Woodlands, drinking his tea - Chris Coleman, a friend of my Dad's for many years. "A great character who will be sorely missed," said Chris.

Just a few weeks later poor Chris was dead himself. And with those words I end the story of my father's family. Now I will turn to the Babell family, on my mother Megan's side.

Penmaenmawr Road, early 1900's.

the viaduct and the old Telford Road before Pen Clip was built. Photo taken c. 1905.

Station Road. Photo taken in 1905 with the sewage pump building, it was demolished in the 1960's.

Llanfairfechan sea front, early 1920's.

S. Winifred's School 1920's.

Class rooms in S. Winifred's early 1920's

Shop Mrs Price 1929 (Britannia House).

*Mrs Elizabeth Pilling was at the shop on Shore Road from 1930 - 1933.
She had previously held the license at The Llanfair Arms.*

Norman Thomas co cowner of Mona Garage in the 1950's.

The village from Pen-y-Bryn 1988.

Part 3

The Babells

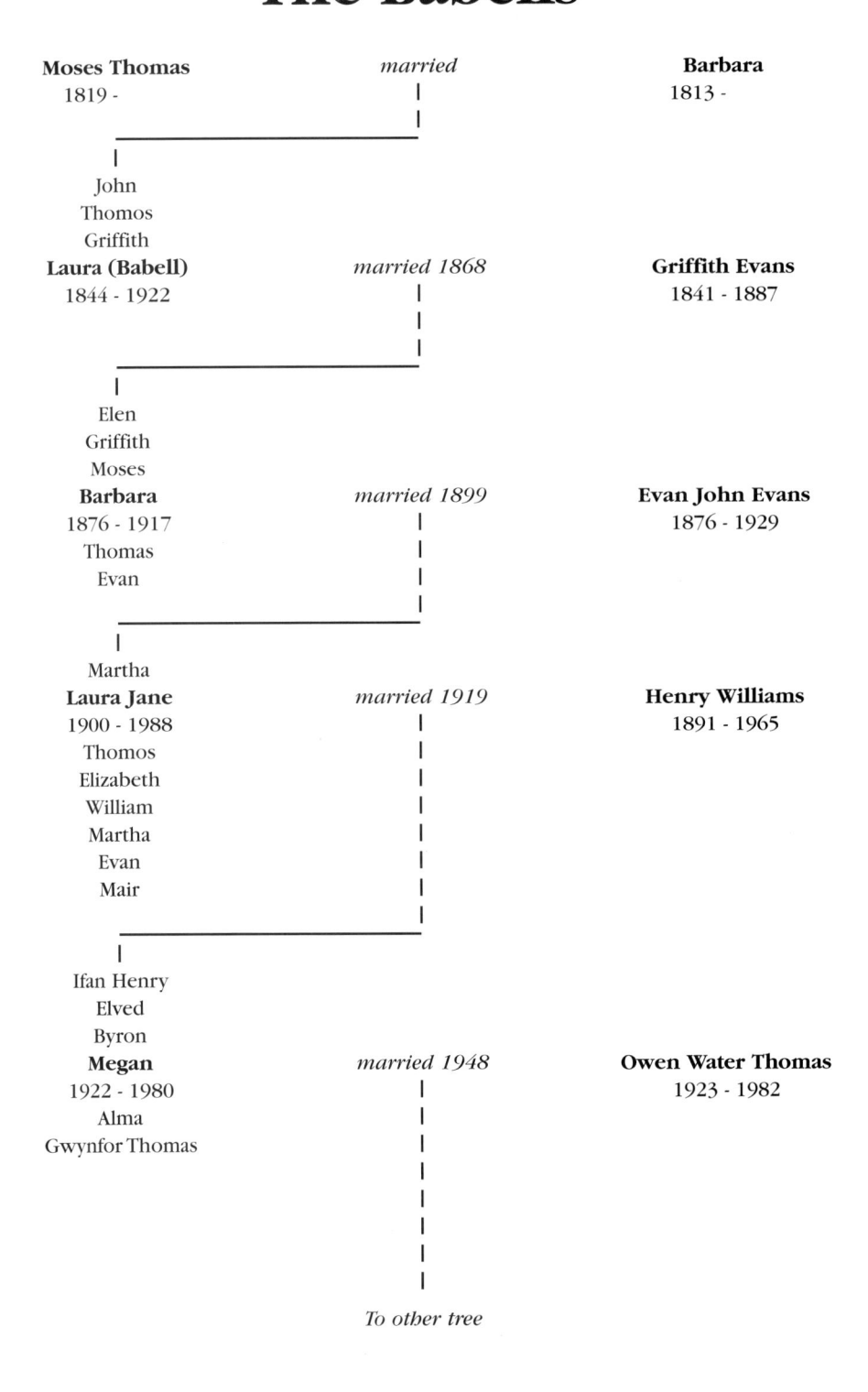

Moses Thomas 1819 -	*married*	**Barbara** 1813 -

John
Thomos
Griffith

Laura (Babell) 1844 - 1922	*married 1868*	**Griffith Evans** 1841 - 1887

Elen
Griffith
Moses

Barbara 1876 - 1917 Thomas Evan	*married 1899*	**Evan John Evans** 1876 - 1929

Martha

Laura Jane 1900 - 1988 Thomos Elizabeth William Martha Evan Mair	*married 1919*	**Henry Williams** 1891 - 1965

Ifan Henry
Elved
Byron

Megan 1922 - 1980 Alma Gwynfor Thomas	*married 1948*	**Owen Water Thomas** 1923 - 1982

To other tree

BABELLS –

My Mothers family – the great-great-great-grandparents

My great-great-great-grandparents on my mother's side Moses Thomas (1819 - ?) and Barbara Thomas (1813 - ?) were both born in Llandwrog near Caernarfon.

When Moses was 55 years old he lived in Tal y Maes, Nebo, with his wife Barbara and their four children and two granddaughters. Tal y Maes was a farm, although Moses was a slate quarry miner. In the census of 1881 Moses, aged 62, and Barbara, aged 68, lived at Tal y Maes Uchaf in Llanllyfni, Caernarfon. It was a farm of 12 acres, and living with them was their son John, a quarryman aged 25, and two nieces, Margaret and Mary, a scholar aged 13; also living with them was a general servant aged 17.

Em and I went to Llanllyfni to look for Tal y Maes Uchaf. We found it! There are two dwellings there, known as Tal y Maes Bach and Tal y Maes Mawr. The two houses are actually in Nebo – a little hamlet, with most of the houses and cottages scattered around the mountainside. It's a lovely place in summer but very bleak in winter. I had the cheek to knock on one of the doors and a lady answered, barely peeping around the door. I explained what I was doing. Of course she was a little nervous, with a stranger at her door; I asked if she would rather I went away and she said: "No, please wait while I go in and see if I can find a copy of something that might be of interest to you." She closed and locked the door; I waited for a few minutes in a rather run-down garden, then she came back and said: "I am very sorry, I can't find it." She asked for my phone number and we swapped numbers. It seems that she had just inherited Tan y Maes Bach from some elderly relatives who had just died. Her name was Gill and she thought that someone named

Thomas had gone from there to live in America many years ago. He used to make violins, apparently; we know that in 1901 a Thomas Thomas aged 41 and his family lived in one dwelling. John Thomas (his brother), aged 45, and his family lived in the other one. They were all slate quarrymen. John died in 1913 aged 57 and is buried with his wife Mary in Llanllyfni. There was another son named Griffith who died in 1882 aged 28; he is buried on his own in Llanllyfni. We now know that Moses and Barbara had at least four children.

My great-great-grandmother – Nain Babell and her family

My great-great-grandmother Laura Thomas (1844 - 1922) was born to Moses and Barbara Thomas in 1844 in Llanllyfni. She married Griffith Evans (1841 - 1887) on October 1st 1868. They lived at Babell, a little cottage in Groeslon, until Laura's death in 1922. She is remembered as Nain Babell. She married Griffith Evans in Caernarfon registry office in 1868. She was a widow with a little girl, also called Laura, when she married Griffith and lived at Pontllyfni, Clynnog. Her husband Griffith, also born in Llanllyfni, was a farm servant who lived at Llwynimpia, Clynnog, at the time of the marriage. Evan, his father was a labourer. Griffith signed the register himself but Laura signed with an X.

Griffith and Laura lived in 12 Llainffynnon, Llandwrog, in 1881. They were both down on the census as labourers. They had six children at that time. Times were very hard, with barely enough to eat; they scraped a living off what little bit of land they had and laboured for the neighbouring farmers when they could. Griffith was only 47 years old when he died in August 1887, leaving Laura a widow yet again. This time poor Laura had a house full of children to bring up on her own, although a couple of the older ones would probably have been of some help to her by then. Griffith was buried in Groeslon cemetery where he was joined by his wife Laura thirty five years later, on March 12th 1922.

Em and I found the cemetery in February 2003 – it's only five minutes walk from Babell. The church, now partly demolished, can't be seen from the road. I have yet to see a lovelier, more tranquil spot to have a cemetery. It is surrounded by trees, fields and hills, with the occasional bleat of a sheep. Not a bad place at all to spend eternity.

Back to Laura now. My cousin Gwen has a photo of her somewhere and I remember seeing this photograph years ago. She was a large woman with big chubby cheeks and with her hair drawn back from her face – rather forbidding, I thought.

In 2004 Em and I went to Babell to meet Ceinwen (a lady who lives at Babell now) in the house where my great-great-grandmother lived a hundred years ago. Ceinwen said that there was a lady called Mair Edwards living in Groeslon who actually remembered Laura (Nain Babell), so we called on Mrs Edwards. When this lady was about 10 years old she and her friends used to go to Sunday school (Ramoth – Baptists) and were sometimes invited to Babell for tea. "There was always room for one more round the table," said Mrs Edwards. She remembers Nain Babell as having big rosy cheeks and she always wore a little black cape on her shoulders. "Laura Evans was a kind, hard-working lady who would always make you welcome; she would give us a *bechdan jam* – a jam sandwich and a bit of cake, which was a real treat to us in those days." She went on to say that Laura was a staunch Baptist and never missed going to chapel whatever the weather: you could rely on her being there in her Sunday best. Mrs Edwards was in her 91st year when we met and she has lived in the same house all her life, just round the corner from Babell. We sat with her for a while, a lovely little Welsh lady in a home that was as clean and shiny as a new pin. It was strange, sitting with her, to think that this lady had sat with my great-great-grandmother in about 1920, and here we were chatting to her. Mrs Edwards was really pleased to chat with us and wanted us to explain exactly how we were related to Nain Babell. As far as Mrs Edwards could remember Nain lived on her own at that time, but of course her memory was not what it was, she chuckled. You must remember that this was eighty years ago. She remembers that Nain Babell's daughter (Barbara, my great-grandmother) had gone away to live and had died a young woman. I will turn to Nain Babell's children now.

Laura Griffiths (1867 - ?) Nain Babells daughter from her first marriage

Ellen (1870 - 1950's), or Auntie Nell as I remember her, was a little lady with snow-white hair. Born in Clynnog, she married William Hoyle Senior, a Yorkshire man, and they went to live in Canada. It seems there was a family tiff. Auntie Nell wouldn't or couldn't help with her sister Barbara's children when Barbara died aged 41. Auntie Nell returned in the late 1940's with her son Will. They opened a shop of some sort in Luton. Will, an excellent musician, was quite brilliant on the piano. Auntie Dilys told me that there was also a daughter in Alberta, Canada. I wonder if there are any more relatives out there. I have so much to look into – I suppose that will have to wait a while.

Griffith (1872 - ?), or great-great Uncle Griff was born in Clynnog but went to live to South Wales. In the census of 1901 he was married to Elizabeth and they lived at 8 Tyisha Rd, Ystradyfodiog St John, Rhondda, with their four sons – Griffith John, Willie, Thomas and David. Griffith was a coal miner/repair worker. Griffith John, his son, was a boss of sorts in the coal mine; he married Laura, whom we knew as Auntie Laura South. They lived in 41 Rheola St, Penrhiwcaiber. When I look back I remember that I used to write Christmas cards on my Nain's behalf to most of these people and never even asked who they were! I do have a faint recollection of Uncle Griff and Auntie Laura South coming to 19 Mona Terrace when Nain lived there years ago. Laura had three sons and a daughter, Eunice. She was rather late in life having Eunice.

Moses (1874 - ?) was born in Caernarfon. Nothing at all is known about Moses.

My great-grandmother **Barbara** (1876 - 1917) was born in Tai Court in Llandwrog on October 23rd 1876. I remember Nain telling me that she was a good clean-living woman who did a lot for the chapel. She was a Baptist. I will talk more about Barbara later on.

Thomas was born in 1879 in Caernarfon. I don't know anything else about Thomas yet.

Evan his brother was also born in Caernarfon, in 1880. In the census of 1901 he lived with his mother in Babell and was an engine driver in the slate quarry.

We always believed that Hugh Babell Bach (1892 - 1915) as he was known (owing to being very tall!) was Nain Babell's son, but it turns out that he was her grandson. In the census of 1901 he was nine years old and living with his grandmother and his Uncle Evan in Babell. Uncle El remembers being told that Hugh was good at making things out of wood. Hugh was born in Llandwrog and was killed in the Dardanelles in the First World War. A story has come down to us from one of the Babell neighbours. Hugh was walking down the street without a care in the world, whistling and swinging his kit bag on his back, on the way to the First World War, shouting *Hwyl rwan, wela'i chi y tro nesa* – farewell until the next time we meet. The neighbour's words, apparently, were: S*gwn i os ddaw Hugh yn ol o'r rhyfel* – I wonder if Hugh will return from the war; but no, he never came home again.

With the help of some very kind people I found documents relating to Corporal Hugh Richard Evans, born in Llandwrog. Next of kin was Laura Jones of Groeslon. He died on August 21st 1915 at Gallipoli in the Dardanelles. His name is on the Helles Memorial in Turkey. Hugh's battalion sailed for the Dardanelles on July 14th 1915 on the *Caledonia*. Prior to the sailing it seems the men hadn't been fit enough for overseas service, owing to problems with their teeth, which were in an appalling condition; a mass extraction was considered the only solution, as there was no time for treatment. So all the dentists in the area were contacted and the problem was sorted. Some of the men had all their teeth pulled and some only a few; it was to be a whole twelve months before their new dentures were to catch up with them, while they were in the Suez Canal. It was potluck and as to which set fitted whom.

The *Caledonia* was a passenger ship of 9,223 gross tons with two funnels, and carried approximately 1,500 passengers. She was built in 1904 and was requisitioned in 1914, when she became a troopship. In 1916 she was torpedoed en route to Malta.

On August 9th 1915 she landed at Sulva Bay and before our men could take cover the enemy bombarded them with shellfire; countless young men were killed. The next day, our men fought from dawn to dusk in conditions we couldn't even imagine. Gallipoli was one of the worst battles of the First World War: an estimated one million men were killed there. There were 21,255 British soldiers killed and 52,000 wounded. Men fought in trenches with very little food; their main diet was bully beef and hard biscuits, with no fruit or vegetables. Here were men who needed all their energy and strength to survive in atrocious conditions, yet had to fight with empty bellies. There was no sanitation and fresh water was scarce; the men were often up to their waists in water and mud, and they had to keep their heads down at all times because of constant sniping. Disease and sickness spread all around them.

On August 15th Hugh's battalion was moved to Gully, Suva Bay. Forced to dig trenches through the night, the men were totally exhausted by now. Hugh had six days left to live. What a way to end your days on earth. They were to advance yet again, digging more trenches, having had very little sleep since they landed. Saturday August 21st was to be the last day of Hugh's life. How did he die? Did he suffer? Did his thoughts turn to his family back home in Wales during those last few moments? I am sitting here writing about a man I never knew; a man that had died thirty years before I was even born; I can't believe that I feel such strong emotions. My heart was heavy and my stomach was churning when I received this information about him. I was so upset – I felt as if I have lost a friend as well as a relative.

Em's Uncle Owen, a lay preacher, was shot in the head in the Dardanelles. Badly injured, he was sent home before the war was over. Having returned home to Bangor, Owen wrote a poem about the time he was wounded. I have read it many times and think it's so heart-rending. It tells us a little about what he and many others like him must have gone through in the Great War.

1914 – Y Milwr – 1918
Gan Owen Lewis

Eisteddais fy hunain – do ganwaith, meddyliais am ddyddiau a fu,
Pan oeddwn yn filwr y brenin, pan oeddwn yn iach ac yn gry.
Fe roddwyd y dryll yn fy nwylaw, achosodd i'm calon roi llam,
Wrth gofio'r cynghorion a gefais, cyn gadael fy nhad a fy mam.

Ac allan i'r frwydr fe'm gyrrwyd, agorwyd fy llygaid gan fraw,
Wrth weled rhai annwyl yn syrthio, a'r gelyn yn dod ar bob llaw.
Fy meddwl mewn eiliad am gartref, fy nghartref pa le rwyt yn awr,
Fy nheulu pryderus gweddiwch, ar Dduw sydd a gallu mor fawr.

Ond dyma'r awr wedi dyfod, yn awr rhaid wynebu'r holl lu.
Safasom gan ddisgwyl y cennad, i ymladd a'r gelyn, mor gry.
Yr arwydd a roed gan y Capten, a bore y Sabboth oedd hi,
Ac ymladd a wneuthum yn galed, ond syrthio i lawr a wnes i.

A cododd y dryll at fy mhen, fe daniodd, a saethodd ei wrthrych.
Mi theimlais fod bywyd ar ben, mi gurais y drws sef drws angau.
Meddyliais mai ofer oedd hyn, ac eilwaith fe gurais nes clywed,
Rhyw lais yn dywedyd yn syn, Dos ymaith pechadur dos ymaith,
Ar fywyd cei chynnig drachefn, dos ymaith a cheisia yr Iesu,
Cyfoda dy groes ar dy gefn.

I have translated the poem as best I can.

1914 – The Soldier – 1918
By Owen Lewis

I sat on my own, yes hundreds of times, thinking of days long gone,
When I was a soldier of the king, when I was healthy and strong.
A gun was thrust into my hands; it caused my heart to leap,
Remembering the advice I'd been given, before leaving my father and mother.

And out to the battle I was sent, and I opened my eyes with fright,
As I saw those dear to me fall, and the enemy closing on all sides;
My mind flew straight to my home: Home, where art thou now?
My anxious family please pray to God, He who is all-powerful.

But here cometh the hour. I must face the throng.
We stood to await the messenger: we had to fight the enemy, so strong.
The sign was given by the Captain, the Sabbath morning it was.
I fought hard, but down I went.

And a gun was trained at my head: it fired and hit me;
I felt my life was ending. I knocked at the door of death,
But I seemed to go unheeded; I knocked again, until I heard
A shocked voice saying: Go away sinner, go away.
Life you've been offered again. Go forth and seek the Lord.
Lift your cross onto your back.

I will turn now to another branch of my family – who are ….

My great-grandfather Evan John Evans (1876 - 1929) was wrongly known by my family as Evan Richard, until I started researching this book. Born in Llanllyfni near Caernarfon, Evan was the second of four children, as far as I know. His siblings were Elizabeth (1874 - 1951) Martha (born 1877) and William (born 1888). The four were left orphans in 1880. It seems that they were brought up by William and Catherine Williams at 1 Madryn Terrace, Llanllyfni. William and Catherine had four children of their own. Later on in life Evan John was to name three of his own children after his siblings. Evan John was a quarryman who worked at the Dorothea slate quarry in Talsarn. He was buried on December 12th 1929 aged 53. At the time of his death he lived at 7 Chapel St, Penygroes. He is buried in Macpelah cemetery with his sister Elizabeth who died in 1951 aged 77. Elizabeth, who walked with a limp, had no children. Also buried there is her husband Robert Williams. Em and I went to the cemetery at Christmas time, 2002, to put some holly on the grave. We were hoping there would be a wreath there, but ours was the only one. So many years have gone by and I don't suppose there's anyone left who cares, or even knows who they were.

Evan John Evans married Barbara Evans in about 1898-99 (My great-grandparents). I can't trace their marriage certificate. Five of their eight children were born in Penygroes. The first born, a girl called Martha, died when she was a few weeks old. Then along came my dear Nain, Laura Jane, born on February 9th 1900. Thomas, Elizabeth and William were the next three children.

There was precious little work to be had in North Wales, and poverty was dreadful, so the family decided to move down south to the coal mines, "to a better life" said my dear Nain. Off went Evan John, Barbara and their family. They moved to 29 Caerphilly Road, Senghenydd, South Wales. They left William with his Nain (Babell); he was brought up mostly by her and thought the world of her.

I remember my Nain telling me how hard those times were in South Wales. They used to keep lodgers and Barbara, being a religious woman, wouldn't tolerate even the slightest smell of drink on the lodgers – they were asked to leave if they transgressed. Barbara was known to say *gwell enw da na chyfoeth oll y byd* – better a good reputation than all the riches of the world.

Evan John and Barbara with their children Tom, Laura Jane (nain) in the back, Lizzie and the toddler is Martha. Senghenydd 1915.

Barbara was to have three more children in South Wales – Evan, Martha (known as Mattie) and Mair. Nain Gwyn (Laura Jane) remembered her father Evan John taking her to hospital to see her mother Barbara when she was poorly; Nain didn't want to go but her father made her. Mair, their youngest child, was only two years old when Barbara died in 1917; Evan was only four. The family got on with it as best they could. I do remember Nain telling me that her father was overly fond of his drink and was rather a nasty man when he was drunk. I searched for a long time for information on Barbara's death. Eventually I received a copy of her death certificate from South Wales. She died in hospital at Bridgend on October 3rd 1917. Her husband Evan was a coal hewer and at the time of her death they lived at 117 High Street, Abertridwr. She died of heart disease. No wonder my Nain didn't want to visit her mother in hospital, with her being only seventeen years old and her Mam in goodness knows what condition. I seem to remember Nain saying that her mother suffered problems with the change of life as well. "There was nowhere in those days to treat people like that," said Nain. How lucky we are to live in these times. Evan John came back to North Wales in the mid 1920's with his two sons Thomas (Uncle Tom) and Evan (Uncle Evan). They went to Penygroes, where Evan

John had family. They ran a bakery in Talsarn. Evan John married again, but I know nothing about his second wife. I will tell you about Evan John and Barbara's children now.

My dear Nain Laura Jane (1900-1988), being the eldest, took the brunt of it when her mother died. Nain never spoke much about those days, except to say they were hard times and she never got on with her father. She always spoke well of her mother and I think she missed her until the day she died. I will speak more of my Nain later on. My heart is heavy, writing about such happy days; it seems like only yesterday when I was sat in my Nain's tiny back room, chatting and laughing with her. Such a small room, so much love in it for so many people.

Great uncles and aunts on my Mothers side of the family

Great Uncle Thomas (1901 - late 1978), or Uncle Tom as he was known to us, went on to marry Auntie Blodwen in 1934. They never had any children. They lived in Llanberis all the years I knew them. We visited them a lot as children – it was a long way in those days on a bus. Having no children of their own, they loved to see us kids. Auntie Blod referred to her husband as *Tom Bach*. They were indeed a quiet, gentle couple who were devoted to each other and always spoke Welsh together. Both of them used to visit us all a few times a year; they came by an early bus so that they could 'do' all the family in one day. One of Uncle Tom's pastimes was writing little Welsh verses; I'm really sorry that I don't have any of them. I can still picture them now in Caledfryn, where they lived: the little back room where they sat, with its tiny window looking onto the back yard. On the little tiled grate were some large brass candlesticks

Uncle Tom and Auntie Blod 1975.

that always sparkled; even with a coal fire in the grate it was still quite dark and damp there. They had a cupboard in one corner with all sorts of chapel books and hymn books, and of course the Welsh Bible. On top of the cupboard stood a well-polished wireless with which they used to listen to their Welsh programmes and especially the hymns and services on Sundays.

A great big Welsh dresser dominated one wall; it was full of willow-patterned plates and all sorts of cherished objects which I loved to look at but didn't dare touch. By the side of the dresser stood a grandfather clock. It was very loud when it struck! The furniture had been passed down from Auntie Blod's mother. I suppose they were left to Auntie Blod's family when she died.

The front room was referred to as *Y Parlwr*. We never sat in the *parlwr* as it was the best room – I don't ever remember anyone sitting in it. I suppose there was a fire in there sometimes but I never saw one lit and the room always smelt damp and musty. As I remember there were three bedrooms, all rather in keeping with the house (very small and dark). In the back was a minute kitchen which Uncle Tom had added onto the house. Val and I used to make sandwiches and wash and clear the dishes there. The dishes were all odd and some were chipped, as if it was a sin to waste money on luxuries. It was spotlessly clean and everything had a place. Just off the yard was the only toilet, and there was also a small shed where Uncle Tom kept his tools. There was no bathroom.

Auntie Blod had really bad arthritis in her hands: her poor fingers were really out of shape and swollen. Uncle Tom worked in the slate quarry, then as a labourer with the council for many years. He liked to work with his hands and did a lot of work on their home until his health failed. Now (my Dad) did some work for them once, but he was one of the most unreliable people I ever met. I don't think he ever finished the job, but he did sub all the money for it in advance. Uncle Tom never bore him a grudge. Em and I used to take our girls to see them sometimes; there's a photo of them both with Auntie Blod when she was in residential care after Uncle Tom died. Uncle Tom suffered with a chronic bad chest, as did my Mam (Megan) and he used to tell Mam: "Don't forget Meg bach, do your deep breathing." I don't think Mam ever did it!

The chapel was very close to their hearts and they did a lot of work for it. Uncle Tom was a lay preacher. He died in 1978 and was buried in Llanberis. We were in Llanberis last year and had a look at their old home. I'm sure they would turn in their grave if they saw it. No shine to the windows and the house is in need of a lick of paint. I phoned Cledwyn, one of Auntie Blod's relatives, to ask him if there was a family Bible I could have a look at. He said that when Auntie Blod died they had a man in to clear the house and all the books and photos were sent to a second hand shop somewhere. What a shame! He did say that maybe Uncle Evan had the Bible. Auntie Dilys said she would have a look.

Great Auntie Lizzie (1903 - 1986) was rather quiet and reserved. I don't think I ever saw her have a good belly laugh. I only saw her in Nain's house once or twice. She married Dafydd John and lived in Capel Uchaf (which has just been renovated) in Gwyllt Road. They had three children: a boy, Donald, who died in 1936 aged 10 months; Barbara, who lives with her husband John and family in Colwyn Bay (I see her occasionally), and Mary, who went to London many years ago to become a nurse.

Uncle Dafydd died a young man (lung haemorrhage) and Auntie Lizzie went on to marry William Hoyle (Junior). They lived in a big house on the hill in Junction. Uncle Will used to give piano lessons there, and he was an excellent musician as I recall. I remember going there as a girl with Mam and Val. Mam would warn us: "Now you remember to be good girls and sit down still." Little children in those days were meant to be seen and not heard. Another thing sticks in my mind regarding visits to relatives; my dear Mam always said: "Remember girls to say please and thank you, and you must never take the last *bechdan* or cake off the plate." To this day I try not to!

Auntie Lizzie became a widow for a second time and moved to Glasinfryn. I remember going there with my parents and Lorraine when she was a baby. We went on a motor bike and side car. The side car was a home-made box that my Dad had made and attached to the bike. Talk about scallywags – we did have some fun though. You wouldn't dare do it these days. Auntie Lizzie is buried in Erw Feiriol with her first husband and their baby.

Great Uncle Will (1902 - 1987) was brought up mostly by his nain (Nain Babell – see Note 19). Uncle El tells me that Will was six years old before he could walk. Why? Who knows? He went to Canada in 1926. He never married. He joined the Calgary Highlanders and fought in the Second World War. He spent a few leaves with his brother Uncle Evan. Auntie Dilys remembers him as a quiet, shy and gentle man who was always clean and tidy; she particularly remembers that she could always see her face in his highly polished shoes. I suppose this was army training! He was good at writing little bits of poetry; sadly, we don't have any copies.

Will didn't come back to this country until the Second World War. When Uncle El was in Holland during the war he came across the Calgary Highlanders returning from the front line. He told one of the corporals that he had an uncle in the Highlanders. "His name is William Evans, he's my mother's brother from Wales," said Uncle Elfed.

"Do you mean little Bill Evans the Welshman?" asked one of the soldiers with a smile. "We had to leave him in Blighty - he's a little too old for this."

"Where is Blighty, Uncle El?" said I.

"It's the home country, ciw," he said laughing at me. I really am thick sometimes! Uncle Will had been left behind in England. At one stage he visited his sister (Laura Jane) when she lived in Lawr Tai (Gerizim Terrace) - now under the expressway as it passes through Llanfair. Uncle El was also on leave at the time and my Nain's house was full to bursting with all the family (remember, it was only two up, two down). When leave was up, Uncle Will had to return to London and Uncle El had to go somewhere else; they left Llanfair station together in a river of tears - I can just imagine my Nain, desperately not wanting to let her beloved son and brother go, but go they had to, as did millions of other mother's sons. They went together as far as Crewe where they had to split up. That, I think, was the last time Uncle Will saw Wales.

Uncle Wil (Canada), Second World War.

I didn't even know there was an Uncle Will until I was in my teens. Uncle Tom kept in touch with him until he died, then Uncle Evan took over. I understand that Uncle Will lived for quite a few years riding the trains in Canada. I suppose you'd call him a hobo, or as we would say, a tramp. He lived the latter part of his life in some sort of sheltered accommodation in Edmonton. Uncle Evan and Auntie Dilys intended to visit him but the doctors said there was no point, since he wouldn't know them. How sad, all that family here in Wales and him so far away on his own. Uncle Will died in October 1987 aged 84 and left his 6 siblings around £30,000 between them.

I will turn now to Great Auntie Martha (1908 - 1991), or Auntie Matt as she was known to us (see Note 20). I remember Nain telling me what a "good girl she had been for her and Taid" when she was young. She had helped with the other children and she had also helped out with money from her cleaning jobs. Auntie Matt married John Richard Evans (Dick). Uncle Dick lived in Nant y Felin when he was a child; his family kept a fox, which all the kids in the neighbourhood loved to feed, at the bottom of their garden. We were always in and out of Auntie Matt's house as we grew up; she was especially kind to Val. Very often Val would take a walk to Nant y Berllan and spend a couple of hours with Auntie Matt. Indeed, some of her children still send Val a gift for Christmas. It's really nice to know that they still think of her. Val always sheds a tear when she gets their cards. Auntie Matt was a regular visitor to Mam's (8 Llwyn y Gog) through all the years Mam was ill in bed.

Great Uncle Evan (1912 - 1993), or Uncle Ev as my mother called him, told me that the family would have been split up many years ago had it not been for my Nain. She was more like his mother than his sister, he said. Evan married Auntie Dilys, who worked at Cerrig Llwyd in Bryn y Neuadd (it was a posh house in those day's she said) as a cook to one of the doctors. They met at the hospital and were married at St Mary's Church on June 8th 1940. Nine months after their marriage he

Evan and Dilys wedding in St. Mary's 1940. Left to right: Mattie, Mair, Blodwen, Harry (taid), Megan (Mam), Tom. Sitting down is Laura Jane (nain). Bride's family on the right.

lost a foot and part of his leg in an accident at work – he was a signalman on the railway; they lived in Walsall by now. He had been told that the railway line wasn't in use and went to do some maintenance on it; all of a sudden he looked up and saw a truck coming towards him. Uncle Evan managed to get down flat on his face between the lines but couldn't move his leg quick enough to save it. He was lucky to be alive.

They lived in Cartref, a big terraced house in Pearsehouse Street, Walsall, most of their married lives – Auntie Dilys still lives there.

There are many tales to tell about Uncle Ev – he was a little eccentric, always liked a joke, and was rather outspoken as I remember. Uncle Elfed and Auntie Heulwen stayed with them on their honeymoon. In the middle of the night, Auntie Heulwen went downstairs for a drink. All of a sudden the alarm went off and gave her the shock of her life; she didn't know where to run to. There was worse to come. She looked up and saw Uncle Ev hobbling downstairs, waving his artificial foot in the air! She nearly died of fright. Uncle Ev was a well known figure in Walsall, riding around on his pushbike. I'm sure his neighbours had lots of fun over the years with him. He was very much the family man. They had one son called Clifford who was very clever on the piano. Clifford won a scholarship to the London Academy of Music and spent five years there, then he went on to the Leningrad Conservatoire in Russia for two years. His parents were very proud of him. These days Clifford lives in Ipswich with his family and teaches music. One day, Uncle Evan and Auntie Dilys went to see Clifford giving a recital in London, at one of the posh concert halls. During the interval Uncle Ev took out his flask and butties but was told very nicely (but very firmly) to "please put those things away, eating and drinking is not allowed in the auditorium sir." I'm sure he had something to say about that.

They kept in close contact with the family despite living away for over half a century; in fact they came back to St Mary's Church to have their marriage blessed in 1990 after 50 years together. We held a family reunion at The Split Willow afterwards. It was indeed a memorable evening. Uncle Evan died a few years later and was buried at Penmaenmawr. He wanted to be buried in Wales. He lies close to his sister Mair, in what I can only describe as a kind of tomb. The grave was dug out and the inside was built of brick. Uncle Ev's coffin was lined with lead. Auntie Dilys, who lives alone now, is a very courageous lady. She had a hip replacement a while ago but she is still as cheerful as ever. She had a chairlift installed and she goes up and down the stairs like a spring chicken. Auntie Dilys was 90 years old in December 2002. She's an example to us all. On her 90th birthday she had over 50 cards and loads of flowers and prezzies. The people from her church are very kind to her. Clifford and his wife were there for the weekend. But within days Auntie Dilys had a shocking experience. She went out with some friends and when she got back her door had been forced. "What a shock I had Margaret fach, there were policemen in the hall, my front door was broken and there was glass all over the place," she said. One of her neighbours thought she was ill because the milk was still out at lunchtime and had called the police. It seems that a couple of weeks previously an elderly man had been found in his house, and he'd been dead for two weeks. So no-one wanted to take any chances. I phone her quite often and she remembers a little more about the family every time.

There was a gap of only seven years between Mam and Great Auntie Mair (1914 - 1989), so they were like sisters, and my Nain was more like a mother to her. Uncle John Morgan says that when she was a girl living in Nant y Felin Mair used to deliver the daily papers with his brother Hwmphra. "She was a nice looking girl," said Uncle John. She married Uncle Jack and lived in a tied railway cottage in Llandudno Junction. They had one son, Elfed Bach. During the war my mother used to work in an aeroplane factory in the Junction. She used to do a lot of singing in the factory at lunch time (she had a good voice in those days) and occasionally she would go to Auntie Mair's for lunch. Uncle Jack worked for many years on the railway. We visited them whenever Mam could afford the bus fares.

One memory stands out, above all others, about Auntie Mair's house. They had what was called a dry toilet. There was no water at all in the little shed at the bottom of the garden – only a tin bucket, with a wooden seat built around it. It was spotlessly clean, but I didn't care how clean it was, I hated it! I loathed going to the toilet there and would wait until I was desperate. In the summer months it was more unpleasant than usual. Every so often someone would go and empty it – about once a week, Gwynfor tells me! Despite the toilet, we loved going there and were always sure of something nice to eat. They would indeed empty the cupboards for us!

Auntie Mair was a nervous woman and everything worried her. She had TB when Elfed Bach was a child and she was in Bryn Seiont Hospital for two years; it was a very serious illness in those days. At this time Elfed Bach stayed in Auntie Mattie's house. When she was finally discharged from hospital she stayed with Nain and Taid in Lawr Tai, Llanfair, for a while. Auntie Mair died a good few years ago and is buried in Penmaenmawr. Uncle Jack was to remain in his own home (Bryn Derw) until he died a couple of years ago. He is buried with his wife in Penmaenmawr.

I will turn now to my Taid (Harry Bangor) and his side of the family

My great-grandmother Margaret Williams (1862 - about 1897), after whom I was named, was born in Dwygyfylchi. She had a sister, Mary, who was about ten years younger than her. Their parents died when Margaret was a young girl. By the time Margaret got married her father was dead. It seems that Margaret moved to Bodeuan in Nefyn. There was a Margaret Jones living in Tyn y Mynydd in 1881; she was a domestic servant aged 19. Was this her? Highly likely, I think.

Margaret married Hugh Williams on November 1st 1882 at Pwllheli registry office. Neither of them could read nor write; Hugh was a set maker. Margaret and Hugh had four children (or so we thought); Uncle Bob, Auntie Nell, Thomas John and Henry (Taid, whom I will refer to as Harry). Having obtained some more information, I have discovered that Hugh, Margaret's husband, died in Penial Ceidio near Bodeuan on

Owen Jones (Bangor) and his wife Mary with their family in Mona Terrace, about 1905. Back row left to right, Harry Williams (taid), his sister Nell, Maggie (Black Lion) and Harry. Uncle Robin (Black) is on his mother's knee and Florrie on her father's knee, Winnie is standing between her parents. The little boys in front are Ludwig and Dafydd John.

February 10th 1890 aged only 27 years old. The cause of death was phthisis (TB). His sister Dorothy Williams registered his death. Some time after Hugh died, Margaret moved back to Tyn y Mynydd Bach with her three children, perhaps to be near Dorothy. Taid (Harry) was born on October 15th 1891 in Tyn y Mynydd Bach. These were two tiny, rather isolated cottages on the side of the road near Bodeuan. We have been very lucky to find a photo of them as they were then. Only one of the cottages remains today.

Poor Margaret was a widow at 27 with three little children. One of them, Thomas John, had some sort of disability since birth and Taid was on the way. It must have been a terrible time for her, with no family close enough to help her. Margaret left the area shortly after Taid was born and returned to Penmaenmawr. Uncle Elfed remembers it being mentioned that Taid was "only a babe in arms" when they all came to Penmaenmawr. Margaret lived for only a few years after returning. I can't find out anything else about her.

Margaret's sister Mary and her husband Owen Jones (Bangor) took in Taid and his brother Bob after their mother died. We believe that Taid was about five years old at the time. Auntie Nell probably went to be a domestic servant somewhere. Thomas John was sent to the workhouse at Conwy and died there in the early 1920's, probably. As yet I can't find any trace of him (see Note 21). I'm sure it can't have been easy for Mary and Owen Jones, with a house full of their own children and two more mouths to feed. Taid was so lucky to have a family to bring him up as one of their own. Owen Jones worked in the quarry – he was the trumpet blower who warned the men, with a blow on his trumpet, when they were ready to blast. We have a good photo of him with his trumpet. Mary and Owen had seven or eight children and I remember a few of them myself. I'm told there was a son called Henry – he was a little younger than Taid, so one was Harry and the other Henry. When they were playing in the garden and Mary used to call them in she would shout Henry! Henry! Harry! Harry! *i'r ty yma rwan* – come in now! One day a neighbour said to her: "Can't you make up your mind what his name is, woman?" Mary went in giggling to herself. They all lived at 5 Mona Terrace in 1901 – quite a crowd in such a small house! Mary, Owen and the family eventually moved to Lawr Tai, Gerizim Terrace; Auntie Alma tells me that Mary was a dab hand at making *Diod Dail* – nettle lemonade. All the children loved it. At Christmas Mary used to sell it to her neighbours for 2 pence a bottle.

After a while Mary and Owen moved to Arfor, one of the big houses on the beach, now known as Derby House. Mary took visitors for many years. No-one was allowed to use the front door except the visitors.

One of Mary's children, Uncle Robin (Robin Black Lion as he was known) was the baby of the family. Uncle Robin always had a smile on his face and laughed a lot. He loved football. I was with his daughter Betty, watching our grandsons playing football recently, and she told me how her dad used to take her to watch football when she was a girl. "My dad would shout and scream from start to finish," said Bet. She and I did some pretty loud shouting as we watched Aron and Curtis play that day! Robin married Auntie Clara; she was a very cheerful lady and also liked a good laugh. They had four children: Vera, Betty, David and Jean, who all live locally.

My grandfather's brother was Robert Williams (1883 - 1971). He was the first child of Margaret and Hugh. He lived, as I have said, with Mary and Owen. Great Uncle Bob was a heavy drinker once but he saw the light one day and never took another drop. He worked in the quarry office most of his life and was known as "Bulgie" owing to him being a little on the fat side; others called him The Commodore. "He was rather bossy in the quarry," said Uncle John Morgan. His first wife, Charlotte, was an invalid who was confined to a bath chair (wheelchair). Auntie Emily was his second wife and they lived at 12 Mona Terrace for as long as I can remember. They were a very quiet couple who lived for each other and the chapel. I don't think I ever saw Uncle Bob laugh; he was rather a serious man. We called on them often as children with my Mam; Auntie Emily always gave us a welcome. We would have to go through the parlour and we would pass a great big sideboard full of lovely ornaments; there was also a table in the corner on which they kept the wireless, their Bible and hymnbooks. They normally sat in the back room, which always seemed dark to me despite there being a small window with cream net curtains. There was a table with a spotlessly clean tablecloth which always had a matching sugar bowl and milk jug on it, ready for the next cup of tea. Around the table stood a couple of odd dining chairs on which we had to sit very quietly for the duration of the visit. Parked around the fire were a couple of well-covered easy chairs; I don't suppose the original covers ever saw the light of day. A very small fire burned in the tiled grate and standing proudly on the corner of the hearth was a shining brass spill holder, full of spills ready to light Uncle Bob's pipe. Val and I made paper 'sticks' while we were there to start the fire; not even the old newspapers were wasted. As we got older Val and I used to make a cuppa in the back kitchen; it was so small you couldn't swing a cat in it. Auntie Emily kept visitors for years during the summer; how she managed in such a small house I don't know, remember there was no bathroom or inside toilet.

Uncle Bob was a diabetic for many years and used to inject himself two or three times a day. Mam would tell us how she had to run home from school to boil a cabbage for his tea. He would drink the cabbage water, which was supposed to be good for diabetes. When I was about 15 or 16 we lived in Britannia House. Uncle Bob would go for his pension on a Thursday and call to see us. My Mam used to pray that he wouldn't stay too long in case Dad came home the worse for drink. What a life!

He wasn't a generous man, Uncle Bob. I can't remember him ever giving Val or me a couple of coppers for sweets. Uncle Elfed doesn't remember him and his siblings ever receiving even the smallest gift at Christmas. It's a joke in the family to this day that if you don't want to spend, you're like Uncle Bob. After Auntie Emily died he used to go to Nain's (Laura at No 19) occasionally to watch a little telly of an evening. This, of course, pleased my dear Nain no end! Uncle Bob spent the last days of his life with some relatives of Auntie Emily's in Pen. He is buried with his two wives in Erw Feiriol. Uncle Bob had no children.

Taid's sister, Great Auntie Ellen (1885 - 1960's), was Margaret and Hugh's only daughter. Auntie Nell, as she was known, lived in Accrington with her husband Albert; it is thought she went there as a young girl to work. Dilys Eames used to go to Auntie Nell's on holiday and remembers being there when war broke out in 1939. She remembers getting the train home, and all the houses had stacks of sandbags. "God knows how anyone thought a sandbag was going to help," said Dilys. I myself remember going there as a girl with my Dad and a chap called Dyfi Humphries from Penmaenmawr; I think he was a builder who was friendly with Dad. We went in Dyfi's van, with him driving, but he couldn't see very well at all. So it was up to Dad and me to find the way. Talk about the blind leading the blind! We had loads of fun, laughing at each other's mistakes all the way there. I don't really remember why we went there; I suppose it was to get some furniture for one of the family – we were always swapping and changing with each other. Auntie Nell and Uncle Albert used to come to Llanfair regularly to stay with Uncle Bob. Auntie Nell was a small, rather stout lady with a very red nose. She was always cheerful and ready to laugh despite having a very bad chest. Uncle Albert worked in a slaughterhouse at the back of their house, which wasn't as clean as it might have been, I'm told.. I assume that Auntie Nell is buried in Accrington. Her husband Albert remarried. They had no children.

I didn't know that Taid had a brother called John Thomas (1888 - ?) until Uncle El told me when I was in my teens. He died in Conwy Hospital between 1910 - 1920 (we think). He had some sort of disability from birth.

My loving Taid and Nain (Gwynfor)

My dear Taid, Harry Williams (1891 - 1965), was the last of Margaret's children. Taid was to be known as Harry Bangor. He went to Penmaenmawr School for a short time, but I don't know much about his childhood. My husband Em remembers Taid telling him a story just before he died. Apparently, when he was a young boy he needed a new pair of trousers but there just wasn't enough money to go round because there were so many children in the family. So he asked his brother Bob if he would buy him a pair. By this time Uncle Bob was working, but he refused. Taid never forgot this.

In 1910, when Taid was 19, a friend of his from Penmaenmawr bought him a return ticket to South Wales. With no work in the area, Taid took a chance and off he went to the coal mines; it was to be many years before he returned.

There was a massive explosion at the Universal Colliery in Senghenydd on Tuesday morning, October 14th 1913. The night shift had only just gone home when a huge blast ripped through the shaft. There must have been close to a thousand men down the mine. The alarm was sounded and crowds of people ran as fast as their feet would carry them to the pithead, among them wives, children, mothers and fathers, with their hearts in their mouths. Despite the smoke and flames and great damage, rescue work went on relentlessly. With smoke pouring out of the mine shaft, some of the lucky survivors came out into the daylight to be met by cheering crowds who stood waiting, watching, and praying that the next face they saw was the familiar face of their loved one. It took many weeks to bring all the bodies up. Some men and boys were so badly burned their own families didn't recognise them. Some bodies were never recovered. Over four hundred men and boys lost their lives that day. It was the worst pit disaster Britain had ever seen. It is said that almost every family in Senghenydd lost a loved one that terrible day. Lots of families lost their main breadwinner.

Taid was one of the lucky ones. He said: "I was coming off the night shift when the alarm went off. We all went back to see what we could do – there was a terrible chill running through the men, as most of them had sons, brothers or fathers on the opposite shift." Taid was one of the rescue workers that day.

Taid joined the Royal Welch Fusiliers at Wrexham on Sept 1st 1914. He later served in the Manchester Regiment. He was a private in the Royal Army Medical Corps when he was discharged on February 10th 1919 after serving 4 years and 9 days with the Colours and 154 days with the Army Reserves. Taid was retired on medical grounds – he had malaria.

My Taid, Harry Williams, married Laura Jane Evans on April 14th 1919. My dear grandparents! You never really get over losing people you love. You just get used to living with it. There is such a lot to say about Nain and Taid Gwynfor (as Val and I always called them). Where do I start? I suppose I will shed a few tears before I finish telling you about them. I owe them so much; they were like second parents to my sister and I.

Harry (Bangor) and Laura Jane Williams wedding day. Pointypridd 1919.

I suppose I should start at the beginning. My grandparents met in South Wales in 1915, when Nain was 15 years old; maybe Taid was on leave. Taid was demobbed in February 1919 and they were married soon after in Pontypridd. They lived in apartments when they were first married. By this time Nain's mother Barbara had been dead for two years. After they were married all Nain's brothers and sisters went to live with them, leaving their father on his own. So Nain and Taid had a ready-made family. Nain was 19 years old and Taid took on someone else's family – what a special couple they must have been.

As I have said, Taid was a coal miner. By this time Uncle Tom also worked in the mines. Times were hard. In 1920 my grandparents had a son, Ifan Henry (Uncle Harry), followed in 1921 by a second son, Elfed. They lived at this time in apartments in 72 High Street, Senghenydd. I have a letter written by Taid to Auntie Nell (his sister) and Uncle Albert, who had just got married. It tells of very hard times: he'd been out of work for many months (there had been a strike on) and their baby boy Elfed had been born at the same time. "We should have called him

Striker," said Taid, who went on to say: "It will take a long, long time for us to get over these hard times, but it will come alright again late or later."

In 1922 my dear mother Megan came along; she was born with a bad chest and nearly died with asthma when she was very young. As we can all imagine it must have been very crowded, but knowing my Nain and Taid I'm sure no one went short of love.

Uncle Elfed remembers that when they were kids Auntie Mair and Mam used to share a room. Uncle Harry and he shared the room next door; there was no door – only a hole in the wall to go from one room to the other. Uncle Harry used to have them all in stitches with his antics and stories. In those early days in South Wales there were 14 members of the family. Uncle Elfed told me recently that he is the only one left now.

Uncle Tom and Uncle Evan came back to North Wales with their father Evan John some time in the early twenties. Their father went back to Penygroes; Tom and Evan went to Nantlle or Talsarn, where I'm told Nain Barbara had a good friend called Kate, who was like a sister to her. There was a bakery run by the family and Tom and Evan worked there. I'm told there was a Baptist minister; his name was Robert Evans and he was a relative as well. I have not looked into this as yet.

Taid was a member of the Senghenydd Welsh Miners Choir and in June 1926 the choir spent three months in Ireland, collecting money for the coal miners who were on strike. It must have been an exceptionally hard time for Nain, with three of her own children and her brothers and sisters to take care of. In 1927 their little son Byron was born but he lived for only four weeks. Nain used to say he was born without a constitution; I'm not sure what she meant by that. They had moved house by this time and lived at 72 Stanley Street, Senghenydd. Byron was buried with his grandmother Barbara in Abertridwr on February 21st 1927.

In 1928 Taid worked in the Llanbradach pit just outside Senghenydd. Working conditions were atrocious. Taid said the men used to work in sludge and water up to their waists. Even at that time Taid had a bad chest. Eventually he said *Dyna ddigon* – that's enough! He decided to come back to Llanfair. He came on his own and stayed with his Auntie Mary and Uncle Owen (Owen Jones Bangor) in Arfor, on the Promenade. Once again the family was there for him! Taid worked for months to save the train fare for Nain and the children to come to North Wales.

The children were all so excited; they couldn't wait to get on the train, to see their beloved father again. The great day arrived and off the train got Nain, Uncle Harry, Uncle El, Mam and Auntie Mair. Uncle Harry was first to spot Taid. "Dad, Dad!" he shouted as he ran to his father. All was well with the world again. All the children were devoted to their mother and father until the day they died. In fact Uncle Harry outlived his mother by only six weeks. They all stayed at Arfor for a few weeks until their bits of furniture arrived and then they took a flat in Min y Don on the Promenade.

Afterwards they went to live in Well Street, Rachub. I think Auntie Al was born there. By this time Auntie Mattie was married and had baby Irwel; they lived next door to Nain and Taid. How long they lived in Rachub I don't know. Then they moved to Llwyn Ysgaw in Nant-y-Felin. Taid was working in the quarry and times were a little better for them by then, probably. In 1936 the baby of the family, Gwynfor Thomas, was born. Nain and Taid were nomadic and moved quite a few times before finally settling down in 19 Mona Terrace,

Coming from Senghenydd 1928. Back row: Mair and Harry. Front: Elfed and Megan.

Nain, Auntie Alma and Gwynfor. About 1938.

which they bought in 1945-1950, from the quarry owners, for the grand sum of £227. It was a three-bedroomed terraced house with a very small back kitchen and a little middle room in which we all sat when we were there. It had a parlour with a lovely red three-piece suite that Nain had struggled to pay for and then had covered quickly "just in case it got dirty". People in those days wanted to cover everything they bought, probably because there was no money to keep buying new things. The kitchen had only a cold-water tap and Nain had a geyser put in – a little gas water heater on the wall over the sink. The house had no bathroom and the only toilet was in the little yard that had a connecting roof. There was a wash shed in the yard with a big white sink which was scrubbed religiously. Nain was a firm believer that cleanliness is next to godliness. I remember Nain used to have a dolly and tub in the wash shed. The dolly was like a broom handle with three little legs attached to the bottom; she would rotate it or bang it up and down on the wet clothes in the washing tub. A metal washboard was used for scrubbing the very dirty clothes, and since the men worked in the quarry there were lots of dirty clothes. Later came an aluminium gas boiler and then a brand new twin tub washing machine (by this time my dear Taid had died). In the back was a very large garden in which we spent many hours playing.

My Dad, I recollect, did a lot of work for them although he wasn't at all reliable, and I'm sure he didn't do it for nothing. I recall the time he put a new toilet in the back for them. He went out to get some materials for the job but they didn't see him again for a week. He came back with no materials or money, with some big excuse as to what had happened to the money. When I was a girl it was so good to go to Nain's house in Mona Terrace – the only one of their many homes I remember. We were a close family and went there very often.

Taid was a foreman in the quarry with a couple of gangs under him; he was also a union official before he retired at 65. He sat on Llanfair Town Council in the early 50's. After his retirement he worked as a caretaker in the snooker club in Castle Buildings on Station Road; it is still there today (above the estate agents). I used to love going there with him. I would help iron the snooker tables with a large brass weight of some sort. Val has reminded me that Taid used to clean an old chapel in Mona, used by the Masons; it was very grand inside and I went along sometimes – of course, I was on my best behaviour. Taid was also a caretaker for the recreation ground on the beach for a while, when I was girl. I didn't really like this: I used to think I couldn't do as I liked in case Taid saw me. I do remember one occasion when Taid saw my friends and I climbing onto the old green wooden shelter on the beach and shouted to me: "Margaret, come down at once." Of course, I was down like a shot. In those days you didn't argue. Taid never told Mam.

One of Taid's favourite pastimes in his later years was to watch wrestling on TV. When they first had the TV their children all gave them 2/6 a week towards the rental. Nain used to tell Mam occasionally: "Don't worry del, you keep the 2/6 – you need it for your little family." None of the children was well off, but dear Mam had a little less. Em and I used to go there on a Saturday afternoon when we were courting in 1963-64 and the wrestling would be on. Taid used to be a bag of nerves and he would tremble with excitement; I can still hear Nain telling him to turn off the TV – the doctor had said it was bad for his heart. Taid also loved a cigarette – he smoked Players or Senior Service. He didn't smoke a lot, and always had one or two to give to Mam. Taid suffered with chronic bronchitis so the cigs really didn't help. Later in Taid's illness Dr Bellis local GP (whom Nain and Taid thought the world of) used to tell Mam: "Mrs Thomas fach, let him enjoy a cig or two – it won't make much difference now." Once again I have a tear in my eye. Oh! Those happy days. I only really remember Taid after he retired from full-time work.

I am going to wander off the track for a while now and tell you a bit about my cousin John from Australia – Uncle Harry's son. John was at home for a month in October 2002, for the first time in 23 years. He came to see his mother Auntie Mildred who hadn't been well. Anyway, we were remembering the old days and John came out with something I had completely forgotten about. Our Taid always wore a metallic spring on each shirt sleeve, half way up his arms, to kept his sleeves up (I suppose they were like garters), and Taid always wore a grey waistcoat with little slit pockets in the front which were always full of cigarette ends; they came in very useful when he'd run out of cigs – and that was very often in those days! He used to split the stumps and mix the baccy that was left over, then roll it into cigarette papers and smoke away! He used to roll the baccy in strips torn off paper bags when he had no proper cigarette paper. How unhealthy was that then? John also told me how it stuck in his memory that Nain used to stroke the back of Taid's head when he sat in his chair by the fire. They were indeed a devoted couple.

I spent countless hours playing with my friends Tegwen, Audrey, Glenys and many other children in Pendalar during the summer holidays. I especially remember playing in the 'jungle' and climbing the old quarry buildings which had been left in ruins; we had many a good den there! There is a community centre there now. We would climb up the old levels and track ways on the scree leading up to the quarry – it was quite a steep climb. Having reached the last level (about the fourth or fifth) it was time to make our way back down, which was even more fun. We slipped, tripped and skipped our way down, unable to stop until we reached the next level; there was many a scraped knee on those adventures, I can tell you! Nain would have had a fit if she'd seen where we went. I spent many, many happy hours in my Nain and Taid's, eating them out of house and home. One of the things my Taid used to say to Nain was: *Gwna'n siwr bod chdi'n llenwi boliau'r plant bach 'ma Laura* – make sure you fill the children's bellies Laura, and she always did. Many a time Nain and Taid put food on our table after my Dad had spent his wages on a horse, or on too much drink, or because he couldn't work owing to bad weather. When I started work it was one of my greatest pleasures to go to Nain and Taid's and slip Taid half a crown (worth about twelve pence today). Taid's face would light up, as if I was giving him a fortune. His words would be *diolch yn fawr ciw, mi brynai baced o Players efo fo* – thanks chicken, I'll buy a packet of Players with it. But what he did with it, actually, was to slip it into his waistcoat pocket and give it to Nain later, or pass it on to some other member of the family in need. That was the kind of thing we all liked to do as a family. Em used to come to Nain's with me; he would sit with Taid in the parlour. Em was so quiet – he hardly said a word, only speaking when spoken to. What changed Em?! Em and I went to Bolton by train in 1963-64, when we were about 17-18 years old. It was a big journey for us then. I remember Taid telling Em to look after me, saying it was a long way to go, and warning him about the English fogs, which he reckoned were bad for the health. Taid didn't drink as far as I know, although I do remember it mentioned in the family years ago that he would call at the Black Lion (a pub on the outskirt of Llanfair, towards Penmaenmawr) for a quick half.

In the early 1960's Taid suffered a few heart attacks which were quite serious. I remember one occasion, late at night. Someone must have phoned the doctor on Nain's behalf: very few people had a phone then, but there was a kiosk in Pendalar. Anyway, after Dr Bellis had been to see Taid and made him as comfortable as he could, he told Nain that he would inform my mother. We lived in Britannia House at that time, and the doctor called on us to tell Mam. She immediately rushed to Mona Terrace, where she found Nain very upset, as you can imagine. Taid wasn't allowed downstairs for a while after the attacks. I never heard him complain; he was a very brave man and his biggest worry was over Laura fach, his dear wife. The last few months of his life were really hard on Nain; she always felt that she didn't do enough for Taid, which was ridiculous, of course. She wore herself out trying to do everything she could for him.

I have clear recollections of those last months of my Taid's life, as Em and I prepared for our wedding. We were married at Bangor Registry Office on March 20th 1965 and we held our reception at Spiers (on the crossroad - it's a hairdresser's now and was a bank before that). We went to see Nain and Taid before catching a train to London. Taid was in bed in the back bedroom propped up on pillows. His words to me were: "You look beautiful ciw, thank you for coming to see us." Em and I were starting our married life as Nain and Taid's was coming to an end. How the wheels of life keep turning!

I went back to work after our honeymoon in London. One day I saw my Dad in Bryn Road, looking down at Mandy Modes (a sewing factory near the river in Bryn Eirin). I can see him there now. *Mae'r hen greadur wedi mynd* he said - Taid was dead. It was March 30th, ten days after Em and I were married. My dear Taid had lost his battle for life and had died that morning aged 73. He used to say of sick people that if they saw March out they would be OK. What a loss to us all. It was the first time I had lost someone close to me. Once again my eyes are tearful - the years go by so quickly, and so many people dear to me have gone. Dad used to say what a good man Taid was and that he (Dad) had caused Taid and Nain a lot of worry over the years. That's a story for another day. Years later, when Mam was very ill, she believed strongly that she would meet up with her father again. I like to think she got her wish.

Taid always said he didn't want to be buried in Rhandir Hedd because there was a lot of water there. When he died it was decided he would be buried in Conwy because his son Harry and daughter-in-law Mildred and their family lived there.

I remember well the day of the funeral. All the family were sitting quietly in the front room at 19 Mona Terrace when in walked Em's mother with a bunch of flowers for Nain. She kissed her on the cheek and said: "Sorry to be late, but I just had to come and see you." She had walked from the village, and as ever Naini May - as she was known to our girls - couldn't be on time! But my Nain was very moved.

Gwynfor, the baby in Nain and Taid's brood, told me recently that if he ever won the lottery he would have Nain and Taid moved home to Llanfair cemetery "where they belonged."

My Nain (Laura Jane)

A few words now about my lovely, kind-hearted and gentle Nain. Her name was Laura Jane Williams but Val and I always called her Nain Gwynfor. Our daughters always referred to her as Naini Joey because she had a budgie when they were little. Nain was a quiet lady who lived for her family. Nain was never one for going out much; in fact, I can't ever remember seeing her in the village. She was a very private person and kept very much to herself, only ever wanting to have her family around her. I never heard her raise her voice to anyone. She always told me: "If you can't say anything good about anyone don't say anything at all." Another of her sayings was: "A still tongue keeps a wise head." Nain was a very gentle, inoffensive lady – and without a doubt she was a lady.

When Taid died she carried on as bravely as possible. They had been married nearly fifty years and she had lived for her husband; it must have been a great shock to be without him – we can only imagine what it was like. Nain wanted a headstone for his grave and she saved up for it herself; she was a very independ-

nain in 19 Mona Terrace, early 1980's.

ent lady. A year after Taid was buried there was a headstone in place and Nain was content. The children, as Nain called them, were so good to her; nothing was too much trouble for any one of them. I remember that Nain wanted her parlour papering when my girls were small. I decided to do it for her and we had a lot of fun. I really enjoy papering and it was doubly enjoyable because it was for my dear Nain. She never took anything for nothing and always slipped me a few bob (which, I must say, was a big help in those days). Her garden was in rather a mess and needed tending. All her children were busy working and looking after their own homes, so Nain decided in her wisdom to get a man in to keep it tidy. Em's dad Owen Roberts (Now Tan Bonc) used to keep the garden in order for her.

Her sons would go there after work. Auntie Alma and Mam went as often as they could. It was easier for Mam, living in the village. Auntie Al moved to Colwyn Bay not long after Taid died, so it wasn't so easy for her. We had loads of fun when we were all there together. The house was always full of very loud laughter! Nain spent most weekends in one of the children's houses. Gwyn and Jean were the first in the family to get a car, in the late 1960's, and they used to take Nain every weekend to one or the other of her children. When we first had a car Em and I used to take Nain on a Friday night to Uncle Harry's in Conwy and Gwyn would pick her up and take her the rest of the way to Auntie Al's house. "You could drive Nain at 100 miles per hour, she wouldn't notice and would just go on chatting," Gwyn used to say.

When I was expecting Lorraine I was overdue. My Mother, Nain and I were having dinner in the small back kitchen in 19 Mona Terrace when Nain said: "There is only one thing for it del, you'll have to take this." It was cod liver oil! I can still taste it. Mam bach, it was terrible! Nain put some cold water in a glass, added the cod liver oil, and stood over me while I took it. I was heaving and making all sorts of faces and noises over the sink. My dear Mother was in the other room, rolling with laughter as only she could, her laughter ringing through the house. She knew I was a big baby when it came to taking anything like that. I managed to keep down a small amount. "Good girl, you won't be long now," said Nain. I was in labour for nearly three days – it didn't make a blind bit of difference. Auntie Alma and my Mam were in 19 Mona Terrace the night Lorraine was born. Auntie Alma kept running back and forth to the kiosk, phoning the hospital. So much water has flowed under the bridge since then.

The years passed and my Mam wasn't well; she wasn't able to do much for Nain, so we all did what we could. Auntie Alma had already lost her dear husband, Uncle Alwyn, aged only 38, leaving her with two little girls to bring up on her own. I used to go to Nain's a couple of days a week to help with her shopping; on other days Val or one of her children went, so Nain never went more than a day or two without seeing one of us. It was easier when I passed my test, although Em was very good and took my Mam and Val there when he could. Val would go to Nain's by taxi from Gadlys Garage and take Nain back to Mam's (8 Llwyn y Gog) when Mam was too ill to go out. They would spend a nice day together. Dad was first rate and would make them all a bit of dinner. Mam could barely walk and spent most of her time in bed. Nain used to sit on a stool by the side of her bed and have dinner there. Dad always called Nain Mrs Williams, although sometimes, for a bit of fun, he called her Laura Jane.

Thursday was pension day; I would go for Nain's pension and get her a bit of shopping. Nain liked loin chops from Jack and Emlyn the local butchers; nothing else would do, they had to be lean with no fat on them. She loved a nice bit of streaky bacon from the Co-op, without any fat of course; in those days it was sliced there and then for you. Uncle Elfed her son used to tell her: "Mam Bach, you must have eaten many a pig in your time." She had a small uncut loaf about four times a week. I can picture her now, sitting by the fire, having a buttie and a banana or a bit of bacon with HP sauce. I miss her still. When my girls were small we didn't have much money and I used to borrow a few shillings from Nain on pension day. She wouldn't always take it back!

When one of us went there for dinner, Nain always had something ready for us to eat. She herself used to have meals on wheels twice a week. I used to do Nain's Christmas shopping, and of course there had to be something small for everyone. It was quite a big family by then and Nain wouldn't miss anyone out. She used to see to her own children herself. I suspect she would give them all a couple of pounds each. "Never let your right hand know what your left is doing," was another of her sayings. There were loads and loads of cards, and lots of letters to write. Nain would dictate to me and I would have to write exactly what she said. I am so sorry now that I didn't ask more questions about the people I used to write to on her behalf. She was a funny little lady, I suppose. I remember one of her little tricks - she would take her white hankie out of her pocket and put it on her head to cover her face; I can't even begin to explain why she did that - it was just the way she was. She was afraid of thunder and lightning, and she would lie on the sofa with a blanket over her head until the storm passed.

Nain loved singing hymns. On a Sunday she would sit and prepare herself for the 6pm service on the radio, with her hymnbook in her hand. She had a lovely sweet voice and she would sing her head off. She would then sit and watch *Songs of Praise* on the TV. She also loved to listen to her favourite Welsh singers, David Lloyd and Stuart

Burrows, for hours. Over the years Nain spent Christmas with all her children in their turn, but she spent the last couple at home on her own; it was her choice, of course. Em and I took her a Christmas dinner one year; she was all ready for it, and she'd set the table nicely in the back kitchen. She looked like a queen. One Christmas she came to our house, but as soon as her meal was finished she whispered in my ear: "I want to go home ciw bach," she was a home bird. I will tell you later about her latter years, in her daughter Alma's home in Colwyn Bay.

One day I was at work in West Coast Knitting when I received a phone message from a neighbour. No-one was answering the door at 19 Mona Terrace (Nain's). I was shaking like a leaf; you know how it is when you get a call like that. Kash, Uncle Ned's daughter, went with me to Nain's. I was afraid to go in, afraid of what I might find. We had moved Nain's bed downstairs a few months earlier. I had my own key so I let myself in; there was my dear Nain, on the floor in the middle room, half under the bed. She'd been there all night; she was freezing cold, and crying. What a long night it must have been, with poor Nain in her eighties and on her own. She was loved so much by so many people, but at the end of the day, when you close the front door you're on your own. We called an ambulance and took her to hospital. Her children rushed there as soon as they heard. Nain was OK, thank God; after an overnight stay she was ready to go home.

Here's a little poem that Nain copied on a scrap of paper. I found it among her possessions. I don't know who wrote it, but it's very wise, I think.

The Clock of life

The clock of life is wound but once
And no man has the power
To tell just when the hands will stop
At a late or early hour.
To lose one's wealth is sad indeed
To lose one's health is more,
To lose one's soul is such a loss
As no man can restore.
The present only is our own
Now is the time you own.
Live, love, toil with a will
Place no faith in the morrow:
For the hands may then be still.

For months, Auntie Alma had been trying to get Nain to move to Colwyn Bay to live with her. The time had come for the move, for a trial period only. So Nain had to leave Mona Terrace, what a sad day for us all. After the trial period Nain decided to stay with Auntie Alma (see Note 22). We took some of her furniture from Mona Terrace, and some of it is still in use today.

Nain was to live in Auntie Alma's for four years. She had her own TV and phone in her room. During Easter 1988 we went to see Nain and spent a little time with her. I had my photograph taken with her. A few days later I received bad news. Once again I was at work when I had a phone call from my cousin Lynn. Nain had been taken ill and was in hospital in Glan Clwyd; it was serious. I rushed home to Woodlands where Em had just received a phone call from Lynn. Nain was dead. My beloved Nain. She was 88 years old – we were lucky to have had her for so long. We buried her with Taid in Conwy. I can still see Uncle Harry, her son, walking up to the coffin in church, kissing his hand and resting it ever so gently on the wood. Six weeks later he was dead too.

My uncles and aunties on my Mams side

I will write a little now about my uncles and aunties, all of whom are – or were – more like brothers and sisters to me.

Evan Henry Williams (1920 - 1988), or Uncle Harry as we called him, was born in Senghenydd in South Wales. He was a real character; he called himself and my mother the black sheep of the family. I cannot think why, because they were delightful, decent people, but of course I am biased! Uncle Harry suffered for many years with a bad chest and for the last few years of his life he couldn't see very much; he had glaucoma. Uncle Elfed tells me that Uncle Harry always had very bad eyesight. Uncle Harry was a cheerful, happy-go-lucky person who was always on the side of the underdog. He had a heart of gold and was generous to a fault – he would give you his last. Is it any wonder that we all thought the world of him? His family meant everything to him, not only his wife and children but his brothers and sisters and their children too. He was a hopeless DIY man and couldn't knock a nail into a piece of wood straight. I remember him trying to do a little job in 19 Mona Terrace once. He put the hammer in his back pocket with the claw side in and couldn't get it out. *Am be ddiawl ydych chi'n chwerthin* – what the hell are you laughing at, said Uncle Harry; he was up a step ladder at the time and he was cross with us for laughing at him. We were all doubled up with laughter. He eventually managed to remove it and he had a giggle with us.

A funny tale about my father, Uncle Harry and Em now. Uncle Harry had been in Conwy having a pint when into the pub walked my father, the worse for wear, having ridden there on a motorbike. It wasn't an offence to drink and drive in those days. They had a couple of pints together, then it was time to go home, but Uncle Harry wouldn't let Dad drive back to Llanfair in that state on his own so he climbed onto the back of the bike and clung on to Dad as they set off for Llanfair. Dad was wobbling all over the road. He didn't normally drive, since he'd decided many years previously not to drive because he was too fond of his drink. Near the former Ship Inn, just before you reached Penmaen Bach tunnel, there was a bad bend. "We didn't make the bend and the sidecar mounted the wall," said Uncle Harry. "I thought it was the end of the road for us, but Now managed to get us back on track and, cool as you like, he carried on with our never-to-be forgotten journey." When they finally reached Llanfair they faced a problem: Uncle Harry had to get back to Conwy. What did my dear father do? He came to our house – we lived at Glan Ffrwd then. It was eleven o'clock at night and we were all in bed when the bell rang. Em went to the front window and Dad shouted up: *Mae Harry eisiau pass adra* – Harry needs a lift home. Em was working 60-70 hours a week in Home Loaf and had to get up early the next morning. He was hopping mad with them both. Nevertheless, he got dressed and after ordering Dad to go home he told Uncle Harry to get on the back of his motorbike – an AJS 600 – and took him home. Uncle Harry remembered it as the fastest trip he had ever made in his life. Hanging on to Em for dear life, they were in Conwy in no time. "How we got there in one piece I will never know. I'm sure we came close to taking off – it was worse than riding pillion with your father," said Uncle Harry, chuckling to himself. Em dropped him off in Conwy and left him to walk the rest of the way to Gyffin. "I was never so glad to get both feet on the ground again," said Uncle Harry, who had a way of telling this tale which made us all laugh every time he told it.

Uncle Harry had been posted to France in the Second World War, as had his brother Elfed. Anyway, each knew that the other was somewhere in Normandy. Having been told that another battalion would be drafted in soon to one of the large battlefields, Uncle Harry lived in hope that he would see his little brother. At last, the new battalion arrived. "We were all worn out, soaking wet, and far from home – carrying our heavy kit bags carelessly on our backs," said Uncle El. "We were just glad to be able to lay our weary heads down anywhere."

Harry and Elfed Williams during the Second World War.

Keeping his eye out for his younger brother Elfed and as soon as he was able he visited the new battalion to see if Elfed was among the soldiers. Finally he found him, after searching for days in the torrential rain, in a field in Normandy full of sludge and mud. With thousands of soldiers milling around them, all going about their business, and miles away from home, the two brothers embraced each other. What a feeling it must have been.

On another occasion during the war Uncle Harry and his best friend Will Bach Tyddyn Ronwy, another Llanfair lad, were on leave in France. They had both enjoyed a few pints, and now - on the way back to barracks - they were lost. When they came to a fork in the road they decided to go left; it was pitch dark of course. The next thing they knew they were both up to their waists in water. They had walked into a rather cold and murky duckpond. This story came to me via Uncle John Morgan who wasn't sure of the ending! Uncle John Morgan isn't really my Uncle - he belongs to one of the families who lived in Nant y Felin at the same time as my parents when they were all kids in the early 1920's.

Uncle Harry married Auntie Mildred from Walsall; they met through Uncle Evan and Auntie Dilys at the church. The quarry being the main employer at the time, Uncle Harry worked there for a few years before going to work at Oakwood Park, a hospital for the 'mentally handicapped' on the Conwy side of the Sychnant Pass. We'd say learning disabilities today. He worked in the kitchens there, but spent many hours chatting with the patients, and was well thought of and valued by them. It was to close down in the early 1970's, and most of the patients were transferred to Bryn y Neuadd. Like Em, Uncle Harry also worked at Welsh Home Loaf, but only for a very short time. *Dim dynion y mae nhw eisiau yno ond blydi mulod* - they don't want men there but bloody donkeys, Uncle Harry told Em. Harry and Mildred had three sons: John, Byron and Gareth. Later on they had a long-awaited daughter, called Venice. They were blessed with 11 grandchildren.

Em, Uncle El and I used to visit Nain in Colwyn Bay most weeks, calling more often than not on Uncle Harry and Auntie Mildred. The fun we had, laughing and joking! There was always a warm welcome there; in fact, it was just like home.

Uncle Harry, a strong Labour man, used to love to put Margaret Thatcher and the Conservatives in their place; we would spend hours talking politics and he loved it. I could go on forever with these little tales but I hope you have a picture by now of the kind of people Uncle Harry and Auntie Mildred were. In 1988, just six weeks after his beloved mother died, we lost Uncle Harry. He died in Llandudno Hospital. What a loss to us all. Em and I were in Tunisia on holiday at the time and couldn't get back to attend the funeral. These people seem to come alive for a while when I write or talk about them. I can hear Uncle Harry's voice in my ears now: "Hello sweet, how are you?" were always his first words to me.

Em and I have been to see Auntie Mildred at Llandudno Hospital; she is very ill I held her hand and chatted for a while. I'm sure there was a flicker of a smile as I talked about the days - happy days, when we were all younger and a lot healthier. Auntie Mildred died just before Christmas 2003.

Elfed Williams (1921): My Uncle El was the second son to be born in South Wales; he was named after a preacher for whom Nain did some cleaning just

Penmaenmawr General Construction Company.

Llanfair, Pen, Bethesda and Trevor Boys in the Royal Engineers in Gabraltar building the airdrome in 1942. Amongst them is back row far right Peter Evans (a tailor). Second row from right to left: Ivor Burno, John Lloyd, ?, Eddie O. Bottom row third from left: Hugh (blondie), Owen Roberts (Em's dad with a ciggie in his hand).

before he was born. He lives in Penmaenmawr with his wife Heulwen. He was a chapel deacon until his health failed him. Uncle El was in the Army during the Second World War, as I have already said. He went home one day and said to his father: "I am going to join the Army, dad." "Over my dead body – who do you think is the boss in this house?" said Taid Gwyn. Having been in the Army in the First World War himself, he wasn't happy. But he relented eventually. Uncle El had his way and he joined up. Uncle Harry was out one night with his mate Will Bach Tyddyn Ronwy. They had gone to Penmaenmawr and later on Uncle El decided to join them. Uncle El doesn't drink – he has always been teetotal. Uncle Harry, who was a little worse for wear, didn't like his brother to see him in that state. Uncle El, being the gentleman he was, turned on his heel so as not to embarrass his brother. "I always told Harry off about drinking too much," said Uncle El, "you'd think he was a raging alcoholic! Do you know, I miss him every bit as much today as I ever did," he said with a tear in his eye. Like most of the young men who survived, Uncle El went to work in the quarry after the war.

One Christmas morning, when my sister Val and I were very young, I recall Uncle El coming up to Tan Bonc with two parcels. Val and I were very excited and rushed at him shouting: "Which one is mine, Uncle El?" He gave us one each – they contained the most beautiful dolls I had ever seen, dressed in the same little mustard-coloured coats and hats. Uncle El married a girl from the Conwy Valley, Heulwen, daughter of Morfudd and John Stanley Jones. Elfed and Heulwen have four daughters: Gwen, Marion, Alwena and Ellen, who are all married with children and live locally. The chapel has played a big part in all their lives. Uncle El was a member of a Welsh choir for many years.

A little story about Uncle Elfed. Em worked for the health service once and was en route to Colwyn Bay with a large van. In those days Em's back was fine and he could lift anything. Anyway, Uncle El met him in Mona Terrace; they wanted to move a glass cupboard from Nain's. The cupboard wasn't safe in the van so Uncle El had to sit in the back to keep it steady. It was a boiling hot day with not much air, and they had to go through Conwy as the expressway wasn't built then. During summer the traffic through Conwy was so bad you'd often have to sit in traffic for an hour or two; tailbacks used to reach from Conwy to Penmaenbach tunnel or even further, so they were in for a long wait. Finally they arrived at Colwyn Bay, where Uncle Elfed fell out of the lorry, his face as red as a beetroot, his teeth in his hand and tears streaming down his face. Uncle El never swears but I'm sure he came close that day. *Mam Bach, paid byth a gofyn i mi symud rhywbeth i chdi eto, rwyf jest a marw* – don't ask me to move anything again, I'm half dead! The family were absolutely hysterical with laughter when they heard the story. I am laughing to myself as I write this; it had been so hot in the back of the van he'd felt ill, and he'd removed his teeth in case he was sick. We saw Uncle El recently and when he remembered that day he said laughingly: "I thought I would never see the light of day again ciw."

Unlike his brother Harry, Uncle El is a very good DIY man and loves to make things out of wood in his shed. When we went to visit Uncle Harry in Conwy he and Uncle El would compare legs to see who had the best pair. They would pull their trousers up and wave their legs around jovially. Uncle Harry was really quite skinny and Uncle El would say *coesau dryw sydd gennyt ti was* - you've got legs like a wren, boy. "Never you mind boy, they've carried me all my life," Uncle Harry would answer, waving his skinny legs around.

A little about my Auntie Al now. Alma Jones (1929) was born in Well Street in Bethesda. She worked in Colwyn Bay Woolworth's as a young girl, and was a frequent visitor to our house in Tan Bonc. She and a friend came visiting one day; coming in sight of the house, she started shouting and waving to a person whom she thought was my Mother in the garden. It turned out to be the clothes on the washing line! Auntie Al's eyes were as bad then as they are now. The hole in our ceiling in Tan Bonc came in handy when Auntie Al and her friend babysat while Mam and

Gwynfor Williams (Uncle Gwyn) and Mrs Alma Jones (Auntie Al).

Dad went to the pictures: Val and I used to peep through and then jump into bed giggling! We had so much fun! Auntie Alma married Uncle Alwyn from Penmaenmawr. He was a quiet, pleasant man, a printer by trade. When Em and I lived in 2 Glan Ffrwd, Uncle Alwyn came and papered a ceiling for us; Em was helping him when he noticed that Uncle Alwyn had cut all the strips of paper short. Em didn't like to say anything, thinking that Uncle Alwyn knew best. When Uncle Alwyn realised what he'd done he was hopping mad with himself – needless to say, we had a lot of joints in our bedroom ceiling. He was mad on football; I can see him now, standing outside our door with his mackintosh on his arm, having stopped in Mam's first to call for Dad. His face was as red as a tomato; he had run up all the way from the bus stop, not wanting to miss the start of the game. He had come to watch the World Cup final in 1966 between England and Germany. Auntie Al has two daughters, Ann and Lynn, who live locally with their husbands and children. Auntie Al never remarried and still lives in the house she bought with Uncle Alwyn.

Gwynfor Thomas Williams (1936) is the baby of the family, exactly ten years older than me, and he still tells me to this day that I should be calling him Uncle Gwyn. Some hope, Gwyn! When Gwyn was about two years old he had a bad accident. One hot August day, when they were living in Bodlondeb, my Mam Megan decided to go collecting bilberries. Looking for something to hold the berries, she found an empty jam jar. Nain shouted: "Don't take glass Meg, it's too dangerous – I'll get you a tin." Off Mam went, leaving the glass jar on an outside windowsill; unfortunately, the wind blew it to the floor and smashed it. Gwyn found his way to the yard and fell on the glass; he started screaming and Nain ran out to him. There stood Gwyn with a sliver of glass sticking out of his eye. John Dick the newsagent rushed him down to the surgery in his car. Gwyn lost the sight in that eye but they managed to keep the eye so that he didn't need a glass replacement. I was talking to Mrs Williams, Mr Pugh's daughter, recently and she told me that she remembered a little baby falling on a piece of glass. She knew he was related to me, but wasn't sure how. "It still gives me the shivers when I think of that little baby," she said. Fancy remembering that, after all those years. Gwyn is indeed a character; he pops in to see us quite often, but like me he doesn't stay anywhere for long – a cup of coffee and off he goes again

Calenydd Williams (a childhood friend of Gwyn's) was telling me recently that when they were young men, a crowd would get together and sit on the benches in the village of an evening and have a good old fashioned sing-song. "We did have a good time. Gwyn and the others had good voices but sadly I was the only one of our crowd to go on and sing with a choir," said Calenydd, who still sings with a choir.

Gwyn married Jean, whom he met as a young girl on holiday from Oldham. She was staying at Plas Menai Christian Hotel. Gwyn and Jean eventually settled in Colwyn Bay; they have two married children, Dawn and Steven, and two grandsons.

And so, back to Mam

What more can I say about my wonderful, brave and caring Mother that I haven't said already? Megan Thomas (1922 - 1980) was born in Senghenydd in South Wales. I have spoken at great length about my dear mother. She was born with a weak chest, as I have said. Her parents and siblings were a great support to her throughout her sometimes very difficult life. She was devoted to my Dad – supporting him when he needed it, and there for him throughout their lives together. Uncle Bob's daughter Olwen told me recently that she

Megan Thomas (Mam) aged 21.

remembers my Mother as always being dressed very smart in a costume, like a princess; she had a kind word for everyone, said Olwen. Mam was around 5 ft tall and quite slim. She never left the house without a little red lipstick on; when she ran out of it and couldn't afford a new one she would stick her little finger in the tube to scrape every bit out. She used dinky metal curlers to keep her dark hair neat and tidy. But when I got older I used to perm her hair and Nain's and my sister Val's too with Prom; it did have a terrible stink!

My Mam was honest, kind-hearted, reliable and hard working and despite many obstacles she managed to always keep smiling. Mam was a great inspiration to my sister Valerie and myself; she taught us right from wrong, and the meaning of a strong family life. She taught us that honesty is always the best policy. I hope Em and I have passed those values on to our two daughters. Dad's words were: "Megan brought our girls up, and it is thanks to her that they have turned out the way they have." That, I think, wasn't strictly true; my Dad also had a great influence on my life. Another of my Dad's favourite sayings was: "The hand that rocks the cradle rules the world." My heart is heavy once again, remembering those happy childhood days so long ago. When I sit here writing this I feel as if my parents were in the next room, but of course there is no-one there. In my heart they have never left me; I carry them both with me wherever I go.

As she got older my Mother derived great pleasure from our daughters, Lorraine and Karen; how she loved them – they brought sunshine into her life. Did I say older? My Mam died when she was only fifty-seven years old and what a gap it left in all our lives. I don't think you ever have the same outlook on life once you have lost your parents, however old you are.

My sister - Val

My sister Valerie Thomas was born on March 23rd 1946 at 3 Pen y Bryn, Llanfair. She is one year and two days younger than me. There being only the two of us, we have always been very close. From an early age I have always tried to look out for Val, and indeed still do. She spent more time helping our Mam at home than I did. I was too busy going to work with my Dad. We'd spend a lot of time playing and fighting together. We shared a bedroom and even a bed until we were 14 or 15 years old, when we moved down to Britannia House. We have shared so many sad and happy memories. I asked Val if I could write a little about her and her illness. Her answer was: "OK Mag, but remember to write about the good times as well as the bad. Make sure you tell everyone about how Uncle Elfed brought those two beautiful dolls up to Tan Bonc one Christmas morning," said Val as the tears pooled on her cheeks. It doesn't take much to make Val cry - she can turn the tears on and off like a tap. I remember those dolls very well myself. Mam always made sure that Val and I had everything the same. I remember us having two floral cotton dresses each for our fifth or sixth birthdays; to this day I can still smell those lovely cotton dresses, bought from a catalogue. Of course there was no money to buy things outright in those days. "You can't wear them yet girls," said my wise Mam. "Never cast a cloud till May is out." We had to wait six more weeks to wear them.

My sister Val aged 7.

Val was always quite a nervous girl and not as noisy as I am. She was a good bit taller and very thin, even though she ate like a horse. I recall Mam telling me that Val was rather a cross baby and cried a lot. Our parents took her to see a specialist when she was a baby and he said she would grow out of it. Although Val had a nervous disposition she was braver than me; she wasn't afraid of the dark. She never worried about my Dad and his drinking, as I did - it seemed to go over her head. Val would come home from school and say: "Mam, I saw Dad in the village and he gave me some money for sweets." "What did you get del?" Mam would ask. "How was Dad - had he had a drink?"

"No Mam, he was OK and said he'd be home for his tea before long," Val would answer. It was a joke between Mam, Val and I - she never could tell if Dad had had one over the eight; in he would come half an hour later, three sheets to the wind.

On a summer's evening in the 1950's, Dad was crossing the road on the way home from the Castle Hotel and was knocked down by a motor bike. His leg was smashed to bits, with bones sticking out through the flesh; a compound fracture, they said. The doctors put him in a heavy plaster from his ankle to the top of his leg. Take it easy, said the doctors - you must be very careful. A few days later Dad, Mam, Val and I were up the mountain collecting bilberries. I remember one of

Dad's crutches getting stuck in the mud; oh dear me, we had so much fun trying to pull it out. The sweat was running down Dad's face as he shouted at us because we were laughing. So dangerous really, we shouldn't have been there – he could have done a lot more damage to his leg. How he walked up that mountain I don't know; Dad was a very determined man and as stubborn as a mule.

One Christmas, Val remembers Dad picking up our capon from Will Parry, who used to keep chickens, geese and ducks where the car park stands today, next to the river, just past Pandy Bridge. Mr Parry would kill the fowl a day or two before Christmas but we would have to pluck it and prepare it ourselves. When Val mentioned it, I do recall watching my dear Mam standing outside 6 Tan Bonc with the capon on the wall and her hand inside the poor thing, pulling its insides out. There was Mam with tears running down her cheeks, wrenching and heaving. Dad, Val and I were in our doubles, laughing at her and keeping well away; not one of us could do that horrible job, only Mam. The job of plucking the feathers I didn't mind, although you had to be careful because you weren't allowed to rip the chicken's skin. It was with mounting excitement that we watched Mam stuff the fowl with her home made stuffing and fetch a darning needle and cotton "so the stuffing doesn't fall out and spoil it," as Mam put it. A capon was a once a year treat for us: there were no frozen chickens in those days. That done, Mam would turn her hand to cooking the beef or pork, and whatever else – we had plenty of everything at Christmas. In later years my parents always had three meats at Christmas; how people managed without a fridge I don't know. Val and I helped with the mince pies on Christmas Eve; Dad went out for a pint and there was always a kiss and *God Bless* for his two girls before he went, with a warning: "You be good girls for Mam now. Bed early tonight, no watching out for that sledge over Garreg Fawr, or Sion Corn won't come." So many happy memories, so long ago.

Soon it was time for bed and up we'd go, holding one of Dad's socks to be hung on the bedpost, and shouting to Mam: "Don't forget to let the fire out early or it will burn Santa's feet." We would peep through the hole in the floorboards while our lovely, caring Mam was busy preparing all the veg for Christmas dinner. When I look back I can't think where my Mother hid our presents. We didn't have as much by a long chalk as they do now, but still you needed somewhere to hide things. Anyway, Val and I would finally fall asleep. Dad had come home from the pub and all was quiet in our home. Once, we woke suddenly when we heard what sounded like a ball bouncing down the stairs; scared and excited, we shouted: "Dad, has he been yet?"

"No del, go back to sleep, I think I hear the sledge coming over Garreg Fawr – remember, he won't call if you're not sleeping." Nearly everyone, I suppose, remembers Christmas as magical when they were kids, and indeed ours was no different. I would wake up at around 5am and hear the crinkling of my stocking on the bed. I would whisper to Val: "Come on you lazy thing, he's been!" We would scream and shout as we went into Mam and Dad's bed in the freezing cold. But who cares – it was Christmas morning and we had hundreds of things to look forward to; always at the bottom of the stocking was a tangerine, some nuts, sweets and chocolates, a few little games. Stuffed in also were knickers (navy blue), and of course new socks. There were small tins of Bluebird toffees with lovely pictures on the lids, plus snakes and ladders, a copy book, a pencil and a fountain pen, and a small bottle of ink if we were lucky. *We were lucky!* Being members of a large extended family, we used to have quite a lot of presents. Mam would have left the fire in all night so that the oven was hot enough to cook the fowl. There was a lot to prepare. Dad always helped Mam to prepare for Christmas dinner – he loved it, after he'd had a few hours extra in bed of course! We would eat at exactly twelve noon – in fact we had every Sunday lunch dead on twelve. One Christmas I remember having a scooter. We were so thrilled; we couldn't believe our eyes when we went downstairs. There they were two new and shiny red scooters. There weren't many cars on the road then, so we would fly like the wind down Valley Road; we thought we were the fastest things on wheels.

New Year's Eve was important to Mam; we'd all wait up for the stroke of twelve. Out of the back door my Mam would go, carrying a lump of coal. And then in through the front door she came, shouting and laughing as only my Mam could. "A happy new year to us all," she would say. It was meant to be good luck for something black, or someone dark, to be the first thing through your door on the first day of the year. Another tradition I remember well was getting up early on New Year's Day to go and collect *calennig*. Whatever the weather, Val and I would be up and ready to leave the house at 9am. We would start at Mr Roland Jones and Auntie Louie's house; we were always sure of a warm welcome there. *Blwyddyn newydd dda Auntie Louie* – happy New Year, we would say. She would give us a couple of coppers and a few sweets. Off we went happily to the next house and say the same again. We would keep this up for the next three hours. Having completed our morning's collection, Val and I would return home excitedly to count our money. Most of the money of course went to help our Mam, but we were allowed to spend a few coppers at Auntie Nell's shop further down Valley Road. Most kids in the neighbourhood did the same thing. I am sure the people of the village were fed up of answering the door on New Year's morning.

My mind goes back to another new year, in 1979 – the last one my Mam was to see on this Earth. After bringing in the New Year at home with Em and the girls I went over to Mam's to wish them a happy new year. My dear Mother was sat up in bed – she looked like a queen in a pink nightdress which I'd made for her. "Remember Mag," she said, "promise me that whatever happens you will go to Canada with Em and the girls as you plan." The four of us were going to Canada in May for a month to visit Em's relatives. Mam could hardly get her breath; she had canisters of oxygen by the side of her bed. She used to say that she felt as if she had walked up Garreg Fawr when she had only walked to the toilet. "I sometimes wish I had a big hole in the top of my head to let the air out," she would say. Dr G Bellis had asked her to go into hospital on numerous occasions but she'd refused. She knew how ill she was and was afraid that if she went in she would never come home again. "There is nothing they can do for me Mag Bach." She was so brave; never complaining, always laughing.

To return to my sister Val: in our early years Val had a few friends, Glenys Owen and June (Gwyndy) amongst them but if I remember correctly, she never went out to play much. I have always thought of Val as needing protection from the world; she always seemed to be so innocent and vulnerable. Even as a child, Val was rather timid and clingy. I was a year older, so she always looked to me for support. The time came for me to move schools, from the village school to the secondary modern at Pant y Rhedyn. I didn't want to go to the Grammar School at Bangor, so there was no question of me even trying the eleven-plus. My friends were at Pant y Rhedyn and that's where I wanted to go. In 1959, two years before I left school, there was a total of 79 children at Pant y Rhedyn School; 41 were Welsh speaking, 25 had some knowledge of Welsh, and 13 were non-Welsh speakers. These children were between the ages of 11 and 15. There are twice as many children at Pant y Rhedyn School nowadays, all between the ages of 7 and 11. The year I left Pant y Rhedyn (1961) it became a primary school and all children aged from 11 to 15 went to Conwy School. These days you can choose where you send your children. In those days it wasn't considered so important for girls to get a good education and my parents never pushed me to do what I didn't want to. Looking back, I suppose they should have given me more encouragement. So it was Pant y Rhedyn for me until then Val and I had always been in the same school, so it was a big change for us both. Whereas I loved school, Val did not and she had one more year left in the village school. She got through that year all right, but as the academic year came to an end she started worrying about going to Pant y Rhedyn. This was becoming quite a problem. It was around this time that Val started to suffer from mental health problems. "Perhaps it's puberty," said the doctors.

Val felt that she didn't fit in with her peers, and at times she became withdrawn and subdued. There was a stigma attached to the words "mental health" in those days, which was another reason for protecting my sister. Poor, poor Val, poor Mam and Dad – it makes me so sad to think that my dear sister has been through so much in her life. I remember the first time Val was taken to the North Wales Hospital, Denbigh – she was just eleven years old, and had just started at Pant y Rhedyn School. The thought of moving school had upset Val all that summer. Over the next few years Val was to have quite a few nervous breakdowns and she lost a lot of schooling.

When it was time for Val to move up to Conwy School, Mam bought her a new uniform but she didn't go there much – she spent most of her last year at school in and out of the hospital. I suppose there would be a lot more help and support for her today. Denbigh Hospital was built in 1848 closed down in 1995. She hadn't been well for many weeks, but my parents managed to care for her at home and they had been taking her weekly to see a psychiatrist in Bangor. The day came when the doctors said she really needed to be in a hospital, for her own safety. One day a hospital taxi was arranged to pick us up at Tan Bonc. At this time Val didn't even know us, she wasn't speaking and she ate very little; she was so thin, around the five stone mark as I recall. She had withdrawn into her own little world. Val sat between Mam and I and Dad sat in the front. I was twelve years old and here was my little sister going to a "mental hospital." I cannot begin to tell you what we all thought, how scared we were. Val didn't speak a word all the way there – she didn't even know where she was going. We were driven to the Main Block, as it was called. The hospital was an old Victorian building and in its heyday provided care for around a thousand patients suffering from all kinds of mental illness. The hospital was set away from the town of Denbigh, in lovely grounds – an ideal setting for a hospital (or should I say institution). There were many different buildings: for instance Gwynfryn, or Bryn Hyfryd, where Val would spend some time during her illness. As we approached the massive building there were lots and lots of people wandering around the gardens aimlessly, some of them accompanied by nurses who wore white uniforms. I remember being scared to death and trying not to show it.

In we went to admit Val. We were taken to the Main Block and it was the first of many shocks that day, I recall. Val being admitted to the hospital was the worst shock; she sat between Mam and I while Dad went to speak to someone. A nurse was called and took us through long, winding, narrow corridors that never seemed to end, with doors leading off them, and high ceilings. The walls were tiled in light green. Hospital smells are the same the world over, I suppose. That pungent smell, a mixture of antiseptic, sweat, urine and people will never leave me. It's strange how the memory of some odours stay with you for ever. Our footsteps echoed on the floor as we walked slowly down the corridors, afraid of what was in front of poor Val. "How can we leave her here," said Dad. Patients were standing here and there with lost looks on their faces, one or two asking if we had a cigarette they could have. Both my parents smoked Woodbines in those days and they gave the patients a ciggie or two, after first asking a nurse for permission. At last we reached the ward; it seemed that we had been walking for hours! I couldn't believe what I saw. In front of me there must have been at least fifty elderly ladies wandering aimlessly around a huge day room, some talking to themselves, some screaming, and some sitting quietly. Most were dressed but some were in their night clothes. Perhaps not all of them were old ladies, but to a child everyone over twenty seems old. My parents were horrified at the thought of leaving their little daughter there, and asked if they could see someone in charge. The nurses were very kind to us and understood how my parents felt, but there was nowhere else for Val – the country just wasn't equipped to deal with children that young. Val wasn't aware of where she was, or indeed that we were leaving her in this strange place. We settled her in the ward, and put her bits and pieces in her bedside locker. Her bed was in the middle of a large dormitory with many other beds. My dear mother couldn't say goodbye to her, she was so upset. With breaking hearts we had to leave her there, so lost and vulnerable.

In those days the hospital taxi would wait to take us home. I will never forget that first time in Denbigh Hospital. Thank God there are places where the mentally ill can be cared for, but I never got used to visiting Val when she was at Denbigh. Dad tried everything to get Val moved, but where indeed could she be moved to? I asked Val recently what she remembered about the time she was ill at Denbigh and her exact words were: "I remember that the doctors and nurses used to put wires on my head to try and see what was in my brain to try and make me better, Mag." So sad, that my dear little sister should have memories like those to look back on. She was of course talking about electroconvulsive therapy (ECT). This was used to treat people suffering with depression. It would, I recall, be given about twice a week for a course of six to twelve treatments. Over the years Val had many of these treatments but I don't think they did her much good. I remember visiting her once just after she'd had this shock treatment. She looked at us with such a sad and vacant look in her eyes; she failed to recognize us for quite a few minutes, and then she started to cry. "I am sick Mam, can I come home please?" She was totally disorientated. How could we take her home in such a condition? There were a couple of times when Dad saw the doctors and they said: "Don't take her home yet, if you do she'll be back in a few weeks," but Dad said: "She's coming home with us and we will take care of her ourselves."

Sometimes this worked and Val would improve at home. "She will at least have a few months at home instead of that bloody place," Dad would say. There was very little support given to us as a family, but in those days there were no services for children with mental health problems. Our main help and support came from our extended family, not forgetting our local doctor who was always there for Val and my family. My dear Mother was her main carer; how Mam coped with everything I really don't know. What a journey it was to Denbigh in those days, starting on the 12.15pm bus from the crossroads in Llanfair every Sunday. Sometimes the bus would drop us off at the bottom of the hill at Denbigh and we would have to walk about a mile and a half up a very steep hill to the hospital, loaded with goodies and clean clothes for Val. Sometimes we stopped half way up for a cup of tea and a sandwich. We would spend a couple of hours with Val; perhaps we would take a walk in the grounds (weather permitting), or go to the hospital cafe. The patients in those days didn't have their own rooms, so we would have to sit in the dayroom with all the other patients. Our bus would get back to Llanfair at around 6pm. It was an exhausting day, not only because of the travelling, but also because of seeing Val in that condition and having to leave her behind. Val was diagnosed as schizophrenic in the early days of her illness and then the doctors changed their minds. I think they were at a loss as to what to do with her. These days I suppose her problems would be described as behavioural, although I cannot believe that all Val's suffering over the years has been caused by a behaviour problem. All that could be done for Val, really, was to have her taken care of until the crises had passed – a matter of weeks or even months. What a position to be in, your child so ill and not much help out there for her. Many times I heard my dear Mother crying. She would ask me: "Margaret fach, why does Val seem so much worse than anyone else?" What could I say? Val was given good care in the hospital over the years; some of the doctors' and nurses' names she remembers to this day. It was a haven for Val when she wasn't well. I think she had more of a social life there than she had in Llanfair when she got older.

There was a dance once a week in the hospital hall and she loved to go to it (if she was well enough). She would also go to Occupational Therapy (OT as she called it). There was a hospital shop where she could get her bits and pieces. Sometimes she was allowed to walk down to Denbigh to do some shopping (her favourite pastime); she used to really enjoy that. There were times when my parents were glad that there was such a place as Denbigh Hospital. It was a relief to take Val there and know that she was being cared for. "It doesn't matter how much you love your child," said Mam, "there is only so much you can do and there comes a time when you need help from the outside – and although we feel a terrible guilt and hopelessness, we have to take Val to hospital and hope that this time they can help her."

As we grew up Val didn't seem to worry about the things I thought important, such as there being no money in the house, or Dad coming home drunk. Val and I would go to bed, and while Val fell asleep I would stay awake until Dad was home safe and sound. I suppose Mam and I would try and protect Val by not telling her things.

After Em and I were married Val was a regular visitor to our house; our girls loved to see her and she would play with them for hours, telling them all sorts of stories which they would listen to with wide eyes. Val loved our girls and I'm so glad that they still go and see her when they can. My Mother used to say to me: "Remember Mag, when Dad and I are dead, all you can do for Val is make sure she's looked after and don't worry too much about her." I hope I have done what my parents would have wanted for Val. Together with Em and our daughters I hope we have always done our best for her.

Mam, Dad, Val, Lorraine and Karen. Llwyn y Gog, Christmas 1976.

For three months after our Mam died Val found it difficult living at home. Dad was out at work all day and life became lonely for Val. With the support of the family doctor and Val's social worker, we as a family decided that it would be in Val's best interests for her to go into a residential care home. Val didn't really want this but agreed to give it a try. It wasn't a success – Val wasn't happy there, and we weren't happy with the care she received. Val went back home to Dad, until a more suitable place was found. While all this was going on we were still grieving for our Mother; it was as if someone had taken the heart out of the family. It was a very hard time for us all. Thank God I have such a good husband, a strong marriage and two wonderful daughters; they were a great comfort to me. Em was also a very good friend to my Dad, although sometimes you needed the patience of a saint with Dad.

Eventually we had to look for somewhere else for Val and we were very lucky to find her a lovely, caring home in Llandudno. Val lived there for many years, but as with all of us, sometimes it's time to move on and she now lives at another really caring residential home a little further away. Over the years she's had her ups and downs with her health and we as her family have always supported her in any way we can.

I was discussing the book with Val recently and showing her what I had written. Of course we ended up crying, so what's new! Anyway through her tears she said "do you remember Mag when Dad was late coming home Mam would laugh and say don't worry girls he will turn up in a minute like a bad penny" Val recalled what happy times we had as a family going up the mountains or spending the day in Nain Gwynfors. "I used to meet Mam from work every Saturday morning when she cleaned for Mrs Bellis. Calling to Spiers for a couple of cream cakes on the way home." Val said. "Dad was a heck of a man and did not always behave as he should have but he was Dad and we loved him didn't we Mag." she said.

Dad had a favourite saying which he would quote all the time to my Mam: *Ti wyddost beth sydd yn fy nghalon* – you know what's in my heart. Yes we did know, Dad!

Here I am with some more of my memories

Born on March 21st 1946, I was the apple of my father's eye. He would rock me to sleep in his arms of a night time. Mam used to tell me that I never cried much, but when I did Dad was up like a shot to pick me up; many times my dear Mam told me: "Dad used to spoil you, Mag."

I will add some stories about myself now, and a few more memories as they come back to me along the way; memories which are important to me and no-one else, I suppose. Memories like sitting on the floor in front of a roaring fire in Tan Bonc, Mam putting rags or pipe cleaners in my hair because I

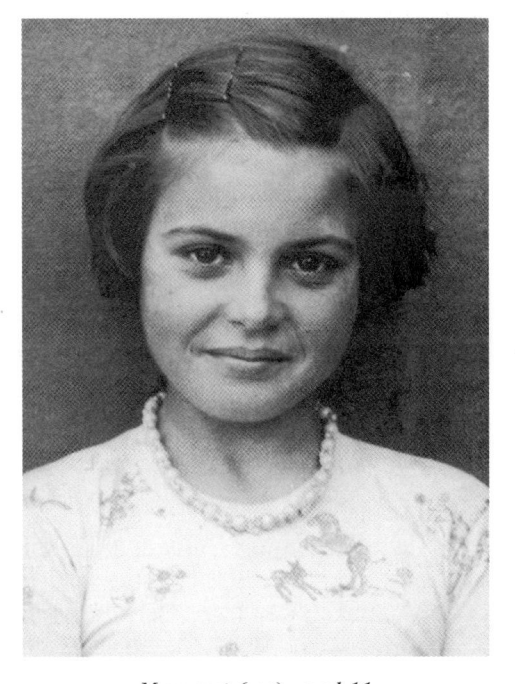

Margaret (me), aged 11.

wanted curls. The nights we sat by candlelight, or an old paraffin lamp, going to bed by candlelight because we didn't even have a shilling to put in the meter, or perhaps the electric cables had been blown down in the mountains. Sitting there with Mam and Dad telling us all sorts of tall stories. Watching the flames leap up the chimney. It was indeed an idyllic childhood. There was an awkward bend in our chimney and I remember that Mam used to fire it in order to clean it. It was like fireworks night; we would run outside to watch the sparks and smoke go rushing up into the sky. Firing chimneys was a done thing then. Some mornings we would get up to discover that soot had been blown down, covering everything – what a mess!

We had a gramophone that we used to wind up. I don't know where it came from but we loved it, especially dear Mam. It was in a green leather case with His Masters Voice written on it. She would sing along to records like *Galway Bay* and *That Lucky old Sun*; her favourite was *Oh My Papa* – her eyes would fill up every time she sang that song, because it made her think of her father.

Even as a child I had a weak chest. I recall having lots of coughs and colds during the winter months; bronchitis was something I was well used to. "Remember

Tan Bonc as it is today, there is very little change in the row of cottages sincce I lived there in the 1950's.

to wrap up warm when you go out into the yard to play," Mam would shout as I left the house for school. I would be wearing a vest and a liberty bodice, which was rather like a vest but thicker and it had little white rubber buttons going down the front. Why the buttons? I never did find out, but my Mam used to tell me it was "one of the most important garments for keeping the cold out" so I was never to go without one. I wasn't allowed to shed that hated liberty bodice until the last day of May.

I used to have lots of boils which would appear overnight; sometimes in my ears, sometimes up my nose, but the worst ones were the ones on my bottom! I couldn't sit properly, they were so painful. I remember my dear Mam putting bread poultices on them; Mam would wrap some bread in a clean white cloth, soak it in boiling water, then put it on my bottom! The poultices were supposed to draw out the pus from the boil. I don't recall if it worked – I only remember yelling when I had it done.

I recall the sense of security and warmth I felt as my dear Mam tucked me up in bed, rubbing Vic on my chest when I had a cold 'to help with your breathing'. "Have you said your prayers girls," she would ask. As if we could forget! We had to jump out of bed and get on our knees – and this was the prayer we said every night of our childhood:

Rho fy mhen i lawr i gysgu
Rho fy enaid i Grist Iesu.
Os fyddai farw cyn y bore,
Cymer dithau fy enaid innau.
God bless Mammy and Daddy and everybody, Amen.

I'm sure many of you will know that prayer, *As I lay me down to sleep*, from your own childhoods.

Later on, when we had a new TV of our own, how we loved watching programmes such as *Sunday Night at the London Palladium* and *Take your Pick* with Michael Miles. One of my favourites was *Wagon Train*. I don't remember any soaps being shown in the early days of TV!

Here's a poem which Dad used to recite to us kids all the time. John (Australia) recalls Dad reciting it to him and his brothers also. I don't know who wrote it, but it goes something like this:

The wind on the hill

No one can tell, nobody knows

Where the wind comes from

Or where the wind goes

It's flying from somewhere

As fast as it can

I couldn't keep up with it, even if I ran.

But if I stopped holding the string of my kite

It would blow in the wind for a day and a night

And if I could find it

Then I would know

Where the wind goes

But where the wind comes from

Nobody knows.

Dad would make us fancy bowls by putting old vinyl records in the oven and then molding them into all sorts of shapes and sizes, and we would spend hours painting them with odd bits of old paint. Long before we had modern crisps, Dad would slice potatoes very thinly and pop them in the oven for a short time – and what we had then was home made crisps!

I had a hooped petticoat that would occasionally need stiffening; we couldn't afford to waste money on starch, so my Mam use to soak it in sugar; what a good job she made of it! I will never forget the smell of red carbolic soap; Mam used it to wash the lino and the slate front doorstep. A big bar of green Fairy soap was used to wash clothes, or later on Persil if we could afford it. I remember that we used washing powder to wash the dishes; there was no washing up liquid in our house! Mam would buy scented soap (toilet soap) and that was what we used to wash our hair. Later on little sachets of shampoo came out.

Mrs Twisaday lived a little further down than us. She was a seamstress and when we needed something altering she always found time to help. I remember I must have been about 14 at the time and was courting Em. We were going to Chatsworth house on a school trip and I had a new dress for the occasion. It was white with big red roses on it and I looked like a princess. However, it had one problem the neckline was to low "I would definitely not wear it like that!" I said. Mam went to ask Mrs Twisaday if she could do something with it. Mrs Twisady immediately reached for her sewing machine and my dress was ready for our trip to Buxton! Shop Nell was on the top of Nant y Berllan steps and many is the time I ran down from Tan Bonc to the back door of Auntie Nell's shop to fetch something we had run out of. I never remember Auntie Nell refusing to serve anyone even though the shop was officially closed.

Then there was our favorite postman Mr Jones, who lived in Nant y Felin and along with a big smile he never failed to produce a polo mint or two out of his pocket for us kids.

Also in Nant y Felin there lived a lady with a pet monkey in the garden. Tied around it's neck was a long piece of string and this in turn was tied to the apple tree where the little monkey spent it's day running up and down. It was such a funny little thing with a long tail but I used to love just standing there and watching it.

Will bach detective I remember was a little man that lived with his sister and as I recall they were not the best of friends so poor old Will would spend the day in and out of the local shops keeping out of her way. He was known as Will detective on account of him being everywhere and watching everything that went on in the village.

Gwenda a friend of mine lived in Mynyddfa in Valley Road we walked home from school many times together making plans for the evening. Gwenda is Noel (Australia's) sister their dad Dick Gwyndy used to do a lot of reciting in eisteddfodau all over Wales.

Eisteddfod Nant was a yearly event and a very important night in the life of our village it was held on a Friday night in Horeb school room. Most of the children of the village and further a field would compete against each other and it went on until as late as 11pm although by this time it was the adults that were in competition with each other and we little ones had long gone. In order to get a seat you needed to be there early and all the children were sat in the front rows bubbling with excitement and waving to their parents in the back rows.

It would also be an important part of our girl's lives. Lorraine, our eldest, could recite anything and really excelled at it, in fact we took her too many Urdd eisteddfods under the guidance of Mrs Blaney- a school teacher in the village school. Karen our youngest daughter was about 5 or 6 years old when she went on to the stage with her class. It was time for our little girl to do her recitation **Dim Parcio Yn Fan Hyn**- No Parking Here was the title and she had been told to shout so that the people in the back could hear. She had been practicing for weeks and knew her lines well she bellowed it out and could I'm sure be heard from the outside let alone from the back! I was crying. Em looked ten feet tall we were so proud of her. Of course all the little children were excellent and had a ribbon.

Another big event was the carnival it was a brilliant day and the village was packed. I remember when I was 14 years old and in the Morris dancing. Miss Parry our gym teacher from Pant y Rhedyn was in charge of the troop we had been practicing for weeks in school and we were all so exited. I can still see the people now lining the streets all the way from the village to the beach shouting and cheering us on as the bells on our snow white pumps were in direct competition with the brass band that was in front of us making an almighty noise as the big drum went **boom boom boom** and I loved it. All the estates and schools had worked their socks off for weeks preparing for the big day. It was always a great success. We would finish school on the last day of term especially the summer term. Oh, but it was great to think of all those days in front of us and our favourite song as we all linked arms walking home form school was:

Morris dancers at the carnival in 1960. Left to right June, me, Lillian and Brenda.

Pant Rhedyn Pant Rhedyn's battle cry.

Pant Rhedyn Pant Rhedyn will never die.

Bring out the teachers let the pupils in.

Even if the place is full of ryddy din.

I am sure that most of us old pupils from Pant y Rhedyn from that era will remember those words with a great deal of affection.

My dear Mam cooked Sunday dinner while listening to *Family Favorites* on the radio; she'd be singing along with the tunes at the top of her voice. Dad would be sawing some wood for the fire perhaps. Sometimes in the winter months the electric would go off, owing to cables being blown down on the mountain – so we wouldn't get our dinner for hours. In the early days Mam would finish cooking everything on the fire. But what did we care - it was a perfect world, up there in Tan y Bonc. Sunday tea was an event in our house; we all helped to set the table nicely. Dad would tell us all sorts of jokes while Mam prepared the food: a boiled egg or a jam buttie perhaps, followed by tinned fruit and jelly. Val and I had the job of clearing and washing up, though I must admit I'd try to get out of it as often as I could.

I remember how Val and I would take that long walk home from school in the winter months; Mam would be waiting in the house with a fire glowing in the grate and something hot for us to eat.

Miss Nellie Griffiths from Felin Hen Farm was one of our teachers in the infants' school. She taught there for many years. She would walk down through Pandy Farm and sometimes we would meet at the bottom of the road, geese permitting! I used to think I was so grown up - walking to school with Miss Griffiths was a real treat for me. She was quite a tall lady and towered over me, so in my memory I think of her as always stooping down to hear me speak. She was well loved by us all.

One of my first memories of the village school is of sitting in the back of the classroom, freezing cold, and trying to warm my hands by putting them on my neck or by sitting on them. The teacher was at the front of the class of course, close to where the fire was roaring. When it was freezing outside the boys would bring the milk crates in of a morning and put them within the fireguards in the hope of thawing the milk before playtime. Every Monday morning one or two of the boys would come round the classrooms to fill the inkwells on the desks. This was a job Em liked "because it got me out of lessons for a while." On a Monday there would be a sale of National Savings Stamps; you could buy sixpenny and shilling stamps and save them in a little book - it was a way of saving money for a rainy day perhaps. There were lots of those sorts of days then.

Lunchtime in the Village School was fun! Whatever the weather all the kids would walk two by two, chattering and giggling with each other, through the village, up by the back of the Police Station to Bethel Chapel schoolroom (demolished now). That is where our school canteen was; as I sit here writing this I can still hear the echo of our voices and laughter as we walked through the village fifty years ago! I remember one of our dinner ladies well: Auntie Mary - all the kids loved her; she was always very patient and kind, even if we sometimes did misbehave. Years later she and my parents were to become neighbours; Mam and Auntie Mary were good friends.

I still remember wearing Wellingtons, day after day; even on days when there was no rain. There wasn't always money to buy us a pair of shoes. The Wellingtons rubbed and chafed; they would leave chapped, sometimes bleeding red marks across our calves. Em says that if they were lucky enough to have long socks the boys would turn down their Wellington tops and turn the socks over them. It's hard to imagine, in these days of plenty, that we didn't even have one pair of school shoes.

Em's Dad Owen was a conductor on the buses and worked for Crossville for over 25 years. Anyway, there was an occasion when he had to go on the sick with cartilage problems; he was a conductor on the double-decker buses, and it was the constant climbing up and down stairs that had given him the problem. School dinners were free to kids whose fathers were on the sick, on the dole, or who had died. "It was very degrading for kids then," said Em. "All the kids whose dads were working went to the front of the queue, to pay their dinner money. On a couple of occasions I had to go to the back of the queue, and I never forgot how it felt." I myself used to have free dinners quite often so I was well used to it.

Station Road 1958. On the left hand side of the photo is Em's bike he used for delivering groceries for The Pioneer Stores (Thanks to the University of St. Andrews for allowing us to use this postcard).

I was a bit of a chatterbox in class and was told off many times for it. One teacher, who had come to the school for one term only, was heartily disliked by us kids. Anyway, this very unpleasant teacher had warned me a couple of times about talking and then she caught me for the third time. That was it. "Margaret," she shouted across the classroom, her face red, "come here, I have warned you about this constant chattering in my class. Hold out your arm girl." I was shaking in my shoes. She pulled out my arm, pushed up the sleeve of my cardigan, and slapped me three times across my forearm. How it hurt; her finger marks stood out in red welts on my little arm. I remember saying to myself: "I will not cry in front of her." I was about eight or nine years old at the time.

We kids would go to shop at Knights, a tobacconist's at the front and a barber's at the back. It was in Station Road, and on the way to Pant y Rhedyn School we would call to buy a couple of loose fags, costing a penny ha'penny each. It wasn't known how bad cigarettes were for you then, and we thought we were so clever. There was a rush for the toilets or the sheds at playtime. Older kids would congregate to share a Woodbine or two. The outside loos were in a row of about seven, with the girls' loos back to back with the boys' loos. There were no sinks there – we had to go into the cloakrooms to wash our hands, although I don't recollect it being thought so important to wash your hands after the loo then. We used to play in the old sheds when it was raining. The boys used to climb over to the girls' side, teasing and messing around; I well remember Em chasing me around the sheds with a stick. There was a locked boiler house where our caretaker Mr Jones would keep the fire well stoked with coke, for our school heaters.

Playtime was one big game of football for the boys; Em loved the game and was really good at it. I was a fair player myself! Em remembers the school receiving three new footballs from the education authority. The headmaster Mr Lloyd Jones had made an announcement about these footballs in assembly one morning. "We have been very lucky to get them, so make sure you look after them boys," he said. The boys were delighted and couldn't wait for playtime. That very first playtime, what did Em do? He kicked one of the balls onto the railing spikes and burst it. "Mr Lloyd Jones was not pleased with me," says Em.

While I'm writing about Em, I must tell you that from the age of ten he used to carry out (deliver groceries) on a shop bike for Willie Thomas. I remember he was such a busy little boy, always in a hurry. The shop, Pioneer Stores, was in Station Road; it has just been refurbished and now sells kitchens. It was quite a large general provisions and grocery store which sold everything; Mr Thomas owned it and ran it. Sides

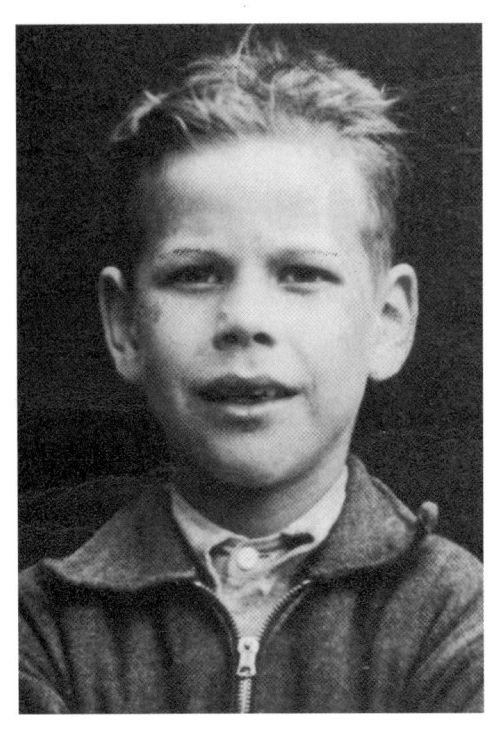

Em. aged about 10.

of Harrison's bacon would be delivered to him wrapped in a sort of cheesecloth and hung in the back room. Sultanas and raisins would come loose, as would most things in those days. Em would put them into bags. Broken biscuits were a favourite. Em would do half an hour's work before school, an hour during the school lunch break, and a couple of hours again after school, with a half day off on Wednesdays. He would work all day Saturday delivering orders, but Sunday was a day of rest of course. One Saturday night Mr Thomas gave Em a ham shank: "I was so proud to take it home," said Em. His mother boiled it and couldn't believe what she saw – floating on top of the pan were loads of maggots! There were no sell-by dates then. Em's wages were £1 10's (£1.50) per week; he would give half to his mother and keep half for himself. Em was the last boy who carried out for Mr Thomas before he got a vehicle.

When Em was 13 he pinched his brother Aelwyn's bike and dodged school. He had always wanted to see Caernarfon Castle; off he went on the bike, a great adventure in front of him. On arriving at Caernarfon he was hungry so he bought some chips and ate them on his way to the castle. The ticket officer asked him how old he was; "twelve" said Em, thinking he would have enough money to get in. "Sorry boy, but you have to be 13 to get in on your own," said the ticket collector. Poor Em had to cycle all the way home without seeing the inside of the castle.

I was caught smoking in Pant y Rhedyn and it was one of the worst things that happened to me in school. There were a few of us caught and we were sent to the headmaster's office. We stood outside, waiting for whatever was going to happen, all of us behaving as if we didn't care, but each and every one of us scared stiff. The waiting, I remember, was nearly as bad as the punishment. Each in our turn we went into that little office at the end of the corridor. We knew what was coming after the first child came out nursing a hand. It was the only time I ever had the cane, once on each hand, and it didn't half hurt. *Cofia ddweud wrth dy rieni am hyn* – don't forget to tell your parents about this, said Mr Lloyd Jones our headmaster. I wouldn't dare tell my parents, but neither could I go to school the next day and lie when Mr Jones asked me if I'd told my parents. What in the world could I do? Next day, I developed a very bad 'headache' and couldn't go to school; hopefully, Mr Jones would forget about the incident by Monday and my parents would never need to know.

We kids would play in Plas haystack; we'd have a whale of a time until we heard the farmer in the yard next door. We would sit there as quiet as you like, with baited breath, praying that he would hurry up with his work and go. Thank God, we were safe until the next time and we would run like mad in case we got caught.

The red post van was a great luxury in our family (for a few weeks). Who knows where it came from! Or indeed, where it went. Dad had been working on the engine on and off for weeks and at last we were going to have a drive in it. He only had a provisional licence and really should not have been driving on his own. There was also no tax or insurance on it. I remember Mam's words "Now bach as sure as eggs are eggs you will get caught." But of course this did not bother Dad very much at all.

It was with a great deal of anticipation that we left the house that particular morning, using the back roads of course to avoid detection. I suppose it was around 1953. Mam was in the front seat and Val and I were sat on a pile of old rags in the back of the van with Dad's tools rattling noisily behind us. Val and I were sick with excitement, a day out in the lovely red van. Off we went, praying that we had enough petrol in the tank (the petrol gauge was broken). Having first been around the back streets of Llanfair and then as a special treat for us girls Dad took us up to Bethesda to see the slate quarry! I remember to this day the narrow roads, the little rows of cottages and my Dad seemed to know everyone. I felt so important to be seen with him. Val and I thought we had been all over North Wales but of course in reality it was only a short drive. Then time to get back, Dad had a job to do at Aber and we finally landed at our destination. It was some sort of a water filtering station (I think) on the right hand side of the road about half a mile before you got to the mountain gate at Aber. Out came the tools for the job. The frying pan, plates and cups were next out (we had brought everything except the kitchen sink). Dad built a grate of sorts and lunch was sorted. An hour later we were sat down eating our frying steak and thinly cut bread and butter. A tin of fruit and cream completed our meal. "That was fit for a king, come on Margiad, Val can help Mam and we will try and get this roof finished so that we can get home" said Dad. Another day in our young lives was coming to an end.

Going to a jumble sale was an event that lots of women looked forward to. They were normally held at 6pm on a Friday (pay day). In my memory they were mostly held in the winter months. I remember standing, on cold dark evenings, waiting in line with great anticipation for the doors to be opened at the Church Institute or one of the chapel schoolrooms. There was a mad rush once they opened! Depending on what they came in search of, everyone darted to different stalls, with us kids looking for anything that was going cheap. Grace Bach (Nain), Auntie Maggie Smith, Auntie Rosie, Maggie Heath, Auntie Rose, my Mam and many others would be looking for some good clothing or shoes: Mam liked to wear shoes with a heel and I'm sure it was from wearing other people's shoes that she had a few corns in her time; she used to cut them off with a razor! Going home with our bags full, we'd have an exciting time rummaging through everything. As I got older, going to jumbles was an embarrassment of course; second hand clothes indeed!

"It's important that you learn to swim girls, especially as we live so close to the sea," Dad would tell us as we walked all the way from Tan Bonc, with our picnic, down to the beach. Val wasn't very keen on the water so she never learned. Mam wasn't a swimmer and she would sit with us at the water's edge while Dad went for a swim. In those days people didn't have the time or the money for the leisure activities we have today. I recall a couple of occasions when Dad didn't even have a pair of trunks and he would have to swim in our navy blue knickers and as for us girls, it was either our navy blue knickers or nothing.

When I was about five or six years old Dad taught me to swim. Not in the sea, as you would presume, oh no. It was far too dangerous for a little girl, my parents would say. With a belt around my waist, my father would walk around the yachting pond, dangling me in the water. With my little arms and legs flying everywhere, I would shout: "Mam, look at me – I'm swimming!" And that was how I learned to swim. I was quite a good swimmer in my youth and loved to go with my friends. As you can imagine, we spent many hours in the sea. What happy memories I have of growing up near the sea. Mr Travers was the manager in the amusements which was a big attraction for us kids. We loved putting our pennies in the one-arm bandits or in the juke-box as we got older. It was great fun jiving to the latest hits; the shame of it was that it was only open during the summer months. Our summers, as I recall, were far hotter and longer than they are today. Once all the visitors had gone home we'd have a hot September if we were lucky. The old folk used to call it *Haf bach i ni ein hunain* – a little summer all to ourselves. One summer, for a treat, my parents took us to the Lido, an outdoor swimming pool at Deganwy. A bus ride, a picnic and a swim in a real swimming pool! Oh, what fun we had that day. During our school summer holidays in the 1950's, the beach was packed with holidaymakers, with not a room vacant in the village. The sun shone brightly in a beautiful blue sky. The tide was in, my Dad and his brother Ned were working on their little fishing boat, and I was doing what I liked best – helping my

Dad. There were crowds of children jumping and diving off the deep end of the jetty, which was very dangerous. Suddenly, the kids started shouting: "Help! Help! There's someone drowning!" Uncle Ned jumped in, half dressed, shoes and all. He swam out to a little girl called Iola but she started pulling him down with her; he soon got into trouble himself. My Dad stripped to his trunks and jumped in after them. He managed to get to his brother and swam back to the jetty with him. "It was instinct, I suppose, to pull my brother out first," said Dad later. Then he went back in to get the girl. By this time things had got really serious, as the girl had gone down two or three times. Dad, who was a very strong swimmer, managed to get her to the jetty and someone turned her on her side and pumped the water out of her. I was so proud of my Dad that day. Iola is still alive today and teaching in Japan. She was the daughter of George Glo Roberts (George Lilac). Mr Roberts came to our house the next day to thank Dad, saying *Dyma rhywbeth bach am lwc i ti Now* - here's a little something to bring you luck. He gave Dad a sovereign; I think they were quite scarce. Of course, Dad didn't take long to spend it!

In the 1950's we used to pick potatoes for a couple of weeks in the late summer. Mam, Val and I would call for Auntie Rose and the kids plus Alice (Fflodiard), Grace Bach (my Nain) and Blodwen (Auntie Rossie), to name but a few. Most were dressed in their husbands' old trousers with bits of string tied around their waists. There would be no time to fiddle with their hair, so most of them had a square headscarf tied up in a sort of turban. Off we went down the village. There was such bubbling excitement among the children you'd think we were going on holiday. Picnics were packed - sandwiches made with dripping, or sugar, or of course the ever-faithful bechdan jam, were among the favourites. There must have been about twenty to thirty women, an occasional man and hordes of kids, all making for the crossroads where a tractor and trailer came to pick us all up by 9am. Having clambered aboard the trailer, with the kids squashed in between their mothers, we were like sardines. Off we'd go, shouting and singing some of the old favourites, such as *It's a long way to Tipperary*, *She'll be coming round the mountain* and *Show me the way to go home*. We were going to College Farm in Aber, or maybe Madryn Farm. There was just time enough for some of the women to light up and smoke a Woodbine before starting their days toil. Times were hard and we were poor; Mam and Auntie Rose often shared a cigarette between them.

While I sit here, writing about days which are buried deep in my memory, it's strange how so many little details come back to me. Ringing in my ears is the sound of one of the women shouting to all us kids: *Eisteddwch i lawr blant rhag ofn i chi syrthio allan o'r hen wagon 'ma* - sit down kids, in case you fall out of the wagon. It didn't matter whose child you were, you did as you were told. If you didn't you'd sometimes get a clip round the ear.

Arriving at the potato field we'd all pile out, each mother looking for her own kids, to sort them out. The farmer would mark out the pitches, counting out his paces and marking them with sacks. It depended on how many pickers had turned up that day as to how long your pitch would be. You'd catch some people moving their sack, to shorten their own pitch (this was always done in fun, I hasten to add).

Now the hard work would start, and believe me, it was back breaking work. All us kids would be very enthusiastic to start with but we soon got fed up and off we'd go to find a playmate. The tractor would drive up the row, opening it as it went. All the spuds would come to the top and it was our job to pick them up and put them into baskets, before transporting them to the sacks at the end of our pitch. Hopefully, this was done before the tractor came around again to open the next row. A welcome sight, in mid-morning, was the farmer bringing round some boiling tea in a large pitcher. The women had brought their own cups and sugar. My Mam always drank boiling-hot water with a drop of tea to colour it. I do seem to remember the weather as mostly sunny and dry. But some days the rain came and you can imagine how muddy it got, so we packed off homewards without much money. At lunchtime everyone sat down in little groups. "Have you got enough butties?" one woman would shout. "Yes thanks!" "Do you need more water?" someone else would shout. "*Oes gennych chi fygyn i sbario* - can you spare a smoke?" Banter could be heard echoing across the field as the day wore on. It was share and share alike. Five o'clock came. *Diolch i Dduw am gael mynd adref* - thank God we can go home, said everyone at the end of an exhausting day: a day full of hard slog and sackfuls of laughter. The women would be able to forget some of their troubles for a few hours, as well as earn a few shillings. It was a rush now to get on the trailer. We would all push, trip, and shove our way onto that old wagon. Having filled our shopping bags with spuds, we still wanted more. We would hide as many as we could down our pants, in our Wellingtons and in our pockets. I'm sure the trailer must have been a couple of tons heavier coming back. The farm hand would take us up to Nant y Berllan Bridge, and if we were very lucky, depending on who was driving, we would get a lift to Pandy Bridge. Another day at the potato field was over, and we'd go home for tea; sometimes Dad was home from work first and had food on the go. If Dad wasn't working he would come and pick spuds with us. We would empty our bags and pockets and fill the sack under the stairs with our spuds, until it got quite full. Perhaps we'd have enough to see us through the winter, although my kind-hearted parents would share their bounty with anyone who called on us. Mam always said: "If you have a few spuds in the house you can always make a meal del."

When I was about fourteen the Sunday newspapers came only as far as Tan Bonc and I would deliver them the rest of the way to Tyddyn Rhedyn Uchaf, a little farm about a mile further up. Brothers Bobby and Goronwy (Hengae) lived there with their wives, Joan and May, and their children. They shared the house, both families having one side each and sharing the kitchen. It was very much a done thing then to share a house while you waited and hoped for a home of your own to come along.

Whatever the weather, it was with great anticipation and excitement I got ready to leave the house at around 10am on those Sunday mornings so long ago. My heart would pound in my chest; I had butterflies in the pit of my stomach. I was off to meet my *cariad* – my sweetheart, Emrys. "Ta ta Mam," I would shout as I went through the door, "see you later." Little did they know that delivering papers wasn't the only thing on my mind. Or did they know…

Em would be waiting for me near Ysgol Nant Sunday School. Off we'd go, up through the drive; there was no-one around at that time on a Sunday morning. We were the only two people in the world! How wonderful it was, to be young and in love. Having given Em a warning to keep out of sight as we got close to Tyddyn Rhedyn Uchaf (I didn't want my parents to find out I had a boyfriend!), I would walk up the field to deliver the papers. After a quick chat with the family I was free for a couple of hours. I was in such a hurry – I didn't want to waste any of our time together. I would trip and slip my way down that field. Em would be waiting for me, and hand in hand, both rather shy of each other, we would walk up to Three Streams; what a tranquil place it was, and indeed still is. Most times we were able to cross the river at Three Streams to Llyn Nant, although this was impossible after heavy rain and we would have to use the bridge near Nant y Coed. Sometimes we would climb up the face of Dinas; when I look back now, I think how dangerous that climb was, with loose stones of all shapes and sizes, but I was as good a climber as any boy, so what did I care. We would look down on our little world of Llanfair and gaze into our future – and what a bright future we envisaged; we made the sort of plans that only the young can make and really believe in. Our courting days in the winter consisted mainly of hours sitting in the cold shelters on the beach, both wrapped up like onions. How well I remember those evenings, especially when the moon was full and it was like daylight. The stars would be blinking at us from high up in that massive dark place we called the sky. Looking back, the stars seemed to shine a lot brighter then. We would sit with our arms wrapped around each other, looking out across the sea, watching the lighthouse winking at us from Penmon in Anglesey, and counting the seconds before the beam came around again. How quickly the hours passed; a kiss or two later it was time to go home. As I got older and Em started coming to our house, our parlour became our refuge during the cold winter months. Sometimes Beaver and his girlfriend sat in with us, and we had a lot of laughs. By this time we had a record player and we would sit and listen to records for hours. *Return to Sender* by Elvis was a great song I recall. Two of the rules in our house were: when we could afford it we had to put two shillings (10p) in the gas meter ourselves, and the other was that my friends had to go home at 10pm.

Boy Scouts came on holiday to Llanfair year after year, to enjoy our lovely little village. The camp sites were up in Tyddyn Llwyfan farm and at Llys y Gwynt, with tents in regimental rows across the fields. How excited all the girls used to be – new lads to chase! The Scouts would march through the village on Sunday mornings, all dressed up in their finery, blowing their bugles. I don't really remember where they were going – to church perhaps.

These are our very own Boy Scouts from the early 1950's. The two scout leaders are Norman Thomas second left and Bob Roberts (stores) fourth left.

Bob (stores) again! Serving behind the counter in the Coop around 1950.

One year in particular comes to mind – the year a little lad was killed on Dinas. It had been raining and the wet, loose stones, some covered in moss, all very slippery, made for a lethal combination. A troupe of boys had been climbing up the face of the hill. The boy slipped on the stones and banged his head. It killed him. For many years afterwards a bunch of flowers was laid on the spot. It was a tragedy that shocked the local people to the core. "But for the grace of God," was said often. I myself was warned: "Don't you dare climb that mountain again, Margaret."

The Co-op in Llanfair was very handy for *tick*. You were allocated an account number – Mam's was 190. You could buy what you liked for three months, whether it be food, furniture or shoes, as long as you cleared your outstanding bill by the quarter ending, as it was called. There would be a bacon side on the massive shiny slicing machines ready to be sliced fresh while you watched. The cheese was cut with a wire that cut off exactly what you asked for. Uncle Bob (stores) and Uncle Col (Colwyn Lewis) worked behind the counter, always with a smile on their faces and perhaps, a few extra bits of bacon put in the paper bag for you. If you were very lucky perhaps they would also put a few bruised apples in a bag. For sure, there was no - buy one get one free in those days. There was not much of a choice in fruit and veg. I remember that at Christmas one Pomegranate each was the most exotic fruit we had and how we loved to pick at it with a darning needle. Mam always gave the people behind the counter a couple of shillings each as a Christmas tip. Uncle Col once told her that it was the people who could least afford it that gave them a tip! The dividend (divi) was paid out once every year. It came in very handy at Christmas. Believe me when I tell you that there was panic in lots of houses at the end of every quarter. You'd pay off your previous bill and immediately start the next quarter with another bill. Mam always made sure that we didn't overspend. I wonder sometimes how my dear Mother managed the money so well with what little she got. I suppose tick was similar to today's credit card. There was no bank account in our house.

It wasn't until a few years after Em and I were married that we opened our first account in Lloyds Bank, Village Road.

Miss Lloyd ran the Music Shop (Gills today) where all we young people made for with our pocket money. I suppose we would have been about fourteen or fifteen. To us youngsters the most important product she sold was records and if she didn't have a particular one in she would order it and hopefully it would be delivered before it went out of the charts! As I recall but she would let you save with her every week until you had enough to pay for what you wanted.

There was a lladd-dy (slaughterhouse) at the bungalow near Nant y Berllan Bridge, run by Jack and Emlyn Hughes, two brothers who owned a butcher's shop in the village. They would slaughter animals and prepare the meat to sell in their shop themselves, and as I remember their meat was the best you could get. If we were very lucky we would be given a pig's bladder to play with. We filled it with water and had a football that hadn't cost us a penny. Jack and Emlyn's shop was across the road from us when we lived in Britannia House. Mam never went anywhere else for her meat; sometimes it was "a bit of home killed beef, none of that foreign stuff mind, a piece off the rump, nice and lean remember," she would tell Val or me as we went to the shop; if Mam wasn't happy with it we would have to take it back and Jack, who was always very obliging, would grumble and tell us in Welsh: "there's nothing wrong with this piece, but if it'll keep your Mam happy I'll cut you a different piece." At other times – when we weren't so flushed – it would be a breast of lamb costing around two shillings (ten pence). Oh, what a lovely Sunday dinner that would make! There was always a side of beef hanging in the shop, or a lamb waiting to be cut up. There were cuts of meat on show on the white tiles in the window and one of the brothers was forever cutting up meat on a huge butcher's block. The knives would be hanging behind the counter, and

Jack Hughes, farmer and butcher delivering meat on his horse Sally in the early 1950's.

they'd be sharpened vigorously before being used. The brothers always handled the meat cleanly. I remember them as always wearing snow-white jackets. I commented to Jack once on the thickness of the butcher's block. "They don't last as long as they used to Margaret, a table like this would last many years but not any more," he answered; this was in the early 1960's. Dad used to like tripe and onions with plenty of vinegar. Yuk! Dad had a greyhound at that time and the butchers would give bones and off-cuts to feed it. *Dos i ofyn i Jack am ben dafad i mi Margiad* – go and ask Jack if he has a sheep's head I can have, Dad would say. A big pan of water was put on the stove in the cellar kitchen, ready to boil the sheep's head. The dogs loved it. The disgusting, sour-sweet smell of the simmering sheep's head went through the house. Even in my bedroom I could smell it.

In 1909 there were over 60 shops in Llanfair. Looking back, Em and I remember about 60 shops here when we were kids in the 1950's. There was a post office in the village, a sub-post office near the beach, and another near Shore Road East. There were loads of pubs and a good few of God's houses. There were three thriving butchers, countless corner shops and of course the Co-op. Four coal merchants made a living here: Llew Bach in Valley Road; John Stocks and Moi, who ran their own business from the coal yard at the railway station, and Georgie Glo, who delivered coal for the Co-op, as well as being the local bookie's runner. I remember taking some bets into the side door of the Llanfair Arms, where Georgie used to work from. Dad liked a bet and he would do accumulators or a round robin (I never understood that bet); mostly he would do an each way bet, because there was a better chance of winning. Betting shops were made legal in May 1961, for the first time in over 100 years, although we didn't have one in Llanfair for a few more years.

There were three cobblers: one was in a shoe shop called Vivian's on Station Road; the other two were Edwin and Meredudd Dafydd Lloyd Roberts, whose father had run a cobbler's shop in the village before them. Meredudd (Dafydd ap's father) had a shop in Station Road, and Edwin's shop was next door to Llan newsagents. Edwin is the one I remember best – I worked with his wife and daughter in the sewing factory. I loved the smell of leather which greeted you when you walked into the little shop; it was no bigger than a hut, really, with a little paraffin heater in the corner, a couple of old heavy duty specialist Singer machines, and a counter that was always stacked high with shoes for repair. There was always someone sitting on the chair near the door having a jangle, and what a welcome you had off Edwin. He would chat about anything and everything as he got on with the job of mending half the villagers' shoes. He put many a buckle on our girls' shoes. "No charge, just keep me any old buckles you have Margaret," he'd say.

There was no real need to go out of the village to do any shopping. If you did, it was more often that not a trip on the bus to Bangor. It seems to me that things began to change in Llanfair in the early 1960's.

A very important thing happened to me when I was fifteen or sixteen years old. Dad found out I smoked! We were living at Britannia House by then, and Chris Coleman was in our house at teatime one day when he turned to me and said: "Margaret, I didn't know you smoked." I couldn't believe my ears; fancy saying that, with my Dad there listening. Chris had seen the nicotine on my fingers. "No Chris, I don't, I've been peeling potatoes and haven't washed my hands yet," said I, too quickly. Poor Chris realized that he shouldn't have spoken – but it was too late. Mam already knew, but not my Dad. He said nothing at the time and went out with Chris to price a job. Talk about worry, I was sick – and I knew Dad wasn't stupid. Mam said: "Don't worry del, it'll be OK, Dad will understand." The evening wore on with no sign of my father, so we knew he'd gone to the pub – and was I worried now! I waited up with Mam until he came in, scared of what he was going to say, but preferring to get it over with that night rather than wait until morning. Dad came home as large as life with twenty Players in his hand for me. "Margiad fach," he said, adding: "I feel such a fool. There was I bragging to everyone that my girls didn't smoke, and all the time you were doing it behind my back. I was going to make you smoke these fags one after the other until you'd never look at another cigarette, but you're old enough – and who am I to preach about smoking?" I have that big lump in my throat again. Poor Chris never forgot that he was the one who dropped me in it with Dad. He and I were to have many a laugh about it over the years. As it happened he did me a big favour.

"The Truck" was a homemade contraption which was very popular with the boys of the village. They would scrounge some old pram wheels from wherever they could, sometimes going to Glan y Mor Elias where our local rubbish tip was. It was indeed an Aladdin's cave. They would put together a truck, with two small wheels in front and two larger ones at the back, with a plank to sit on and a loop of string connected to the front wheels for the steering. "Down Pen y Bryn hill we went, like greased lightning, sometimes two or even three of us on it," said Em. "No brakes – only our feet to rely on. Straight down Village Road we went, to the beach – there weren't so many cars back then." One day, after one of these escapades, he had to go home and face his mother with only half a shoe: the other half lay in bits along the streets of the village. "Did I get a walloping that day," said Em.

Glan y Mor Elias, was a place where many, many people of the village visited in those days. It was our local tip. If you wanted anything, or even if you didn't, you would take a walk along the Cob to the "dump" for a look around. It was infested with rats. There was stinking smoke everywhere, curling up slowly from the bowels of the earth, as if there was some sort of underground furnace there; it came from the smouldering remains of all the rubbish, ash and cinders. Eric Lewis has told me that people used to go there looking for "empties" which the more fortunate would throw away without bothering about the few coppers they could get on the returned bottles. "People would rinse them in the sea, take them back to a shop, and if you were in luck it meant a few bob," said Eric. On one occasion Llywelyn Jones the men's outfitters in Station Road dumped loads of shop soiled suits on the rubbish lorry. "What a damn shame, throwing them away," said Eric, "but don't worry – anything that was thrown on the lori ludw (refuse lorry) in those days was recycled very quickly!"

Em and his friend Adrian Dunkley bunked off school occasionally to go to the tip. They'd borrow a couple of old hessian sacks and make their way to the tip, hoping to find a load of cinders for their fires at home and earn themselves a copper or two. It took a day or so after the lori ludw had dumped its load for the ash and cinders to cool down. Yes indeed, there were rich pickings to be had at the tip if you had the stomach to go and look.

When I started work at the factory I wanted a sewing machine and couldn't afford one. "Don't worry del, we will get you something," said Dad. As if by a miracle there was a terrible rainstorm and the river swelled: *y llif Awst* – the August flood, as we called it. The sound of the river passing our house was like thunder; large stones and rocks would fly down as if they were pebbles, bashing the foundations of our house as they went on their journey towards the sea. Old iron bed-heads and springs, tables and even some old chairs would go flashing past. The amount of rubbish that floated past was unbelievable. It was as though everyone who lived on the banks of the river, and even some who didn't, used the occasion to dump their rubbish. This was the time for us all to dispose of any unwanted junk.

After the rain had stopped there would be all sorts of junk stuck here and there on the riverbank. Dad went out to see if there was any damage to our house, but all was well. When he came back into the house he was carrying something in his hands. "Look what I have found – go and get Mags," he shouted. Would you believe it – among the branches and old rubbish he'd discovered an old Singer sewing machine. I was thrilled to bits; I knew Dad could fix it.

When he came home one day, after a day's foraging in the dump, Dad had a big smile on his face. He had found an old treadle sewing machine bench. I was on my way! Mam cleaned it all up for me. I can see her smiling face in front of me now – she was so pleased. Dad fixed it all together and set it up in the parlour at Britannia House. I was to spend many happy hours on that old machine, making all sorts. Eventually I part exchanged it for a new electric machine from a little shop on Bryn Road called Wenroe. It took me three years to pay for my new machine at eleven shillings (55p) a week, but by this time I was on piece-work and earning a little more money. Every Friday I would call on my way home from work with my club card and wages.

After I left school in 1961 I worked at Mandy Modes, a sewing factory on Bryn Road, just off Bryn Eirin, making clothes for mail order firms. It was owned by Mr and Mrs Wilson from Manchester. In those days you got some sort of grant if you brought work to the area so the Wilsons moved lock stock and barrel from Altringham. There were about twenty to thirty of us working there and we had a great time. Most of us were local, so we knew each other's business; we were more like a big happy family than a factory workforce. Among the other workers were George Rycroft and his wife Pat from Manchester. He came for the job of cutter in Mandy Modes and ended up as a manager at West Coast Knitting. I remember buying a cot off Pat when Lorraine was born. The first time Em and I went on holiday, in about 1980; George let me use his credit card to book the holiday over the phone. We were working at West Coast

Mandy Modes, sewing factory carnival float - early 1970's. Front row left to right: Sheila, Joan, Beryl, Auntie Louie, ?, Barbara, Auntie Mair with the spinning wheel. The float - represented sewing through the ages.

Knitting at the time and did not possess such a thing as a credit card. George and Pat were to remain friends of ours until they died a few years ago.

Miss Woolly, a quiet, inoffensive little lady, came from Manchester for the job of forewoman; she was not suited to the job, but stayed on as a sewing machinist. She loved the village and was to remain in Llanfair until she died.

In those days we were on piece-work, and believe me when I tell you that what you earned is what you got! We worked very hard. There was Auntie Louie, my great Uncle Robin's wife, who was our supervisor for many years, and her son Philip, who was our van driver, delivering goods far and wide; I recall that during lunchtimes in the factory we used to sit and tell each other all sorts of stories. Auntie Louie was a Yorkshire lass and she met Great Uncle Robin during the Second World War, or maybe just before; anyway, they had a whirlwind courtship and she came to Llanfair to live. Now someone had died in the village and it was tradition then to visit the home of the deceased with something small towards the wake. "I didn't want to go Margaret," said Auntie Louie, "but Uncle Robin said it was the done thing so I went along with him, taking a quarter of tea and a bag of sugar, which we could ill afford I might tell you! We knocked at the door and waited; after what seemed like hours the lady of the house answered. Uncle Robin gave our condolences and she kept us standing on the doorstep; taking the tea and sugar out of his hand, she said 'thank you very much' and closed the door in our faces. I never paid a visit to anyone in those circumstances again!" said Auntie Louie.

Also there were Auntie Mair (Stores), Auntie Edith and her daughter Pat, Auntie Molly and her daughter Ann, Mrs Fenton, Auntie Megan and Pauline (Teiliwr), Auntie Joyce, June; the list goes on and on – far too many to name here, but all those people and the memories we gathered are deeply engraved on my heart. We made pyjamas and girls' dresses for mail order firms. We had loads of fun there. Auntie Megan must have been like her mother Maggie, a bit of a comic. She was always up to something and she kept us all in stitches – I mean laughing, of course!

I will go back to Easter 1961. It was my first job and I hadn't been there for very long; I couldn't wait to leave school and earn some money. I was so proud and excited. I was going to be trained as a sewing machinist; training, I might add, that has been a great asset to me all my life. I was 15 years old and working. One day a member of staff sent me upstairs to the cutting room to get a *long stand*. I was rather quiet and shy in those days, and didn't like to draw attention to myself. After a while I was worried that I would get into trouble for being such a long time away from my work. Knowing Auntie Meg well, I naturally went to her and asked her quietly in Welsh: "Can you get me the long stand please Auntie Megan?" Yes, you're right – I was on a fool's errand. Auntie Megan said, as she shook with laughter, *Dos i lawr a dywed wrthyn nhw dy fod wedi sefyll ddigon hir rwan* – go back down and tell them you've stood for long enough now. I felt such a fool, but I got over it.

By the way, my first wage packet was £3. After tax and insurance my take-home pay was £2.14/5 (£2.73p) – £2 for Mam and 14/5 for me. I was rich. I remember giving my dear Mother that first £2; she was so proud of me she cried.

Working on a Saturday morning, cleaning the factory from 9am till noon, earned me an extra half a crown (12p). But oh! What fun we had, all friends together, trying to earn a crust. Mam used to work most Saturday mornings. If Dad was out I would keep an eye on Val when she wasn't well; I used to take her with me to the factory, under protest I might add.

Em and I got engaged on my eighteenth birthday. That same year, 1964, we bought 2 Glan Ffrwd – a little semi-detached house a few hundred yards from the village. I should say Em bought it. He had been saving a few pounds a week for a deposit and had reached the £200 required. Mr John Bellis and Co did the business for us and Em's mother signed as a guarantor - we were too young to get a mortgage; you had to be 21. John Bellis had an office in Trigfan (next door to the library) in those days. We bought our new home from Uncle Harry and Auntie Mil, and paid £1,200, which was £300 less than the market value. The house had tenants in at the time, so they paid us rent for the first twelve months. It was a help towards the mortgage. The cost of an average house in 1965 was £3,600 and the average weekly wage was £21.

We were married on March 20th 1965. My father Now paid for our wedding reception at Spires, the bakery and café on the crossroads - it was used for wedding receptions in those days. We had a small wedding with 38 guests in all. My Dad had paid Mr Spires the £25 for the reception weeks beforehand, but a fortnight before our wedding he asked for his money back. He wanted the money for materials to do a job, or so he said! Mr Spires returned the money. With just two weeks to go until our wedding, what could I do? £25 was a lot of money then. Once again, Uncle Harry came to our rescue - he lent us the money. Em and I paid him 5 shillings (25p) a week until it was paid off. I might add here that Uncle Harry and Dad were always the best of friends, more thanks to Uncle Harry than Dad, I'm sure. No! I tell a lie - they thought the world of each other. Uncle Harry would really lay down the law to Dad, and Dad would listen - then he'd do as he liked anyway!

We didn't have much money but we managed to furnish our new home with bits and bobs from all the family. We had 114 wedding presents. I can't believe that I remember that, after all these years. Requesting your present was not the done thing then; you took what you got and said thank you very much. My mother laid out all our gifts in the front room of Britannia House, with the cards we received so that people could see what we'd received and from whom - another thing that was done in those days. In the weeks leading up to the wedding everyone who came to our house was shown proudly into the parlour by my Dad. *Dewch i weld y presantau* he would say - come and see the presents.

Meirion (Em's brother) gave us £50 for a wedding present and off we went to spend our money. We bought a small cottage suite, a red Formica topped kitchen table with four matching chairs, and some jute carpet for the stairs. We had a lot for our money, and we were so excited. Em's parents bought us a new sideboard at a cost of £20. Mam and Dad gave us some money towards a new gas cooker. Dad and Em did some structural work on Glan Ffrwd.

Em and me in Birmingham 1967.

The day of our wedding dawned and Bangor Registry Office was where we had decided to do the deed. I can still see Mam and Dad looking so proud, Mam crying quietly into her hankie. That was it, I cried all through the ceremony too! If there was any one reason why I wouldn't have a church wedding, that was it – I knew I would get upset. I have never been one for a fuss. The immediate family saw us off at the station, all waving and shouting. "We will miss you del," whispered my dear Mother through her tears as we boarded the train. We planned to honeymoon in London for five days, but stayed only three – for two reasons, really. The first was that my dear Taid Gwyn was very ill and I was worried about him. The second was that we had our little home to get back to and we couldn't wait. We were only nineteen and twenty respectively, we were rather green and we didn't like the big city very much. When we arrived home from London it was quite late and all the shops were closed, except School Shop (the off-licence today). Mr and Mrs Davies ran it then as a sort of general store. It sold food, sweets, cigarettes and all sorts of everything. That is where we bought our first weekend order. We were so glad to come home to our very own little house.

Four years and two daughters later we decided that Glan Ffrwd was too small for us and Bryn Glas came on the market at £2,000. There was a lot of work to do there. Em and Dad worked very hard, it was like a building site for months. How in the world we lived there with two young daughters I don't know.

Em kept of pigeons for a while, until he decided to go shares on a couple of greyhounds with Dad, and then the birds went. They had the dogs for a few years. Every Friday evening they would go to collect enough meat to last the week from an abattoir in Bangor. After picking up the dog food they would make their way up to The Royal Oak in Llanllechid near Bethesda and enjoy a game of dominoes with the locals. My Dad used to tell me that "How Gets (the nickname for Bethesda people) are the salt of the earth Mags, there is still a real sense of community there." Dad loved dominoes and was a dab hand at the game. He so looked forward to going with Em on Friday evenings. It was the highlight of his week. He'd go home after work, have his tea, and then he'd have a quick wash and change – Dad liked to look smart when he went out. Mam loved to see Dad go out with Em. "I know Em will look after him, although how poor Em tolerates your father after a few pints I will never know," she'd say laughingly. Every time I tell them a little tale, our girls ask: "How in the world did poor Nain stick Taid all those years?" Before going, Dad always came to see our girls first, with a pocket full of sweets for them, of course. When Easter came around Dad would go to the paper shop and buy two of the biggest eggs in the shop for our girls. By this time in Dad's life he had calmed down a lot and used to say: "My years working at Home Loaf and Hotpoint were some of the best years of my life. There was a certain stability about having a job inside, something I never felt when I worked outside. The years I spent as a roofer are long over – it's a young man's game." Despite Mam's failing health those years were happy years.

In the early days of the dog partnership they would go up to The Royal Oak on Em's motorbike, in all kinds of weather, on Friday nights. Up they'd go, along the winding, narrow roads to Llanllechid. Em remembers one very wet night in the middle of winter. They arrived at the pub, soaked to their skins, and had only just thawed out in front of a roaring coal fire when it was time to go home – three hours had flown by. *Noson dda iawn*, said Dad – a very good night! Em and Dad never spoke English together. It came to chucking out time, about 10.30pm, and on went their waterproofs. They weren't looking forward to the journey home at all. Their waterproofs were old and tired and let more water in than they kept out. Before Dad got on the back of the old AJS he'd pull out one of the clean, white, home-made handkerchiefs I used to make for him out of old sheets, to dry the seat. "The rain was coming down in sheets and the wind was roaring in the trees as we drove down the little lanes," said Em. "*Yr oedd yn ddu fel bol buwch* – it was as black as a cow's belly, and I could hardly see a thing. Now was holding on to me like a leech," he said. They'd both had a few pints but there was no worry in those days about drink driving – it was the done thing to have a few pints and drive afterwards. Em was never one to drink too much so I didn't need to worry. To top the lot, the driving rain had got to the lights and they started flickering. Onward they rode, fighting against the wind and rain, along those dreadful roads. By the time they got half way home the lights had failed altogether. Managing to get as far as Gypsy Corner near Tal y Bont in complete darkness, they came across a street lamp at last. *Diolch i Dduw am olau* – thank God for some light, said Em as he jumped off the bike to have a look. There was nothing much they could do without tools, and since there wasn't a single vehicle on the road to flag down, they decided to take a chance, while praying a copper wouldn't come along. They drove home with no lights; the roads back then were nothing like they are today. Needless to say, they got home safe and sound, even if they did look like a pair of drowned rats.

Decimalization was introduced in 1971: Em was working in Hotpoint at the time and used to have 1/6 a day for soup and a pudding. I didn't have a clue what that was in new money. Our insurance man used to call for his money every week and he sorted out Em's dinner money for me and put it on the grate ready for morning – it was 7p!

Em and I were on a walk around the top of the village back in 1976. We descended past the golf course, down past Llanerch, and came to Woodlands. It's a bungalow next door to the golf clubhouse. There were a couple of palm trees in the garden, the flowers were in full bloom, and the sun was peeping from behind a cloud as if it was trying to shine on Woodlands itself. "That," I said, "is my dream house. I would love to live there."

"Some hopes," said Em. What happened next I can only describe as fate. The next day Lorraine came running into the house yelling: "Mam, Woodlands is for sale!" "How do you know, del?" I asked. Lorraine was friendly with Dewi and Cynthia's daughter Morfydd – at the time they lived at Bwthyn, next door to Woodlands, and they'd heard that Woodlands was for sale. What a coincidence!

Having spoken to Em about it we agreed that if it was no more than £16,000 we could afford it. I was knocking at Woodlands' door before I drew breath. "I hear you're putting the house up for sale," I said to Mr Gordon, the owner. "How on earth do you know? I only decided yesterday," he said. "Well," said I, "this is a small village and you can't keep things under your hat for long here."

"I've heard about the jungle drums but this is ridiculous," he answered. "As you're here you might as well come in for a look," he added. Mrs Gordon had just come out of the shower and was drying her hair. I had a look around and fell in love with the place. I knew that once Em had seen it he would feel the same. The big question was; could we afford it? "How much do you want for it?" I asked. "No offers, we want £17,250," said Mr Gordon. That was a little bit more than Em and I had agreed on. I asked when it would be convenient for my husband and children to view it. "Any time," they said, so we arranged a time for the next day.

After Em had seen it we did our sums and we offered them the asking price; they agreed to give us a week to sort out a mortgage. Not long you might say, but Mr Gordon was a businessman first and foremost, and time was money. "Remember," he said, "we will wait a week and then it goes on the open market." There was no way we could sell Bryn Glas in a week so we had to look at other ways of borrowing the money. We wanted that house; I suppose I was the driving force, and I was lucky that Em said: "OK, if you think we can manage the repayments, go for it." And that is exactly what we did. I spent the following week not eating, and sleeping very little. I drove myself and everyone else mad, especially poor Em, but as usual he was there, helping and reassuring me. Eventually, the waiting was over. The Abbey National had agreed to lend us the money. By the end of the week we were in a position to make the Gordons a firm offer - £17,000 for the bungalow and £250 for the curtains and carpets. The Gordons knew how much we wanted the bungalow and were delighted for us. "Your little girls are the first children to live at Woodlands," said Mrs Gordon, smiling. Now for the difficult bit - we had to pay for it! We still had a mortgage of £1,300 on Bryn Glas, on which we were paying the grand total of £73 every six months. Our mortgage was with the council, at a fixed rate of interest, which meant that it never fluctuated. Bryn Glas took a whole year to sell so we really struggled to pay the bills. When we bought Woodlands it had oil central heating, and we thought it was great, since there was no central heating in Bryn Glas. For the first few months we were lovely and warm, the heating going full blast. We came down to earth with a bump and spent the next few months sitting in sleeping bags and blankets - we couldn't afford to fill the oil tank. Much to the delight of our daughters we also took over the Gordons' phone. Our girls were constantly on it; I remember putting a lock on it once, but they soon found a way around that!

Em and Dad used to go to Winsford racing the dogs - by this time we had Rebel, whose racing name was Woodland Baby. One day, Em recalls, Rebel had come second and they were going to the pens to pick him up after the race. Another race was coming to an end and it was a photo finish. "As you know," said Em, "your father couldn't see further than his nose. But he was close enough that night to see who the winner of the photo finish was, so he rushed to place a bet - on the nose, so to speak! - and won £10."

At last, Bryn Glas was sold and we could sort out our money. We put our deposit on Woodlands and kept £1,000 back to go towards a holiday in Canada, visiting Em's family. We were able to do some work on Woodlands now; Em built a garage there and put a new sewerage system in. We made lots of alterations over the years. It was indeed a happy home. Both Em and I like to go on holiday and we have travelled all over the world, but we're always glad to come back to our little corner of it - Llanfairfechan! In 2005 we celebrated our fortieth wedding anniversary and our daughters surprised us with a trip to London, to the same hotel where we went on our honeymoon - The Gresham Hotel near Marble Arch. It was an odd experience. Em said: "It's strange, really; the last time we were here we were planning our lives together, looking forward to going home and working on our house. Here we are forty years later, with most of it behind us." Where have all the years gone? It's my body that keeps getting older, not me. I am still only sixteen years old, really.

Our Daughters

Our lovely little girl Lorraine was born in St David's Hospital in Bangor on August 11th 1966. She was given that name simply because Em liked it. She was dark skinned with lots of dark hair and was the living image of Em. I remember looking at her when she was only minutes old and thinking that we were the luckiest parents in the world to have such a beautiful, healthy baby. I think it was one of the most moving times in my life. When I looked down at her, all wrapped up in that hospital blanket and saw her little face all red and wrinkly she was beyond doubt the most perfect thing that I had ever seen in my life. And she was ours! Em came in to the labour ward seconds after she was born. He was as proud as punch; it wasn't such a done thing then for the father to be present at the birth so I don't even remember it even being in question. Val was the first to see Lorraine. "Well Mag fach fancy you being a mother" said Mam, she was so exited and relived that everything went well. "Only two to a bed please" said the nurse as the ward was invaded by Em and my family.

Em and Lorraine 1967.

It was the first night that Em had driven his new (second-hand) motorbike, bought from Emlyn Hughes the butcher for £5. That old 125cc BSA Bantam had been in Emlyn's field (at the back of Glyn's chippy) for a long time and it was a complete wreck. Em fell off the bike that night and ripped his new imitation leather jacket. I'm not sure what he was most excited about – the birth of his first child or his new bike! Dad and Em had been working on the bike for weeks and Em was so excited when he got it on the road. Over the next few years our front room at Glan Ffrwd would periodically become a motorbike shed. Any trouble with the engine and out came the newspapers and old sheets to cover the carpet; the beloved bike would be kept in the warmth for a few days while Em and Dad worked on it. Em had a couple of motorbikes – a 500cc AJS and a shining blue Sunbeam that was shaft driven. Em also had a sidecar at one time and he would take my Mam and Val for a spin – my mother was game for a laugh and boy, did we have a lot of laughs!

I remember Auntie Mair (Stores) and Auntie Molly coming to Glan Ffrwd to see us only hours after we arrived home bringing with them two little matinee coats, which was a good job as I couldn't knit! Lorraine hardly ever cried, she slept through many a feed, she was such a good baby. "You won't be as lucky next time" said Mam but she was wrong! A new baby meant lots of washing. I had no washing machine in the early years so it was a hard struggle keeping up with all the nappies. I recall that I used to boil the terry nappies in a galvanized bucket on the gas stove. Later on I had a second hand gas boiler and I thought it was brilliant.

Lorraine was always an outdoor girl. She would call at my parents' house on the way home, after a day with her mates on the mountains, and Dad would cover for her if she was late! Lorraine loved the mountains and when she was about 14 and we had the greyhounds she would spend hours with Em and my Dad at the old golf links, watching the dogs coursing hares. I recall she brought a seagull with a broken wing home "Can you fix it Dad" she said and another time there was a sick rabbit. She was always very soft hearted and hated seeing an animal suffer. When Lorraine got older and started working in Plas Menai (the Christian holiday hotel) she often called on Dad on the way home to slip him a couple of shillings. She remembers occasions when Dad would meet her off the school bus; he would walk home with her and her friends, and they'd have loads of fun with him. Lorraine had a mind of her own and was as stubborn as a mule (like me says Em) she was and indeed still is generous to a fault and always liked to help people.

She would try and do some baking with my mother shouting instructions from her bed, but it was never very successful. She looked forward to going shopping in the village with my sister Val; calling for fresh bread at Spiers was the first task, with a drink and an iced bun in the café, perhaps. Going to the jumble sale with myself and Auntie Val was another thing our girls loved until they were older! They used to enjoy listening to Dad's stories, and he'd tell them that when they were older there would be more to come. It is only now that they hear the end of some of those stories! I remember a time when Lorraine was going to confirmation classes. As usual, she was late one day. She ran down in her Wellingtons and playing clothes; on arriving at Bethel Chapel she ran up the stairs to the balcony and saw that there was something special going on. To her shock, her friends were all dressed up – it was the actual confirmation ceremony and she'd forgotten all about it, and forgotten even to tell us! There was no time to dally now, so she ran to June and Richie's house, Epworth Villa – they're good friends of ours. "Can I borrow some of Julie's clothes please?" she asked as she explained the situation. After a mad dash back, she made it just in time. And that was Lorraine's confirmation – Em and I missed it!

Carnival day had been a big event in the village but for some years there had been no one to organize it. Then Sylvia and Wendy came along and decided to revive it. How excited our girls were when one year Lorraine won a prize for dressing up as a gypsy and Karen won a prize for the best dressed dolls pram. Later on they were both in the Morris dancing, Zandra Williams spent hours organising and teaching the girls. I remember one year making twelve dresses for one of the troups and if I do say so myself, all the girls looked lovely! Em used to fetch my parents to our house and with Em's parents they would sit on the steps of Bryn Glas watching proudly as their granddaughtes went by in the procession. How glad and proud we are to have helped make these wonderful memories for our girls to look back on. Taidi Roberts (Em's dad) would call every Sunday before the girls went to Sunday school bringing with him some sweets or perhaps 10p each for them to spend. My mother-in-law (Naini May) would pay us a visit, always in the evening, and she would stay for a couple of hours. That was my ironing time; while we jangled away I got on with the endless ironing of our girls' dresses; I even used to iron their socks and knickers – was I mad or what! Every Christmas Eve Em's parents and his brother Meirion came up to our house for their supper. It came to be a tradition that went on for many years. They would call to the Social Club (Heath Home) for a game of bingo perhaps before making their way to our

May and Owen (Em's parents) in our house 1982.

Lorraine and Jason

house. So it was normally rather late on them arriving and I had already sorted the girl's presents out and of course they loved to see everything laid out ready for the girls for morning. Goodness me they did have a lot of stuff!

Lorraine didn't enjoy school and couldn't wait to start a job. After one or two other jobs she went into nursing. Along came Jason and that was it. "You and Dad have been good role models and I wasn't going to settle for anything less than you have." She told me recently. Jas has lived in Llanfair since he was about twenty years old; he has learned our language and loves living so close to the sea and mountains. Jason and Lorraine were married on September 6th 1996. I suppose you could say that he has adopted Llanfair, or perhaps Llanfair has adopted him. Jason has two daughters from a previous marriage, Hayley (19) and Nicola (17), and they have grown up to be lovely young ladies. Hayley is off to Manchester University in September and Nicola is at Llandrillo College studying art. Jason is a nurse, and supports Spurs, and worse than that even, he's a Cockney! Regardless of all that we're very proud to have him as a son-in-law. He is a good man! After Megan their second child was born Lorraine went on to train as a mental health nurse. "Do it while we can help with the children," is what Em told her at the time. The three years training went quickly for Lorraine. She now works as a nurse in the community.

Nicola and Hayley 2006 (Jason's girls).

Our beautiful daughter Karen was born on November 15th 1967 in Glan Ffrwd in that very same room that had housed the old motorbike. Karen was in a hurry to come into this old world: I was in labour for only a few hours with her. She was born in the early hours of the morning and weighed 8lb 4oz she was fair skinned with quite dark hair and once again we had a lovely baby girl. I was so high on gas and air that I felt as if I was up on the ceiling looking down at myself in bed. Mam shouted up to Em, who was upstairs: *Mae gennyt ferch arall Em, tyrd i lawr* – you've another daughter Em, come down! He was down like a shot. Nurse Moody, a midwife from Penmaenmawr, was with me at the time, and told Em to get rid of the afterbirth. He was so excited and nervous he said: "Can I give it to the dog?" "Don't you dare, go and burn it in the garden," she answered. How could we have been so lucky Karen was every bit as good a baby as her sister and we had very few sleepless nights with either of them.

Karen and me on the beach in 1968.

Karen has a carrycot to thank for her name. It was a second-hand cot that Em had bought from a mate at work for 10/- (50p). Karen was only a couple of days old when Em was settling her down for the night. She was so nosy – she picked her little head up and strained her neck to look at the back of the cot, which had Karrycot, the make, written on it. "Karen" came into Em's head and that was it, our beautiful daughter Karen Elis was here. Our family was complete. I had always wanted two girls. With only fifteen months between our girls there was always loads of washing and ironing so I was kept very busy.

When we decided to buy Bryn Glas Karen hadn't been christened so I asked Mr Emlyn Williams the preacher at Bethel and a friend and neighbor of my parents if he would baptize Karen at Glan Ffrwd before we moved house. It was a lovely service and so special to have her christened in the house where she was born.

I was talking to Mrs Williams recently and she told me a story about her late husband. Mr Williams was going home past the Llanfair Arms one evening, having been out on some ministerial work. My father was walking rather unsteadily across the bridge towards him, looking the worse for drink. They stopped for a chat, and Dad told Mr Williams that he was off to kill his brother. After a bit of gentle persuasion, Mr Williams caught hold of my Dad's arm and led him home. *Nos da Mr Williams a diolch yn fawr am y cyngor*, said Dad as he went in – goodnight, and thanks for the advice! There were many such incidents as this, far too many to put on paper.

Em was working nights in Home Loaf so Sunday was our family day and was very important to us. It was a day that we tried to keep for our girls and ourselves. Karen bach as I call her (she doesn't like it) was as perfect a child as you could wish for. She always did as she was told, and she wasn't one to go out a lot. Karen was a home bird and would enjoy cooking and cleaning; she spent a lot of time helping me around the house.

She was always Daddy's girl and loved to follow Em around the garden. One year, when Karen was around 5 years old, we had a bonfire in Bryn Glas and Em was lighting the fireworks. Karen screamed her head off – not because she was scared of fireworks, but because she feared her Dad would get hurt!

Our girls wanted a budgie so we went out and bought them one. All was well until we let it out for a little fly around the front room. Karen ran to a corner and she screamed and screamed until Em caught it and put it back in its cage. We had to get rid of it; she wouldn't go into the same room as it again. My sister Val or Dad used to baby-sit for us sometimes and how the girls looked forward to those nights – there would be sweets galore! Like her sister, Karen went to Pant y Rhedyn and then on to Tryfan. There was a little cafe at that time on the way up to Aber Falls and Karen used to work there during the school holidays. She and her friend Ruth would be dressed as Welsh Ladies serving teas.

Em went to Hotpoint to work in the early 1970's owing to one of the many one-day strikes he would always clean our gas oven (I hated the job); making sure the girls did their share of housework too, he would tell them to "do your bedrooms before you go out to play." Karen would do as she was told with no bother but there was always an argument from Lorraine. On school holidays I would take the girls up to Mam's before I went to work, and how they loved it there. Karen would jump into bed with Mam and snuggle up to her, calling her "my beautiful Nain." Lorraine made a beeline for the black and white TV. I remember one occasion Karen wanted to wash her doll's clothes and Dad made her a little string line to hang them on. "But Taid," said Karen, "there's no wind to dry them." "Don't worry del," said my father, "I will sort it for you now." Dad went to get the vacuum and put the pipe on blow. Lo

Karen 2003.

and behold, a great wind came along! Karen was delighted; she remembers it to this day. Another of her memories of Nain and Taid's house is that she made her first-ever cup of tea there, in response to a request from Taid, "Make me a cuppa, del."

She married Ian on June 6th 1987 and they were divorced in 1995. Taidi Roberts was taken ill the day before the wedding and was taken to hospital. He died suddenly of a heart attack, two days after the wedding. Poor Taidi Roberts died as he lived, very quietly. When her boys were old enough Karen went to Bryn y Neuadd to nurse people with learning disabilities; she started her nurse's training in 2004 and passed her first year exams with flying colours. A few of her friends are doing the same course, so they all support each other. A three year course will not be easy, but I know she'll do well.

Our Grandchildren

Karen and Ian's first son, Paul Emrys Davies, was born on September 29th 1988; he will be 18 this year. He was our first grandchild, and we were so thrilled. I can't understand where all the years have gone. He left school last summer and started at Llandrillo College, doing a course in Public Service. He is a pleasant, quiet, no-nonsense young man who loves to play football and golf. His teachers always commented on his infectious, hearty laugh. Paul completed his life-saving courses in swimming by the age of thirteen. A local paper round earned him pocket money from when he was thirteen and he did that for nearly three years. "Thank God I've finished it Nain," he said last year, as he gave us a thank-you card for helping him sometimes. He moved on to work with our cousin Alex, roofing for the summer. Then he had a summer job with his friend Jay, working in a confectionery factory in Llandudno. Paul told his mam recently that Sion and Megan are more like his brother and sister than his cousins.

Paul, aged 16. *Aron, aged 14.*

Aron Ian Davies their youngest son, was born on November 17th 1991. Coming up fifteen, Aron is a lovable, lively young lad, who goes to Friars School in Bangor, as did his brother Paul. Aron is also into his football and golf. He and Paul play football for their local team. He loves to swim and he gained his gold badge when he was ten years old. "It's good to encourage them in all sorts of activities," Karen says. Like their father, both boys are big, big supporters of MUFC. However, I think they do have a little soft spot for Bolton Wanderers! Aron is a great fan of the old TV programme *Only Fools and Horses* and he can act Del Boy to a tee. He and Sion entertained all the family last Christmas with a sketch; we were all in our doubles. Em was speaking to one of his teachers recently and her words for Aron were: "He is a lovely lad." How nice to hear something like that about your grandson.

Lorraine and Jason's son, Sion Elis Devereux, was born on April 20th 1995 and goes to Pant y Rhedyn School; he will be moving up to Friars this year. As well as being cousins, he and Aron are best friends. Sion is a quiet, thoughtful little lad who will do anything for you. He loves to play football and as well as playing for Llanfair under tens (his Dad, Jason is the manager) he also plays for the Bangor Academy. We were at Aberystwyth last summer and had a brilliant day watching the Academy team play in the Ian Rush Tournament. Bangor did really well, winning five out of six games. Sion scored five goals. There's only thing wrong with Sion – he supports Spurs!

Sion, aged 10. *Megan, aged 7.*

Jason injured his knee recently playing football, and was in a lot of pain, so he strapped it up. We all told him he was too old for football, but would he listen? Anyway, a black cat crossed their paths when he and Sion were coming out of the car, so they were both allowed a wish. Jason made his wish and then asked Sion if he had wished to be a professional footballer when he grew up. "Oh no," said Sion bach, "I wished your knee would get better Dad." How thoughtful was that then!

Born on December 14th 1998, Megan Ellen Water Devereux, the baby of the family, is a lovely bubbly little girl. Seven years old, going on seventy! She was named after her two great-grandmothers and great-great-grandfather. What a treat – a little girl! Megan wants to do everything the boys do and she certainly likes to be the boss! She is as bright as a button and runs rings around us all. She loves to play with her dolls; she's a proper little mother – at just seven years old! She and her little friend spend many happy hours playing house together with their dolls. Megs (as we call her) moves up to Pant y Rhedyn School this year. She always has a pencil and paper in her hand. I think she's going to be a writer!

I couldn't begin to tell you how much pleasure Em and I have had from our grandchildren, and how proud we are of them. Em has especially enjoyed and encouraged our grandsons in their love of football, taking every opportunity to watch them play, and taking them to stadiums like Wembley and the Millennium Stadium at Cardiff. Em's first love, of course, is his beloved Bolton Wanderers and the Reebok.

I always say that you have a little more time to spend with your grandchildren, and a little more money to spend on them, than you ever did with your own kids. We have been so lucky to have them all living close by. It has been such an honour and a privilege to watch them grow and develop. Hopefully, if we are very lucky, we will be able to see them all reach adulthood. "The children," my dear old Dad used to say, "are what life is all about." How proud Em's parents and my own would be of their grandchildren and great-grandchildren. It's one of the great sadnesses of my life that our parents never knew our grandchildren.

All in all, I feel that I've lived a charmed life. I was born to loving parents whom I adored, in a village I love. I have a loving sister, Val. Being brought up within my wonderful extended family gave me such a feeling of warmth, love and belonging, and that was worth far more than any treasure you could buy.

I was to be even more fortunate – I found my dear husband Emrys. Em had two back operations in Walton Hospital when he was in his forties; over the years he has suffered a great deal of trouble with his back, but despite all that we've had a good life together and I wouldn't change him for the world (but please don't tell him I said so!).

We have two lovely, healthy daughters whom we are immensely proud of and a son-in-law who is second to none. Our four grandchildren: Paul, Aron, Sion and Megan, and two step-granddaughters, Hayley and Nicola, have been the icing on the cake, so to speak.

I am coming to the end of my work and I have no idea how to finish it, or even if I want to finish it. I will miss the writing. I feel that I have got to know my ancestors personally and I will miss them all. I have shed many, many tears through it all; I have been able to sit in my little computer room and 'speak' to my parents and grandparents, and feel as if they were really here with me. It has brought so many of my family, some of them long gone, back to me. My dear Mother and Father, I know, would be proud of me and so pleased that I have been able to write down what I know about our family.

I have written lots about my Dad, Owen Water (Now) – some of it not always to his credit, but life is not always a bed of roses. Dad used to say: "Always have the courage of your convictions, Margiad." So, when I decided to write all this, I felt I had to tell it as it was, good or bad. This has been a great feat for me, one that I have enjoyed immensely. I have met so many interesting people, young and old, all with a tale to tell. I hope I have been able to tell my story with integrity, honesty, and sensitivity. Most of all I hope that you have enjoyed reading it as much as I have enjoyed writing it. I started this as a record of our family, for our family, in the hope that they will never forget where they came from. Then, one day, our daughters Lorraine and Karen took it home to read and spent a couple of hours crying their way through it. "Mam, you must try and get it published," is what they said after reading it. So despite being really nervous about it all, I am going to do just that. Years from now, when I am long gone, I hope that other members of our family will take up where I have left off; maybe they will enjoy reading a little about their ancestors who have gone before.

I will finish with a Welsh verse that Lorraine wrote and read – through her tears, on the day of her wedding. I am going to give the English translation first.

Longing

How we long for the ones that once were.

How we long for their presence here today:

Their voices and laughter; today they would rejoice

To see their children, their warmth and happiness.

Today they would be proud.

Hiraeth

Hiraeth am y rhai a fu.

Hiraeth am eu presenoldeb hwy heddiw:

Eu lleisiau, eu chwerthin hwy.

Heddiw mi fyddent yn llawenu

I weld y plant:

Eu cynhesrwydd a'u hapusrwydd –

Heddiw mi fyddent yn falch.

Village School late 1950's. Elizabeth, Avril, Laurence, Miss W. Hughes (Mrs Parry), David.

Front row: Margaret, Emrys, Brenda, Michel, Elwyn. Second row: John, Gwylfa, Margaret, Rhiannon. Backgroup not sure of and miss Morgan.

255

Front desk L to R: Janice, John, Margaret. Second row: ?, Patsy, David, Brian, ?, John and Gwylfa. Back row Miss Morgan, headmistress (Mrs Granger Smith).

Pen y Bryn Football team, early 1970's. Left to right - backrow: Chris, Alan, Gwyn, Mike, Meirig, Embo. Front row: Kevin, Peter, Roy, Sonny, Malcolm, Gwylim.

Llanfairfechan boxing club 1961. Vince, Dafydd ap, Ade (Bach), Alwyn, Embo, Elwyn and their trainer Dereck.

*Boxing club. Back row left to right - Adrin, Dafydd Ap, Embo, Hugh, Aelwyn, David.
Middle row: Alwyn, Elwyn (post), Derek, Vince.
Front row: Trevor, Robert (Fredrick), Peter, John, Spud, Gareth, Jake.*

Darts night Castle Hotel early 1960's. Amongst them is John Water (grandson of John Water of the flood), Twm (Penbryn), his wife Loui and son Glyn. Bobby Gregson, Leslie Griffiths, John (Tyn Llwyfan).

Llanfair quarry men early 1950's. Back row left to right: Joe Williams, Quil Owen, Carl, ?, ?, Mr Bailey. Middle: Will Tyddyn Angharad. Front row: Bob (Cabaidd), Teddy Ferins, Will (Tyddyn Rhonwyn), Harry (Bangor junior), Idris Dafydd Lloyd.

Pant y Rhedyn School 1949-1950. Top row: Wynn, Cemlyn, Margaret Coopre, Myfanwy, Gwyneth Jones, ?, Brian Burns. Middle: Miss Parry, Rhoda Williams, ?, ?, Doris Jones, ?, ?, Hilary Fisher, Miss Jones (form 1). Front row: ?, Gwynfor Williams, Lesley Griffiths, Glyn Taylor.

Village School early 1950's. Back row left to right: Trevor, David Jones, Richard Vaughn, Francis Travers, Michel Thomas, Barry Simpson, ?. Middle row: Anthony Williams, Michel Hughes, auline, Jean Roberts, Pauline Hughes, Edward Twisaday, Trevor Owen. Front row: June Jones, Carol, Sandra Owen, ?, Gwyneth, Angela Evans.

Coronation party in Valley Road, 1953. Val and I are amongst the children.

Pant y Rhedyn School late 1950's. Back row left to right: Peter Williams, Alan Hughes, Aelwyn Roberts, Raymond Roberts, Rodney. Middle row: Noel Gregson, Gwynfor, ?, Annette, Menai, ?, Miss Jones (form 1) and Ken Jones. Front row: Ann Hughes, Gwen Jones, Gwen Hughes, Marjorie, ?, ?.

The Virginia Inn at the time of Prince Charles Investiture 1969.
Left to right: Ivan, Arthur Bailey, Will Tŷ Rhonwy, ?, ?, Llew Owen.

Mr Jones and Auntie Kate, the couple ran Nant y Coed tea gardens for many years.

Village bridge day of the fair 1959-60, Owie and his brother, Cyril, Jo, John Henry, Victor and Ivan Bach a Mina.

Pen y Bryn Darts night out in 1979. Back row second from left Deio, Spud, ?, Ken, Peter, Embo and Kevin. Front row left to right - Eddie, Nigel, Mike, Laurence, Arthur and Gerald.

The annual boxing day walk of Llanfair men 2002.

Motor cycle exhibition in the Town Hall in 1977.
Left to right: Gwyn, Gwyn (Always), Gareth, Bruno, Gwyn, Aled, Derek and Vince.

Gladys, Freda, me, Ned and Howard, c. 1980.

Left to right: Alma, Doris, Elfed (bach), Laura, Clifford, Mavis, Gwynfor. Front row: Elfed, Less, Irwell, c. 1990.

Left to right: Embo, Beaver, Noel and Merfyn, 2005.

Carnival float in the 1950's. The ladies dressed in Llanfair Town FC strip. Back row left to right: Maureen, ?, referee in the mask was Mrs. Lewis. ?, Gladys (Gregson) and Mair Morgan. Front row: Olwen Roberts, her son Mike, Betty (Murry), Eileen, Gareth (taxi), Olwen (Williams). My cousin, Laura and Gwyneth (post).

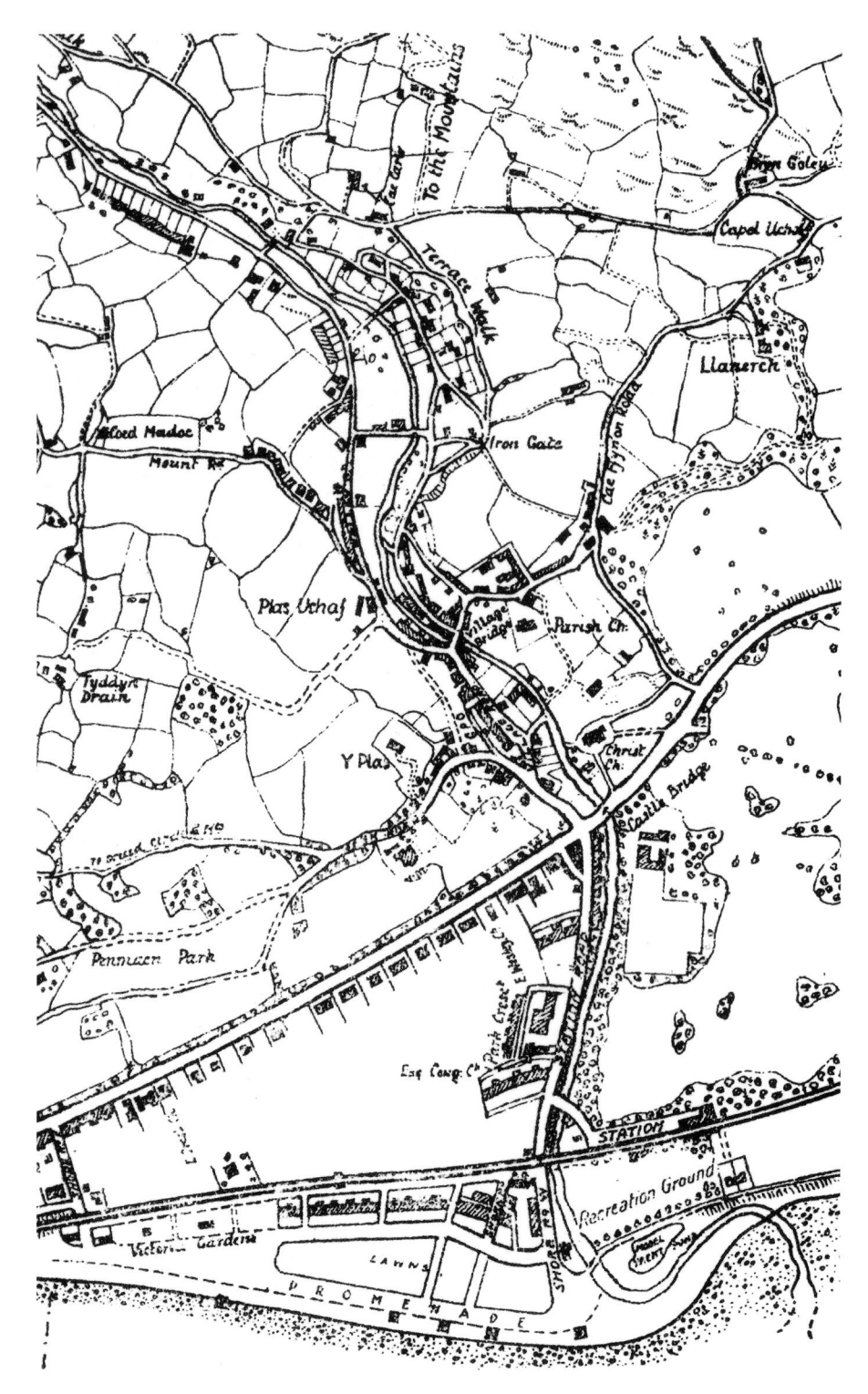

Map of Llanfairfechan c. 1900.

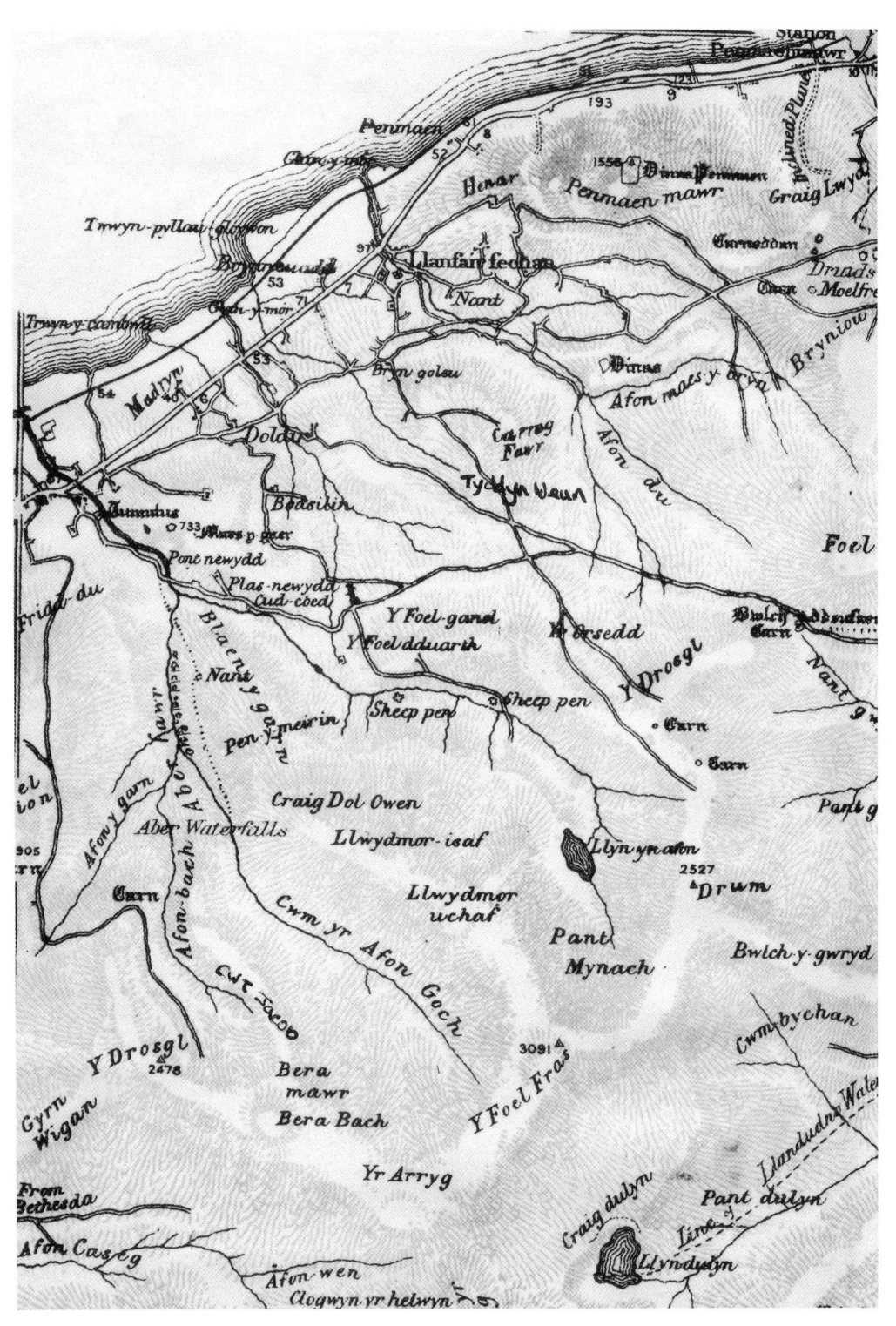

Map of area c. 1900.

Notes

Note 1: St Seiriol Gwyn, born in the late fifth century, retired to what the Vikings called Priestholm, known today as Puffin Island. St Seiriol set up a small community there and spent his old age on the island. St Seiriol and his cousin King Maelgwyn Gwynedd – a ruler in North Wales at the time – are both said to be buried there.

Note 2: My great Aunt Lizzie and her first husband Dafydd John (on my mother's side) lived in number 1 Capel Ucha in the 1930's; Dafydd and their son died there. The houses were inhabited until the 1950's but are now derelict. Capel Uchaf is in the process of being renovated as I write.

Note 3: The Jones family (Maggie Black Lion, my mother's family) lived in Pen Penmaen in the early 1920's – "Which was handy," said Dilys Eames (Maggie's daughter), "as my dad Sion worked at the quarry in those days and didn't have far to walk."

Note 4: Robert Roberts (1) (1776 - 1872) my GGGG Grandfather, married in 1806 to Jane Hughes 1776 - 1863 (my GGGG Grandmother). At the time of his marriage Robert (1) lived in Pen-y-Comins. His wife, Jane, lived in Tan Rallt. Pen-y-Comins (Comins Isa) and Y Comins were two crofts quite close to the sea, in the grounds of what we know today as Bryn y Neuadd. Close to Comins was a small farm of about 30 acres called Wern Bach; Owen Morris and his family lived there in 1841. It was near where our railway station stands today.

Note 5: Hugh Roberts 1793 - 1869 and Elizabeth Williams 1794 - 1873 (my GGGG Uncle and Auntie). According to the parish register 'Hugh bach teiliwr' was christened on 9/6/1793; he was the son of Robert Roberts (1) Ty Coch Y Comins by his wife Jane. The parish register tells us that Robert (1) and Jane were married in 1806. There seems to be a discrepancy with dates here. At the time of his marriage on 19/2/1814 to Elizabeth Williams, Hugh lived in Nant. There were a few Nants in the village, so who knows which one it was! Elizabeth was the daughter of Elias Williams and Ann Hughes of Plas. Their first two children: Grace, born circa 1814, and Mathias, 1816 - 1846, were born at Plas. Ann Hughes, their third child, was born at Bryn Meirion in 1820. This property was also known as Erw Fair/Feirion (Cemetery House). The children of Hugh and Elizabeth Roberts were:

Richard 1823 - 1903.

Catherine 1829 - ?, born Erw Feirion, christened 29/7/1829.

William 1829 - 1831, born Erw Feirion, christened 31/8/1829. William died in infancy and is buried with his maternal grandparents, Elias Williams and Ann Hughes (previously of Plas) in St Mary's.

Margaret 1831 - ?, born Erw Feirion, christened 16/9/1831.

William 1835 - 1904, born in Bryn Meirion, christened 5/7/1835. As well as being a tailor, William was a rate collector for the Parish Vestry, and was a well respected member of the community.

Elizabeth 1839 - 1918, lived with her parents until they died, and then with her brothers; ran the tailoring and drapery business later on when they moved to Meirion House (the old post office) where they let furnished apartments to tourists. Elizabeth was the housekeeper. Living with them was a servant, Mary Williams, aged 17; it was customary for girls to start their working lives as live-in servants (Welsh=gweini). Elizabeth is buried with her brother William in St Mary's cemetery.

Grace 14/5/1814 - ?, born in Plas. Grace had a son in 1837 called Hugh. She was living with her parents at Erw Feiriol at the time of the birth. There is no father named in the parish christening records.

Ann Hughes 1820 - ? (named after her maternal grandmother). Born at Bryn Meirion, christened 29/10/1820.

Robert 1821 - 1885; worked as Mr Luck's ora man (jack of all trades) and lived at Plas Newydd. He eventually settled in Menai Bridge. Robert died December 10th 1885 aged 66 and was buried with his parents Hugh and Elizabeth and brother in St Mary's Llanfairfechan.

Note 6: Robert Roberts (2) 1806 - 1899, my GGG Grandfather (teiliwr). Robert 2 was born in Comins or Corn Coch. I have yet to find out where Corn Coch was. It seems there were two Comins in the village at that time. It probably meant common land. It seems that Robert (2) spent most of his life in Ty Coch Comins Nant-y-Felin.

Robert and Ellen's children:

William (1) was the first born, in Tyddyn Drain in 1831. William died aged 1 year.

Jane, born in Groesffordd (near Erw Feiriol cemetery) in 1833, died when she was 5 years old. William (1) and Jane are buried together at St Mary's.

William (2), named after his brother, was born in Clwt y Groesffordd in 1835. He was also a tailor by trade. I don't know much about William. He died on 16/2/1915 aged 79 and is buried with his sister Jane (my GG grandmother) and her family in Erw Feiriol cemetery.

Robert (3) 1838 - 8/1/1850.

Jane (my GG grandmother) was born in Ystryd y Rhedyn in 1841.

Mathias 1844 - 8/1/1850.

John 1847 - 8/1/1850.

Mary 1850 - 1897.

Elin 1852 - 21/9/1858.

Robert (4) 1854 - 10/11/1855.

Note 7: Thomas Roberts 1882 - 1966. Twm teiliwr, nephew of Robert (2). Any information I have on Twm is thanks to his granddaughter Joan, whom I went to school with. I hadn't seen Joan for forty years. Someone gave me her phone number; I took a chance and gave her a ring. After explaining why I'd phoned, Joan said: "I've got too many photos to send; I'll bring them to you." How very kind of her. Joan lives in Runcorn, and she was due to take some flowers to her parents' grave so she called here and we spent a nostalgic couple of hours going through her family album.

There was speculation about Twm teiliwr's parentage. There could have been any number of reasons why Twm was living with his Uncle Robert in 1891. It was certainly thought in the village that John Water and he were brothers. Twm was a quarry worker and married Ellen Jones. She was a member of the Henar family. They lived in Glen Thorn, Nant y Felin, for many years and had three sons and a daughter, Annellin (Joan's mother). Two of his sons were policemen. John Water (Twm's brother) died in 1904, shortly after he named one of his sons after John. I have been in touch with Twm's other granddaughter Glenys, from Leeds; I hope she'll look for more information. I have found out that Twm teiliwr was probably a cousin to John Water and not his brother, as some believed. No-one seems to know properly how they were related. Twm is buried at Erw Feiriol with his wife Ellen, who died in 1961 aged 79, and their son Thomas who died in 1984 aged 71.

Note 8: Jane Roberts (1839 - 1929) my GG Grandmother (mother of John Water). Jane (one of the teilwriaid) was born in Ystryd y Rhedyn, the daughter of Robert 2 and Ellin. The fifth child of ten, she was christened in 1840. Nothing is known about Jane's early life. It seems that Jane, Mary and their brother William were the only three of Robert and Ellin's children who survived to adulthood.

John Roberts (1839 - 1927) my GG Grandfather and father of John Water belonged to another branch of the family.

John was born on 15/6/1839 in Pentraeth, Anglesey. Son of Robert and Ellen Roberts. His mother Ellen's maiden name was Evans. John's father was a mariner when John junior was born. However, he was a weaver at the time of his son John's wedding and his name on his son's marriage certificate is not John but Robert. In those days it was quite common to get names and dates slightly mixed up, I'm told. John and Jane lived with her parents in Nant y Felin when they first got married. They had their first child Robert (5) in 1864, William in 1867, Mary in 1870, John Water (my G grandfather) in 1874, Jane in 1875, Grace in 1879, Richard in 1881, Thomas in 1882, and Margaret in 1886. There were nine children in all. John was a quarryman. In 1881 John and Jane lived in Llwyn Onn with six of their children. By 1891 they had moved yet again to Nant y Felin with their children. In 1901 they lived in 1 Nant y Felin Terrace. Some time between this and 1904 they were to move to Bryn Meirion. John died in Bryn Meirion in 1927 aged 88 years. Jane died two years later aged 87.

Note 9: William and Elizabeth Roberts' children were Nellie, John (Helen Slack's taid), David Richard (Uncle Dai), Kitchener, Kitty and William. William (Bill Skerries grandson). went to America as a young man, working his way around. Their son William (17/6/1893 - 2/11/1946) fought in the First World War in the American army and became a Naturalized American Citizen in 1918. He came back to Wales after the War and married Ginny Tan Graig. They had two daughters: Betty, who died when she was a child, and Jean (Bach Duda), who emigrated with her mother to America after her father William died. Jean (Bach) has two children, Elizabeth and William. She also has two grandsons, Billy and Steven (thank goodness for a new name). Jean and her partner Ray were in Llanfair on holiday in May 2004. It was the first time we had met them and through Jean we met a few more of the tailor clan from Bangor. So many people, all coming from a little Welsh village. Uncle Elfed (Mam's brother) remembers the family living in Llwyn Celyn with their children. My maternal grandparents and their children lived in Llwyn Ysgaw just across the road from them. Uncle El remembers William (Jean's dad) as being "a very pleasant, fun-loving man, a typical teiliwr." That must have been in the 1930's. I have had some good pictures sent by e-mail from Jean. One of the photos shows a wedding outside the Llanfair Arms in 1922, between one the Roberts family (tailors) and a Quinn. The Quinns ran the Llanfair Arms at that time. Mrs Hugh Lloyd Jones, who was only a child at the time, remembers that the bride wore a lovely cream dress with forget-me-nots on it. The Llanfair Arms, incidentally, was built in 1863 by Mr Hugh Davies for the grand sum of £163!

Note 10: Grace Fawr and John Water had their first child in 1892 - a daughter, Mary Jane. Then came Owen, then my Nain, Grace Bach, then there was Rossie, followed by Hannah, then Maggie, then John (who died) and lastly Annie Waters. All these were Great Aunties and a Great Uncle to me, and I remember them all except Auntie Hannah who went to Australia. Auntie Mary Jane died when I was only 5 years old, so I only have very faint memories of her - or do I just remember being told about her? I was with Blodwen recently and she said that her mother Rossie - John Waters and Grace Fawr's fourth child - was born on a cold November's day and was named Rose because there was a single rose left blooming in the garden.

Note 11: Buried with John Water in 1903, aged 3 weeks, is his son, also called John. Also two of his granddaughters, Hannah Thomas aged 10 months, and Pearl White aged 2 years, and his great-grandson, Ned and Gladys's son, Edward Wyn Thomas, who died in 1951 aged 3 weeks.

Note 12: Auntie Mary Jane married Robert (Robin Llys). Robin had worked at Llys y Gwynt farm at one time. They had five daughters and three sons. One of the sons was named after his grandfather, John Water. I remember John very well and I always thought he looked like my Dad. John died of a heart attack when he was quite a young man. The boys are all dead now; only Auntie Gracie and Eirlys are left. Gwen, one of the girls, died on 27/12/03 aged 69 - a nice lady. Em and I went to the funeral - lots of family and friends were there. Two of her children spoke of their love for their Mam and her unselfishness, forever giving love to the three of them – a love that most mothers possess, I suppose. They were so brave, being able to stand up and talk to us about Gwen. None of Auntie Mary's children wandered very far from Llanfair.

Note 13: Alexander (Taid Thomas's grandfather): on the 1871 census he was down as born in St Asaph and his age was 32. He lived with his wife Jane, also 32. She was born in Llanerchymedd. Living with them were their daughters Margaret aged 12, Marri 10, Mary 4 (my G grandmother) and their sons John 6, and Richard 2. The census of 1891 showed us that Alex, aged 58, born in Bangor, and his wife Jane, aged 56, still lived in Kyffin Square with their daughter Mary aged 22 who wasn't married and their son Robert aged 12. They occupied 3 rooms in 43 Kyffin Square. The records state that Alex died in 1916 aged 89 and is buried with his wife Jane who died in 1910 aged 72. Robert their son died in 1906 aged 27. Their daughter Mary – my G grandmother – was buried with them in 1928 aged 59. She died of "fatty heart, bronchitis and heart failure". Her son (Taid Thomas) registered her death. He lived in 2 Pant y Carw, Nant y Felin, at the time.

Note 14: (another branch) William Thomas (1) born in 1813. William, Taid Thomas's GG grandfather, lived with his wife Mary, born the same year. In the 1841 census they lived at "Back of Bank Buildings" in Caernarfon with their three children Elinor, Mary and Margaret. His occupation was down as a smith. My father remembered a story about a blacksmith in the family. Now I know where they came from.

Edward Thomas Taid Thomas's G Grandfather was born in Caernarfon in 1840. He was a blacksmith. He married Ellen, born in Llangefni, in 1835; they had two children that I could find: William born in Caernarfon in 1863 (G Grandfather) and Ellen born in Llanrwst in 1875.

William (2) Thomas 1863 - 1943 (Taid Thomas's father) was born in Caernarfon. In the 1881 census he was down as a stonemason's labourer aged 17. He lived in Scotland Road in Llanrwst with his parents Edward and Ellen.

William is buried with his son Will, daughter-in-law (Grace Bach), and their son Uncle Bob in Erw Feiriol in Llanfair.

Note 15: Fred's letter see diary May 5th 2003.

Note 16: I don't remember much about Nain Thomas's funeral. One thing does stand out in my memory though. After we buried Nain in Erw Feiriol, I remember Annwen P Hughes coming up to my Dad outside the cemetery gates, giving him a hug, and with tears in her eyes saying: Mae'n ddrwg iawn gennyf am eich colled Mr Thomas – I'm very sorry for your loss, Mr Thomas. My Dad wasn't a person to show his feelings, but that day he broke down and cried. Poor Dad, I have a tear in my eye thinking about him. Annwen was a good friend – we were in school together and she was a great character. In our younger days she used to call my Mam her second mother. Annwen lost her own mother (Grace Price) when she was a young girl. Annwen died in early 1994 aged 47; it was so tragic. I still think of her as a girl, she was so full of life and laughter.

Note 17: How in the world my Dad ever kept quiet about another child I'll never know. I sat down with Dad so many times and talked about life, especially after he'd had a few drinks; he really couldn't keep his mouth shut. What a massive thing in one's life, if it's true – to have a half brother or sister on the other side of the world and not know them. Auntie Freda said Dad wouldn't speak to her about it, even though she'd helped him with the divorce. Who knows what the future will bring. Perhaps one day I will find out.

Note 18: Census population in Llanfair.

1801 – 470
1811 – 472
1821 – 508
1831 – 653
1841 – 749
1851 – 809
1861 – 1,199
1871 – 1,612
1881 – 2,041
1891 – 2,409
1901 – 2,769
1911 – 2,973
1921 – 3,639
1931 – 3,162
1951 – 3,183
1961 – 2,869
1971 – 3,440
1981 – 3,435
1991 – 3,741
2001 – 3,755

No census was taken in 1941 owing to the war. In 1981 there was a change in the way census names were collected. Previously the count included visitors who were staying in the village at the time. From 1981 onwards only the usual residents were counted.

Note 19: Great Uncle Will's money was shared but by that time Nain had died so Nain's share went between her children: Val and I had Mam's share. Whether he left a will or whether his worldly possessions went unconditionally to his next of kin, I don't know. Uncle Evan was in touch with the hospital when his brother died and offered to pay for the funeral but they said that the British Legion was sorting it out. I have managed to trace his grave to Forest Home Cemetery, Ponoka, and he was interred on October 15th 1987. The Reverend Don Miller took the service. There was no list of surviving relatives.

Note 20: Auntie Matt had two sons, Irwel and Les, and three daughters – Doris, Laura and Mavis. Laura came to Tan Bonc quite a lot when we were kids and Mavis (a little younger than me) used to stay the night occasionally. When Auntie Matt married Uncle Dick they lived for a while in Well St in Rachub, next door to her sister Laura Jane. Irwel was born there. I only remember Auntie Matt ever living in 11 Nant y Berllan. When we were kids we would call on Auntie Matt very often with Mam; there was always a *bechdan jam* and a warm welcome for us. Auntie Matt suffered for as long as I can remember with what was known as White Leg and Thromboses in her leg. Poor Auntie Matt had an open wound on her shin that just wouldn't heal; it was constantly in need of dressing and needed a great deal of care. Uncle Dick died in 1955, a few weeks before Doris's wedding; it was a terrible time for the family. Auntie Matt spent the last years of her life with her daughter Doris and would go to one of the other children sometimes for a break. Auntie Matt died in Manchester (where Doris lives) in 1991 and is buried with her husband Dick in Rhandir Hedd. The family remains quite close despite being a little spread out. Aron our grandson came home from swimming lessons recently and said he had a new friend, Levi – Mavis's grandson; amazingly, among all those kids in the pool, five of them were related and didn't even know it!

Note 21: I have spoken to someone at the archives in Llandudno and there's a possibility that they have got some records from Conwy Hospital – or the workhouse as it was known then. I don't know where John Thomas was buried, although Uncle El seems to think that Taid came back from South Wales to the funeral. We have failed to find his grave in the records of Pen and Conwy; I hope to do some more research into this. We have also failed to find any information on him from Conwy Hospital; it seems that some of the records were lost. I find it very sad that my Taid's brother is buried somewhere and we don't know where. We will keep looking.

Note 22: It worked out very well, Nain living in Auntie Alma's, though I'm sure it wasn't easy for Auntie Al at times. We cleared Nain's house. It was easier for me to sort out her things, being the closest. I put bits and bobs into boxes for her children. The family took what they wanted and what was left the council took away. Uncle Elfed handled the sale of the house: a lady from Lawr Tai bought it for around £11,000. Nain's money was shared between her children. I had Mam's share and dished Val her half when she needed it. It was the end of our association with 19 Mona Terrace. How I missed going there. Every week Em and I went to visit Nain Colwyn Bay, picking up Uncle Elfed on the way and calling to see Uncle Harry and Auntie Mill in Conwy. Dear me, we did have some fun.

Notes from my diary while writing this book

January 20th 2003: Em and I went to Llangefni archives today and were lucky to find some additional information on Robert and Ellen (Pentraeth). They lived in Tan-y-Graig in 1851; Robert was now a weaver in wool. He was born in Llanllechid. Nothing else is known about John's family from Anglesey as yet. We went to Anglesey and found Tan y Graig; it is has been a holiday complex for many years.

March 21st 2003: My 57th birthday. Paul our grandson has gone to France with school. They went on the 19th and he'll home on Sunday night. We'll be glad to see him home safe and sound. The war in Iraq is into its third day; it's really getting bombed tonight. God help them all. How many people will be killed before the war is over? I cannot imagine how the families of all those thousands of soldiers are feeling tonight, and every other night until it's all over. There were 12 soldiers killed today in a helicopter accident, four Americans and eight Brits. How are the families of the Iraqis coping, the little children who'll be maimed and scared to death of it all? How many children will be left without their dad? Is the war really necessary? I think not – I'm sure it can't be worth all the heartache and misery it'll cause to so many thousands. We can only hope and pray that it will be all over quickly.

April 20th 2003: Sion bach is eight years old today. Ten of us went to watch Bolton v West Ham yesterday at the Reebok. Bolton won by one goal to nil. Sion's friend Matthew came as Sion's guest. It was a brilliant game; the boys had a great day. Megan was a good girl and sat with her parents all through. We all went to the market first and had dinner at MacDonalds. There was only one thing wrong. We were all frozen stiff. We were sitting high in the stands and the wind was swirling around us. Poor Paul went without his coat and to top it all he had toothache. The cost of tickets, between us all, would you believe it, was £215. What an expensive day out! I would say that between us all, with food and petrol, there wasn't much change from £300.

The war in Iraq is over now, although I think it will take the Iraqis many, many years to get back to anything like normality.

May 5th 2003: Fred Parry sent us a moving letter from hospital in Liverpool, adding that if he came home perhaps we should give it back to him. He called it the The diary of a brain-op patient.

Here is an abridged version of his letter:

Dear Margaret and Embo,

It's now 1.15 in the morning of the last day of April. I recall at some time in March being on the phone with my brother, chatting about a clue in the Sunday Telegraph's easy little crossword: "----- is the cruellest month". Ted said he thought the answer was March but I said no – it's April – a line from a poem by TS Eliot. And so it was. Beware, this letter may drag on and on and my handwriting may deteriorate. The best therapy for me these past days has been to write whatever comes into my head, and also to phone Jo at the Virginia for a little bet on the horses. Mostly I am losing, but it does help for me to have a purpose, looking for the racing results in the evening, on the bedside TV/phone set. When you get to understand them, these sets over the bed are an absolute boon. They can be on at any time of the day or night. I have a feeling that the phone facility is mysteriously switched off somewhere in the depths of the technological dungeons in the wee small hours of the morning to save families at home from being moidering down the phone at all hours. I must get back to the beginning. Let me say that about 1am this morning I experienced perhaps the lowest moment of the whole hospitalisation. I got myself together, rang the alarm bell, and one of the night staff came in to have a chat and to reassure me about matters. And guess what? She had your card in her hand! What a lovely moment. So, Margaret and Em, you are my victims. Nothing is better than writing – for me anyway, to clear my head. And your card arrived at just the moment I needed – what a tonic! Last Thursday was a great day for me, when you all walked in.

Now I am fully aware that I have been babbling away for weeks since they delivered the 'shocks'. I can only apologise to all those who have suffered it. Even the eyes of my fellow patients in the Day Room – some in a far worse mess than I am – tend to glaze over when I start to moider. Now, thank God, I can recognize the warning signs, shut up and creep away.

Some of the cases here are bad. The TV technician, who works for the bed phone/TV company, came to see me for a friendly chat. He's about 30, a nice lad and most important, a Koppite – one of our own! Incidentally, whilst I remember, well done Bolton v Arsenal. I've never known such a season atop or bottom of the Premiership for tight finishes! I ask myself – are these results a fortunate accident, or is the whole bloody thing a fix?

Jamie my Koppite pal was here on Monday 28th April for a little chat, and happened to mention that there's a lad in Caton Ward (that's the next ward) who's been in the war in Iraq. He's been in a hell of a mess – in a tank hit by the Americans with a missile (friendly fire?) and the only one that came out alive. His mates – two or three – all got killed instantly. He has been badly hurt – head, spine, and left leg shattered hip to knee, but apparently (and thank God) only the left leg remains to be surgically finished. I felt an awful sense of pity for this poor young lad. Almost as bad for him as his own injuries, I should think, is the knowledge that his mates (and how close they must have been, in every sense of the word, living in a moving box perhaps 8 feet by 6 feet) have gone to Heaven or Hell in a blinding flash and he will never ever see them again. My God, what nightmares can develop? Perhaps with new drugs and techniques they can help him in the future. Science moves on! Both to cure us and to blast us all off the face of the earth – in the style of this bastard Bush and his bloody bombs. I am beginning to think Bush has now lost his marbles. He is a man who has got Religion, and a man who thinks he has God on his side is a real danger. We will bomb you in the name of the Good Lord!

At this point I am going to take a little break and close my eyes for a few moments. It is now 2.20am, I feel OK again. I must say sorry again for what is a long letter, with some strong emotions. I do not mean to upset you, but it is so valuable to get my jumbled thoughts down on paper and out of my crazy head. Perhaps you could keep this and let me have it when I arrive home.

Here I am again. It's now 2.55am. I've just had a long chat with one of the night staff – we had become enemies through misunderstanding – she was scared of me and I was petrified of her. It went so far as for me to see the ward sister yesterday morning, saying that if she (the night nurse) came within ten yards of me I would phone the hospital bosses and demand a security guard. It's now become clear to me that it's all down to the steroids. Since they discovered the brain tumour on 8th April I have been receiving steroid medication, first at Bangor intravenously, then changed to tablets, 4 times a day, but the 10pm issue is the one that seems to send the worse "changing" elements through the body. Now it has become clear that because they are reducing the steroids the temporary after-effects are worse. All is now clear.

Now it is almost 4am. All is quiet. I have been to the smokers' room, not to smoke – they are all gone – but for therapy to strengthen my legs and breathe the fresh air through the windows.

Yesterday morning, by the way, I went down to the coffee shop for a paper and Coke and afterwards had half an hour in an open courtyard by the fountains. A bit chilly, but I can't tell you what this meant to me. My first time outside since 1st April I, think.

Going back to April – the cruellest month. Yes, I think I agree. It was on 1st April that Dr Walker told me he suspected a mild stroke – well, he was right, that's what it was, but not a normal one – a fake set off by the tumour.

Yes, last Thursday was a great day. Apart from you two, Steve and Gwynoro, I had Helen and James here in the evening, so a busy day. So good to see you all. A visit makes a hell of a difference.

I have met a lad from Felinheli here – he's on the Caton Ward and he's been through a hell of a lot. First rushed into Ysbyty Gwynedd, then straight here (must have been bloody serious). One day here to fix whatever was wrong – could have been haemorrhage – then at 5am in the morning to Manchester (extremely bloody serious). Somehow they have saved the poor bugger's bacon but he has been here for weeks just waiting to see that everything has settled. I thought I had it bad! And he is only about mid 30's. I look into his eyes and see deep pain and anguish but still he is calm and strong as an ox. The first time we met – maybe 4 days ago – he was delighted to find someone from Wales and I was able to explain yng Nghymraeg where I was from. I think it cheered him up. He is a true Cymro – a fit bloke, no fat, jet black hair and eyes. Dwy'n practisio fy Nghymraeg efo'r boi 'ma ac mae'n helpu fi – I am practising my Welsh and this boy is helping me. What he must have been through. His wife comes almost every day – 70 miles! Stays as long as she can. Sometimes she comes in the evenings. He has nothing to do expect try to sleep, and wait, have the odd smoke, wait for his family, and so it goes on. They will not let him go until they are happy that he is free from danger.

This brings me to Friday – a quiet, if a little historic, day for me – I had the operation. I was told to get my gown on for theatre about 11am. I would be called after dinner. I thought it was a biopsy I was having (little did I know, even the German Professor of brain surgery who did the op – there, I've told you, I have met a Professor of Brain Surgery, and he has been inside my napper for a look round – even he didn't know quite what was coming). Anyway, I was in the theatre by 2pm. Quite a rigmarole, with an Egyptian anaesthetist who asked a lot of searching questions.

How many pillows do I have on the bed? Do I get breathless when laid down thus? Can I lie flat on my back motionless for an hour or more? It went on until he was satisfied. I am sedated to a certain point. All is ready. The apparatus is ready and I am relaxed and drowsy. I am happy to be making progress – this is the overriding emotion – happy to be making progress. There is no anguish, no pain. Once you accept it, an op is straightforward and helpful – it's not as bad as seeing your football team lose!

Voices now: "We are fitting your head into the clamp. You relax. Lie still. We will do everything. We will move your head. All you do is relax and listen, OK."

Another voice: "Ready now. Local anaesthetic coming up. Just a sharp sting to right above ear. Another to left ear." Pause. "What is this lump at the back of your head, has it been there long?" Me: "Sebaceous cyst, some years now." OK, two more bee stings, one left, one right – cyst and all! Now begins the real thing. I hear the drill, a long way off. Then a tapping, but it sounds like a sledgehammer. No pain, only interest. Then a voice – the Professor I think, and how I love to brag about my Professor, bloody petty snob! No bloody ordinary brain surgeons for me pal! Anyway, there are two voices murmuring: I found out later it was the Prof and his regular colleague on the team. It transpires that they have been conducting a visual microscopic biopsy as they proceed to take away the tissue, and the Prof decides to go ahead with a quick-fix, one-off, newish "cure" (I hope) which is only possible in a small percentage of cases. This consists of implanting a radioactive iodine seed in my brain. I have a card certifying this which I must keep with me. It will be removed when the job is done (I hope!). I am taking bugger all for granted from now on. Removal 31st May – I hope.

No wonder these brain surgeons (and especially Professors!) are considered top of the heap. They have to be. To have the knowledge and the bottle and the energy to turn a 1-hour biopsy job into a 5-hour full-scale operation based on an instant decision. Could I do that? No bloody way.

Job done, 1½ hours in recovery room. One man dressed in red gear and me. I am babbling away. Cannot make sense of what I am saying. He is calm: "You're OK, I can understand you." I ask him who he is and his history etc. He's about 35 to 40 I guess. "I was in the RAF for 10 years – in the Gulf War – as an aircraft engineer. I came out and had a switch of careers to health." Fair enough. Finally the hour and a half is up. We shake hands. Back to the ward, into bed, slight stings around my head (from local) but nothing else.

Peaceful night, no problems.

Saturday I am mostly alone and quiet. Just routine food, washing, nothing else. About 7pm (24 hours post op) I notice my eyes are puffing up badly, like a boxer who's been 15 rounds with Mike Tyson. Somebody comes. "I don't like this swelling," I say.

"It's nothing to worry about; it's just the pressure on the fluid inside your head, because of the slight pressure of the clamp. It's caused swelling and gravity brings it down, it will be OK."

Sunday: a visit from Helen and James. The poor girl shrieks when looking at my face; I must look bloody awful. But she soon recovers. We have a good laugh - I'm so pleased to see them. Simple little things are sorted out: laundry, I need money, and they bring the post (mainly junk). I tell them briefly what happened Friday - what a doddle it was. A happy two hours, I am able to say, don't worry about next week - I'm pretty sure to be coming home!

Monday a.m. - matron comes in. I think you can go tomorrow. With the op you had, two days is all we need to assess. Then you can come back 3rd May to remove the seed.

One hour later my Professor is here with my general support doctor. The Prof is quiet and looks at me. I rise to shake his hand. It's like that of a baby.

I asked a few questions - satisfactory answers. Then came a slight crunch. "I have a slight suspicion that the tumour we have treated is not absolutely certain to be primary, but possibly secondary, judging by the tissue." So I must have a scan - full body - this afternoon at 2.30. Back to square one, really. There is a danger that I am not out of the woods, but I am going home on Thursday come what may.

It has been a long day's journey from night to day - I mean out of my head and onto the paper. It has helped no end that I am able to release my thoughts like this - it keeps me sane. This morning I woke up at 1am - had slept like a log since 9pm mind. It was horrifying. I got out of bed thinking: "What am I? What have I become? I am inhuman, I am alien."

I have my own en suit room by the hall, room 3. It's comfortable. Embo and Margaret I ask you to be patient - keep this please and I pray none of it is upsetting to you. Please let Jason and the girls read it, to see if they find any part of it interesting to their studies. *Diary of a Brain-op Patient*. You can return it to me when I'm home. If I fail to come home through some technical hitch - keep it.

Tara rwan - goodbye now. Will phone when I get home. Fred.

Regards to all you meet who might ask about me.

PS It's been a wet two days here.

May 2003: Auntie Freda (Dad's sister) has just gone back home to Sutton Coldfield after a week's holiday with us. I think she enjoyed her stay. We saw a few people whom she'd been in school with and hadn't seen for years, so it'll be food for thought for them all. We went to see Auntie Gladys (Ned's wife) and the family. Auntie Glad doesn't look at all well although she's better than she has been. Auntie Freda has been coming to stay with us for a few years now. She is no trouble at all, we love having her. She and Em have some good laughs together and she really enjoys the banter. She is 82 years young and still looks as she did thirty years ago, although she's not able to walk very far owing to a hip replacement a few years back. Her son Derek brought her here by car and picked her up yesterday. She has another son called Glyn. He is not at all well. I'm afraid that he has a terminal illness, poor Glyn. He was telling me on the phone that they have all mucked in (Derek's two daughters as well) and refurbished Auntie Freda's bedroom while she's been here. She phoned us when they got back. She was crying – she couldn't believe what her boys had done, she was so touched. What a thoughtful thing for her sons to have done for her. Auntie Freda brought me a china tea set that had belonged to Grace Fawr and Grace Bach (her nain and her mam). I was thrilled! To think that Nain had used this over fifty years ago. Needless to say, it's in a glass cupboard now!

July 20th 2003: It was Aron's last day at Ysgol Pant y Rhedyn on Friday, bless him; he is really looking forward to Friars. Sion will miss him in school. Megan is moving up to Ysgol Babanod next term and is really excited about it – she can't wait to have her dinner there and she wants homework like the boys. We will really miss her.

September 23rd 2003: We as a family went to an evening reception last week – Sarah was marrying Kevin. Sarah is Kash and Dafydd's daughter (Ned Thomas's granddaughter.) They had the wedding and reception at Hendre Hall, Tal y Bont. It was a brilliant night; they had all sorts to entertain the kids, with bouncy castles and a great display of fireworks. There was a live band there until 4am. The food was great and everyone enjoyed their evening. Sarah and her husband went to St Lucia for their honeymoon.

September 27th 2003: The children are all back at school now; it has been a lovely summer. Meg loves school – we bought her two little toy dogs in a basket on her first day. Sion has settled well in Pant y Rhedyn, and Aron loves Friars, his new school. Our first grandchild, Paul, is fifteen years old today.

October 2003: Sad news about Glyn, he died last week aged fifty. He didn't want to go into hospital so Auntie Freda looked after him at home. He had lived with his mother for 11 years and he will leave a big gap in her life. Karen, Em and I went to the funeral. Lorraine was unable to get time off work. Uncle Ned's children went as well so there was a good turn-out from the Thomas clan. There were loads of people there, mostly Glyn's friends. Em and I had met a few of them on previous visits to Sutton Coldfield. The service itself wasn't morbid or sad; Glyn wouldn't have wanted that, said his brother Derek. The service ended with the song *I Did It My Way*, and Glyn certainly did.

December 19th 2003: Em and I have been to see Auntie Mildred at Llandudno Hospital; she is very ill. Her children Byron, Gareth and Venice have been with her all the time. Gareth has spent the last three nights at her bedside. It's so hard for Venice and her brothers, watching their mother in a hospital bed, so ill. How sad. Auntie Mildred hasn't been at all well for many months and I fear she's lost the will to carry on. I sat with her for a while today; she wasn't in any pain and I think she recognized my voice. Tears were rolling down my cheeks as I thought about Uncle Harry and how much he loved his wife and family; so many happy and sad memories all interwoven. John is so very far away, although his siblings are in constant touch with him. Em and I phoned him on Sunday and had a long chat; he does love to have a natter. "Emrys is the only one I can talk football with," says John, who's a fanatical Manchester United supporter, and as you know, Em loves his Bolton Wanderers so they do enjoy a bit of banter together.

A friend we went to school with, Noel, who has lived in Australia since he was a young man, was taken ill about six weeks ago. He's hoping to go home for Christmas. When we were in Australia in 1990 we stayed the weekend with Noel and Phyllis, they were very kind to us. We hope to return the favour some day.

Dec 20th 2003: Auntie Mildred died today just hours before her son John's surprise visit from Australia.

May 2004: Auntie Freda had her annual week's holiday here this month. As ever it was lovely to have her and she had a great time visiting friends and relatives. She was not as well as she might have been but she was determined not to let it spoil her week. Derek came to take her home and the last thing she said to me as she got in the car was: "I think it will be my last visit, Margaret." She must have been feeling really ill to say that. "Don't be so silly," I said through my tears.

September 24th 2004: We have found Dad's divorce papers. I had been searching vainly for a trace of them in Vancouver. I wrote to the courts in Ontario and Ottawa – still no luck! We had a brainwave. We knew that Mam and Dad were married in Bangor so we decided to look locally for the papers. I phoned the County Court in Caernarfon and after nearly three years of searching there they were. Dad and Vera's divorce was made final on April 7th 1948; Dad was the petitioner. No mention of any children was made on the decree absolute. The court officer in Caernarfon told us that the file had been destroyed years ago and only the decree was kept. The search for a child goes on; although where I go from here I've no idea.

December 28th 2004: A tsunami – a giant wave – struck Asia on Boxing Day. It has shocked the whole world. Thousands upon thousands of people were killed. So many have been made homeless, children losing parents and parents losing children. Whole families were wiped out in a matter of minutes. It's too early to say how many lives were lost. The devastation is unbelievable, with entire villages and communities completely washed away. The TV reports are horrifying to watch; people are walking around in a daze, searching what is left of their homes and villages and for lost members of their families. The suffering and despair felt by these people shows on their faces and it's impossible to imagine what they're going through. God help them all.

May 20th 2005: We were sitting quietly by the fire around 9pm when the phone went. It was Karen in a flat spin: "Can you and Dad come up please?" she said. "What's the matter del," I said. "We've got a bat in Aron's room!" To cut a long story short, we went up and they were sitting in the parlor with the middle door closed. I am giggling to myself as I write this. Karen had heard Aron shout and then he practically flew downstairs, screaming: "A bat just passed my head; I'm not going to my room until you catch it!" Words like bat and hell come to mind! Aron ran into the kitchen to get a brush. "What he thought he could do with it I dread to think," said Karen. Paul was trying to brave it out and went up to help. By this time Lorraine had joined us and Aron said: "I'm going to sleep in your house tonight," and off he went. We spent the next three hours hunting the bat. With Aron's window wide open and the lights turned down low, we left the room and watched as the bat came out of his hiding place and flew outside. But when we went back up it had taken refuge there again. We were hysterical with laughter as we took turns to stand in the darkened room with a sheet over our heads, and holding another sheet in our hands to throw over the bat should it emerge, but it was much too clever for us. Eventually we decided to strip the bed and start moving furniture out bit by bit. Em stood guard, armed with a sheet, as we pulled and tugged at the furniture to look under it. All of a sudden there it was, under one of the cupboards; it looked like a small piece of black fabric. I screamed and jumped out of the way, and Em threw the sheet over it and threw it out of the window onto the conservatory roof. We all watched with baited breath for what seemed like ages; it must have been only a few seconds. Out from under the sheet, into the darkness, flew what must have been a very frightened little bat.

September 24th 2005: A gathering of the clan (my father Now's family). We had a family reunion at the Dwygyfylchi Hotel in Penmaenmawr on Saturday, organised by Dafo and Nia (cousins). It went on from lunchtime until the early hours of the morning. There was face painting, balloon blowing, and football for the younger ones. There were over 150 of us and it was a brilliant day; there were people sharing the same bloodline from all over the UK and as far afield as Cyprus. Jason, Sion and Aron walked over the mountain from Llanfair. We were aged from two to 75, all mixed together at Derek's pub (he is also a relation!). What a good feeling it gave me as I walked amongst our family, some of whom I hadn't seen for 40 years, others whom I'd never met before. What a treat to see the young people all looking so smart and enjoying themselves so much. We were there in force, singing, dancing and rejoicing in each other's company. The food was excellent, the company was grand, and a good time was had by all.

October 2nd 2005: Em and I went to see Val today; she was in good spirits and was very exited about visitors she'd had the previous day: Auntie Ann (Uncle Bob's wife) and her daughter and grandchildren had been to see her. We hadn't seen them for many years until the gathering of the clan! It's so good to have rekindled family ties.

October 12th 2005: Noel and Phyllis have been here from Australia for a couple of weeks, stayed in his sister Marie's home in Llandudno Junction. They have another week to go. They are having a brilliant time and seeing far more of North Wales than most of us have ever seen, I'm sure. Emyr Ty Pitch took them up around Garreg Fawr and Llyn Anafon in his Land Rover. They've been on the train up Snowdon. Carol and Philip took them out on a couple of runs. Many of their family and old friends have taken them around the countryside; they've had a brilliant holiday.

October 20th 2005: Paul started driving lessons today.

October 27th 2005: I had some very sad news today. Auntie Freda died last night. The last one of Grace Bach's brood – and the end of an era. Auntie Freda was 84 years old and up until last week was still going out and about. She was a very determined lady and told me on the phone recently that "I will not sit and rot in the house – I will keep going out as long as I possibly can." It is with a great sense of loss that I write about my Auntie Freda's death; she never got to read the book. Perhaps her granddaughters Leah and Hannah will be able to show it to their grandchildren one day. And so the wheels of life keep turning. On the day of Auntie Freda's' funeral Derek asked me if I would like two large old vases that had belonged to our grandmother Grace Bach. "It seems fitting that they go back to Llanfair" he said.

Bibliography

BORROW, G (1862) *Wild Wales* Collins.

CYHOEDDIADAU MEI (1992) *Lleisiau'r Graig*.

DODDS, AH (1968) *A History of Caernarfonshire 1284-1900* Caernarfonshire Historical Society.

DOYLERUSH, E (1985) *No Landing Place - A guide to Aircraft Crashes in Snowdonia* Midland Counties Publications.

ELLIS, CONSTABLE, E (1988) *Fresh as Yesterday* Cyhoeddiadau Mei.

HUGHES, H AND NORTH HL *The old Cottages Of Snowdonia*. First published in (1908).

HUGHES, Ll (1994) *Teyrnged/A Tribute* Llanfairfechan Historical Society.

JONES, G (1890) *Llanfairfechan and Aber with Historical and Topographical Notes* The Herald, Caernarfon. JONES, JE (1986) Yn Fy Ffordd Fy Hun Gwasg Carreg Gwalch.

LLANFAIRFECHAN (1907) *Llanfairfechan the Gem of North Wales* Caxton Printing Works.

LLANFAIRFECHAN HISTORICAL SOCIETY *Rhwng Pandy a Plas, Essays on The Past of our Parish*.

LOCAL BOARD (1891) *Bylaws of Llanfairfechan* Knight & Co Fleet Street.

PENMAENMAWR WELSH GRANITE COMPANY (1950) *Moving Mountains* C Vernon & Sons Ltd, Liverpool.

PRICHARD, OJ (1962) *Hanes Eglwys Horeb Llanfairfechan* (1772-1962).

ROBERTS, J ap Cenin (1902) *Llanfairfechan Fel yr Oedd, Fel y Mae a Fel y Dylai Fod - Hen Gymeriadau Llanfairfechan*.

ROBERTS, J ap Cenin (1925) *Llanfairfechan* Y Brython.

ROBERTS, Nesta (Editor) (1887) *S. Winifred's Llanfairfechan*.

RODENBERG, J (1856) *An Autumn in Wales* Translated William Linnard.

SILOS, L (1976) *Sixty Years a Welsh Territorial* Gomer Press.